PENGUIN SHAKESPEARE LIBRARY

GENERAL EDITOR: T. J. B. SPENCER

SHAKESPEARE'S HISTORIES

William A. Armstrong has been Professor of English Literature at Westfield College, University of London, since 1967. A graduate of Sheffield and York Universities, he was Director of the British Institute in Gozo (Malta) before teaching at the University College of Wales at Aberystwyth, King's College, London, and the University of Hull. His publications include numerous articles on Elizabethan drama and an anthology of Elizabethan history plays. He is currently helping to edit a new edition of Samuel Pepys's diaries.

SHAKESPEARE'S HISTORIES

AN ANTHOLOGY OF MODERN
CRITICISM

Edited by
William A. Armstrong

PENGUIN BOOKS

Penguin Books Ltd, Harmondsworth, Middlesex, England
Penguin Books Inc., 7110 Ambassador Road, Baltimore, Maryland 21207, U.S.A.
Penguin Books Australia Ltd, Ringwood, Victoria, Australia

—

First published 1972

—

This selection copyright © William A. Armstrong, 1972

—

Made and printed in Great Britain
by Richard Clay (The Chaucer Press) Ltd,
Bungay, Suffolk
Set in Monotype Fournier

CONTENTS

ACKNOWLEDGEMENTS

FOR permission to reprint the contents of this anthology, thanks are due to the authors and original publishers. Full acknowledgements are given on the first page of each extract.

INTRODUCTION

NINE of the eighteen plays that Shakespeare is known to have written by 1599 deal with English history. He returned to this subject when he completed *Henry VIII* near the end of his career, and when his friends Heminges and Condell prepared the first Folio of his plays for publication in 1623, they grouped them as 'Comedies, Histories, and Tragedies'. They arranged the histories, not in the order of their composition, but according to the chronology of the events portrayed in them, beginning with *King John*, following with the tetralogy dealing with Richard II, Henry IV, and Henry V, continuing with the tetralogy about Henry VI and Richard III, and ending with *Henry VIII*. The arrangement adopted in the first Folio has a profounder logic than that of temporal sequence to justify it, but some of the deepest connexions between these 'histories' were not excavated until the twentieth century, and their claim to be a distinctive and coherent dramatic kind has been vindicated only in comparatively recent times.

Eighteenth-century critics found the history play hard, if not impossible, to classify. Nicholas Rowe prefaced his edition of Shakespeare's plays (1709) with a forthright rejection of the history play as a dramatic kind; Shakespeare's plays, he says, 'are properly to be distinguished only into Comedies and Tragedies. Those which are called Histories ... are really Tragedies, with a run or mixture of Comedy amongst 'em.' Dr Johnson likewise thought the history a very amorphous sort of play, but he was willing to accept it as an inferior Elizabethan kind. He describes it in his *Preface to Shakespeare* (1765) as 'a series of actions, with no other than chronological succession, independent on each other, and without any tendency to introduce or regulate the conclusion', adding that 'a history might be continued through many plays; as it had no plan, it had no limits.'[1] Johnson finds compensations for this alleged looseness of structure in Shakespeare's capacity for

1. *Dr Johnson on Shakespeare*, edited by W. K. Wimsatt (Penguin Shakespeare Library, 1969), page 63.

inventing diverting incidents and creating a rich variety of characters, and even suggests that 'Perhaps no author has ever in two
plays afforded so much delight' as Shakespeare has in the two parts
of *Henry IV*.[2]

Coleridge's comments on Shakespeare's histories are relatively
brief,[3] but they show a greater awareness of their distinctive form,
substance, and purposes than those of earlier English critics. He
sees the history play as an intermediate form between the tragic
and the epic, having in common with the latter a concern with 'the
relation of providence to the human will'. At its best, it achieves
unity through causal rather than temporal connexions; 'a unity of
a higher order, which connects the events by reference to the
workers, gives a reason for them in the motives and presents men in
their causative character.' Coleridge realized that the playwright
had to blend fact with fiction to create a unity of this kind, hence he
defines a history play as 'a collection of events borrowed from
history, but connected together in respect to cause and time poetically, by dramatic fiction.' He also makes some useful distinctions
between one type of history play and another in terms of the extent
to which their plots are directed by history as opposed to fiction.
He rightly regards *King John*, *Richard II*, and *Henry VIII* as plays
in which 'history *informs* the plot', and therefore terms them 'purely
historical plays'. In the two parts of *Henry IV*, on the other hand,
historical characters and events are not so dominant; they *direct* the
plot but do not inform it, so Coleridge terms them 'mixed drama'.
According to Coleridge, the history play had the 'great object . . .
of familiarizing the people to the great names of their country and
thereby of exciting a steady patriotism, a love of just liberty, and a
respect for all those fundamental institutions of social life which
bind men together.' This is a rather limited and biased conception
of the aims of the history plays, which emphasize order and obedience
more than 'just liberty'. It makes no reference to the revelation
of the workings of divine providence, which was at least as
important as the patriotic impulse. But Coleridge, as we have seen,
was aware of the theme of providence, and he must be credited with

2. op. cit., page 117.

3. *Coleridge on Shakespeare*, edited by Terence Hawkes (Penguin Shakespeare Library, 1969), pages 241–67.

having demonstrated that Shakespeare's history plays had a distinctive ethos, direction, and unity, and could be endorsed as a dramatic kind without apology or qualification.

Coleridge's valuable pointers were not followed by Felix E. Schelling, the first critic to attempt a detailed study of the Elizabethan history play. In his lengthy book, *The English Chronicle Play* (1902), he asserts that the authors of Elizabethan history plays were 'unselective in their use of material', accepting 'whatever they found' and 'using it as they found it'. He concludes that the 'diversity of subject-matter in these plays is as great as their want of individual unity.' These disparaging generalizations are applicable to only a few Elizabethan history plays, and it is a measure of the increase in our understanding of this dramatic genre that no responsible critic would now endorse them.

An important contribution to this deeper understanding is Alfred Hart's monograph, *Shakespeare and the Homilies* (1934), which shows that Shakespeare's history plays make persistent use of key religio-political doctrines of the Tudor period and are therefore much more than random dramatizations of loose-knit chronicles. These doctrines are eloquently expounded in the collection of Anglican sermons called *Certain Sermons or Homilies*, first published in 1547, and reprinted, with additions, in 1563 and 1574. Two of the most important are 'An Exhortation Concerning Good Order and Obedience' and 'Against Disobedience and Wilful Rebellion'. These sermons were preached year in and year out in Anglican churches. Shakespeare heard them and remembered some parts of them so well that he reproduced phrases and images from them in his history plays.

Hart demonstrates this close familiarity and also shows that certain themes in the history plays are closely connected with five doctrines or ideas expounded in the two homilies mentioned above: (*a*) the doctrine of order or degree, (*b*) the doctrine of the divine appointment of kings, (*c*) the doctrine of the obedience due to appointed kings, (*d*) the sinfulness of rebellion against such kings, (*e*) the vicious characteristics of rebels and rebellion. As applied to history, these ideas constitute a providential theory because they represent nations and men as continuously subject to God's dispensation of rewards and punishments. The system of order and degree is described in the homily on Good Order as a universal one created by God. Just as there are higher and lower orders of angels, so the sun, moon, and stars have their appointed place in the firmament, and kings, lords, and commoners their hierarchies in human society, each with its special vocations and duties. Animal, vegetable, and mineral species were seen in the same way as arranged by God in a descending scale of values. These celestial and terrestrial hierarchies are represented as interdependent and any attempt to disrupt them as an affront to God and damaging to all things. Shakespeare's deep interest in this doctrine of order and degree is revealed by many passages in his plays. The most comprehensive is Ulysses's speech in the third scene of *Troilus and Cressida*, where he proclaims that the heavens, the planets, and the earth itself 'Observe degree, priority, and place', compares the health-giving powers of the sun in the firmament to the attribute of rule in a king on earth, and warns his hearers that when the system of degree is violated, 'The enterprise is sick'.

The homily on Good Order and Obedience also contains the Anglican theory of the divine appointment of kings and their superiority to any other lay or spiritual powers in their domains. 'It is written of God in the Book of the Proverbs: *Through me kings do reign*', states the homily, and from this text its authors deduce that kings owe their power not to the Papacy but directly to God. This doctrine explains why a number of Tudor writers, including Shakespeare, regarded King John not as the worst of English kings, but as a ruler who tried to retrieve from the Papacy powers which rightly belonged to the English monarchy. When John tells the papal legate in the first scene of the third Act of Shakespeare's play that he is 'supreme head' of his kingdom 'under heaven', he is asserting this doctrine and prefiguring Henry VIII's defiance of the Papacy.

A logical sequel to this theory of the divine appointment of kings is the Tudor doctrine of obedience. The homily on Good Order bases its demand for obedience to lawful kings upon St Paul's Epistle to the Romans, quoting the text which states that 'the powers that be, be ordained of God . . . they that resist shall receive to themselves damnation'. Even if a king who has lawfully succeeded to his throne rules badly, he must be obeyed, because, according to the homily, his subjects must have sinned and his tyranny is God's way of punishing them. Only God has the right to punish a lawfully-succeeded king who rules badly. All of these ideas are at work in *Richard II*. When the Duchess of Gloucester inveighs against Richard's complicity in the murder of her husband, John of Gaunt conducts himself like an ideal subject when he replies that if Richard, God's anointed deputy, has done wrong, revenge on him must be left to heaven,

> for I may never lift
> An angry arm against His minister.

I.2.40–41

The doctrine of obedience has as its corollary a wholesale condemnation of rebellion against a lawful king. This is the basic purpose of the long homily 'Against Disobedience and Wilful Rebellion', which represents rebellion of this kind as one of the worst of sins because it is an offence not only against the king but against God and the hierarchial system of order which He has established in the universe. Hence the homily declares that rebellion comprehends all sins against God and man 'heaped together'. Correspondingly, in *Henry V* (II.2.141–2) the King tells the traitor Scroop that

> this revolt of thine . . . is like
> Another fall of man.

One of the most pernicious results of rebellion, according to the homily, is that it produces civil wars in which fathers sometimes kill their own sons, and sons their own fathers. This passage impressed Shakespeare so strongly that in the Third Part of *Henry VI* (II.5.54) he epitomizes the miseries of civil war by introducing an episode representing '*a son that hath killed his father*' and '*a father that hath killed his son*'.

Hart's monograph thus specifies and illustrates some of the main religious and political principles embodied in Shakespeare's history plays. But principles are one thing and their organization into a sequence of cause and effect is another. There is certainly a pattern of cause and effect in Shakespeare's two tetralogies about kings and their problems from the time of Richard II to that of Henry VII. One of the chief merits of E. M. W. Tillyard's book, *Shakespeare's*

History Plays (1944),[4] is that it demonstrates that one of the main sources of the pattern underlying and connecting the two tetralogies is Edward Hall's history, published in 1548.[5] This work has a clear-cut shape and purpose. As its title – *The Union of the Two Noble and Illustre Families of Lancaster and York* – indicates, Hall was a staunch admirer of the Tudor dynasty, and his aim was to show the origin and nature of the period of discord and civil war which had preceded the reign of Henry VII, and how Henry had restored health to the state by bringing to an end the tyranny of Richard III and uniting the Houses of York and Lancaster by marrying Elizabeth of York. Shakespeare's tetralogies deal with the same period; in fact, as Tillyard points out, *Richard II* begins at exactly the same point in history as Hall's history does; at the moment when Bolingbroke's quarrel with Mowbray led to his estrangement from Richard. The pattern that Hall imposes on events from the time of Richard II to that of Henry VIII is a distinctive one, as the titles of his eight chapters indicate: chapters one and two portray the 'unquiet time' of Henry IV followed by the 'victorious acts' of Henry V; chapters three and four follow the same pattern of decline and retrieval, showing the 'troublous season' of Henry VI followed by the 'prosperous reign' of Edward IV. In the latter half of the work, the deepest decline in the fortunes of the nation is followed by the attainment of unprecedented stability and harmony, as the 'pitiful life' of Edward V and the 'tragical doings' of Richard III give way to the 'politic governance' of Henry VII and the 'triumphant reign' of Henry VIII.

Shakespeare did not deal with the reign of Henry VIII until he was nearing the end of his career as a playwright, and his treatment of it is less panegyrical than Hall's, showing how eminent personages came to grief in it, and how the King exhibited human frailties as well as royal virtues. His treatment of the character and fortunes of the eight kings who preceded Henry VIII, however, resembles the pattern laid down by Hall. In his preface, Hall sums up his dynastic theme by declaring that 'as King Henry the Fourth

4. Available in the Penguin Shakespeare Library (1969).

5. A facsimile of the 1550 edition was published by the Scolar Press (Menston, Yorkshire) in 1970. A modernized edition of the parts of the work most used by Shakespeare is planned in the Penguin Shakespeare Library.

was the beginning and root of the great discord and division, so was the godly matrimony the final end of all dissensions, titles, and debates.' The 'godly matrimony' is, of course, the marriage of Henry Tudor and Elizabeth of York, and it is with this prospect of the union of the two houses that Shakespeare chooses to end *Richard III*.

Though Shakespeare's debt to Hall is extensive, Tillyard goes too far when he states that Shakespeare's picture of English history is 'nearly the same' as Hall's. Shakespeare's picture is much richer and more complex than Hall's. He frequently draws upon other sources besides Hall. He augments and modifies the characteristics of historical personages for special dramatic purposes; the peculiar fascination of his Richard III, for instance, is due to a Machiavellian intellect and a vein of sardonic humour not found in any earlier portrait of this king. He adds characters and situations of his own invention to those provided by historians, especially in his second tetralogy, where such fictitious characters as Falstaff, Pistol, Bardolph, Mrs Quickly, Doll Tearsheet, Slender, Shallow, and Fluellen play important parts. Moreover, Lily B. Campbell has argued, in *Shakespeare's 'Histories': Mirrors of Elizabethan Policy* (1947), that Shakespeare devised these plays to provide a commentary on Elizabethan political problems as well as an interpretation of medieval history. In the 1590s, for instance, the Jesuit Robert Parsons was publishing treatises declaring that subjects could justifiably depose their kings in certain circumstances, so Professor Campbell claims that Shakespeare wrote *Richard II* partly to explore this topical question. On the subject of the First Part of *Henry IV*, she argues that Northumberland, Hotspur, and their principal followers are modelled to some extent on the leaders of the Rebellion of 1569, and that Shakespeare is again infusing an Elizabethan issue into a play about a medieval king and his difficulties. I think that she is on firmer ground in her discussion of *Henry V*, when she states that some passages in it reflect a contemporary controversy about the best methods of waging war, because she shows that Fluellen's ideas on this subject correspond closely to those of Sir John Smythe, and are contrary to those of Sir Roger Williams, both of whom published books on the subject in the 1590s. Professor Campbell overstates her case, however, and it is a symptom of this fault that she belittles the importance of Falstaff in the history plays because he has few connexions with her topical analogies. Falstaff has become a controversial figure in twentieth-century criticism for other reasons besides this. In his *Essay on the Dramatic Character of Sir John Falstaff* (1777), Maurice Morgann had defended Falstaff against the charge of cowardice; in his *Characters of Shakespeare's Plays* (1817), William Hazlitt had claimed that Falstaff was a 'better man' than Henry V; and the admiration of Falstaff reaches its climax in A. C. Bradley's 'The Rejection of Falstaff' in his *Oxford Lectures on Poetry* (1909) in which he claims that our 'sympathetic delight in Falstaff' transcends 'moral judgements' so completely that we cannot concur with Henry's rejection of him.

Reacting strongly against Bradley, E. E. Stoll argues in his *Shakespeare Studies* (1927) that Falstaff was conceived in the satiric spirit of the cowardly *miles gloriosus* of Roman comedy and does not transcend ethical criticism. In *The Fortunes of Falstaff* (1943), John Dover Wilson pursues this line of historical criticism even further, interpreting *Henry IV* as 'Shakespeare's great morality play'. In the allegorical Moralities of the early sixteenth century, the central character is sometimes a Young Man or a Prodigal, who ignores the sound advice of his Father, and is tempted by a Vice representing Riot in the form of an old man who is sometimes both witty and cowardly. Wilson claims that Prince Hal, Henry IV, and Falstaff correspond to the Prodigal, the Father, and the Vice. He also associates Falstaff with the traditional Lord of Misrule and argues that the rejection of Falstaff is a virtuous repudiation of disorder. Hal's description of Falstaff as a 'reverend Vice', a 'devil . . . in the likeness of an old fat man', and a 'misleader of youth' in the First Part of *Henry IV* (II.4.435–49) clearly connects this history play with the old Moralities, but it also shows that Hal is highly critical of Falstaff from the outset, and we are never at any stage given the impression that he is likely to succumb to Falstaff's temptations, so the parallel with the Moralities cannot be sustained beyond a certain point. But Wilson's case is supported by the increasing grossness, outrageousness, and rapacity of Falstaff in the Second Part of *Henry IV*, and he has given good reasons for his belief that Falstaff embodies moral frailties as well as exquisite humour and does not stand outside the ethical and historical framework of the plays in which he appears.

Some recent critics, such as A. P. Rossiter, William Empson, and D. A. Traversi, disagree with Wilson's interpretation of Hal and Falstaff. They see Hal as the type of narrow and frigid personality produced by a concern with policy and statecraft. They find positive virtues in Falstaff, and feel that in his second tetralogy Shakespeare became increasingly aware of the value of personal relationships, more critical of the rigid hierarchial relationships imposed on life by the concept of order and degree, and that he turned to a more humane and liberal ethic. In *Shakespeare from 'Richard II' to 'Henry V'* (1957), for instance, D. A. Traversi argues that Hal is designed to show that 'success in politics implies a moral loss, the sacrifice of more attractive qualities in the distinctively personal order', whereas Falstaff is offered to us as a tolerant, perceptive, and 'vivid human commentator on the detached inhumanity which political ability . . . seems increasingly to imply'. The latter remark makes Falstaff more moral and systematic in his observations than is the case; as I see him, he is never altruistic. Against the notion that Hal's career exhibits a moral decline which reaches its nadir when he rejects Falstaff, it can be pointed out that he has sworn a solemn coronation oath to rule justly only a few minutes before Falstaff possessively accosts him at the end of *Henry IV, Part Two*, and that his consequent rejection of him, far from being absolute, is tempered by financial provision for him and the promise of advancement if he reforms.

It is an interesting fact that when Sir Laurence Olivier began playing the role of Henry V at the Old Vic in 1937, he had a strong dislike for what seemed to him its jingoist sentiments and its scoutmaster's sense of humour, but in the course of studying and acting it he found that his misgivings disappeared as he responded to its genuinely heroic rhythm.[6] The last fifty years have witnessed excellent performances of the great roles in the history plays and unprecedented efforts by producers to stage the two tetralogies as closely integrated cycles. Sir John Gielgud's Richard II, as played in his own production at the Queen's Theatre in 1937, ranks next to his superb Hamlet of 1945 among his Shakespearian roles.

6. See Felix Barker, *The Oliviers* (London, 1953), pages 122-3.

Olivier's genius probably found full expression for the first time in his Richard III at the New Theatre in 1944. Falstaff's vast capacity for ingratiation can seldom, if ever, have been so fully realized as it was in Sir Ralph Richardson's interpretation of the part at the New Theatre in 1945.

Convinced that 'the great epic theme of the Histories had become obscured through years of presenting the plays singly', Anthony Quayle successfully presented the second tetralogy as a cycle at the Stratford Memorial Theatre in 1951, integrating it by using the same neo-Elizabethan stage and setting for each play and having the same players act throughout those characters who appear in more than one of the plays. Like many other important plays, the three parts of *Henry VI* owe their recent rehabilitation to Sir Barry Jackson's company at the Birmingham Repertory Theatre, where Douglas Seale directed them singly between 1951 and 1953, and then staged his productions in chronological sequence at the Old Vic in 1953 and 1958. These important experiments prepared the way for the most ambitious enterprise essayed by the Royal Shakespeare Company since Peter Hall became its director in 1960; namely, the production in 1964 of Shakespeare's historical sequence from *Richard II* to *Richard III*, with his three *Henry VI* plays skilfully reduced to two, which were called *Henry VI* and *Edward IV*.[7] It was thus possible for the first time in the history of the English theatre to see the two tetralogies effectively presented as a single cycle. Despite its modish preoccupation with scenes of violence and cruelty, the production was an impressive demonstration of the structural coherence and moral consistency of the sequence. The test of performance, the final arbiter of theories about plays, thus vindicated some of the most important ideas about Shakespeare's tetralogies advanced by twentieth-century scholars and critics.

The aim of this anthology is not to provide examples of all the different approaches to Shakespeare's history plays which have been pursued in recent years, but to assemble a set of comprehensive discussions of Elizabethan theories of history and the history play,

7. The text of this important adaptation of the tetralogy, prepared by John Barton in collaboration with Peter Hall, was published by the British Broadcasting Corporation in 1970.

of Shakespeare's reaction to those conceptions, of each of his history plays, and of some of the main aspects of their stage history, together with an eminent actor's approach to one of their greatest roles.

Professor Irving Ribner's study of 'History and Drama in the Age of Shakespeare' skilfully outlines the medieval, classical, and Renaissance ideas of the purposes of history at work in Shakespeare's time, and argues that history plays are 'those which use, for any combination of these purposes, material drawn from national chronicles and assumed by the dramatist to be true'. Asserting that Shakespeare 'interpreted history aesthetically rather than philosophically', Professor S. C. Sen Gupta's examination of 'The Substance of Shakespeare's "Histories"' is in some respects a reaction against Professor Ribner's definition, and contains an impressive refutation of Dover Wilson's idea that *Henry IV* closely follows a Morality pattern, aptly remarking that Prince Hal, unlike the erring young man in the Moralities, never succumbs to riot, temptation, or self-deception. His reaction against the idea that Shakespeare's treatment of kingship and usurpation is a mere reflection of contemporary orthodoxy is likewise salutary, though some of the inconsistencies which he finds in attempts to relate Shakespeare's treatment of usurpation to that of contemporary political theorists disappear when it is recalled that it was widely maintained among the latter that if a usurper rules justly (as Shakespeare's Henry IV does) the true successor should spare the nation from civil war by holding his claim in abeyance (as Shakespeare's Mortimer does not in *Henry IV*).

Some of the most illuminating of recent criticisms of the history plays have shown that, although Shakespeare was well versed in contemporary chronicles, political ideas, and theories of history, his use of them was eminently creative and original. In his essay on 'The Frame of Disorder – *Henry VI*', for example, Professor J. P Brockbank shows how effectively Shakespeare employed dramatic forms and conventions to express 'whatever coherence and order could be found in the "plots" of chronicle history', particularly by the calculated use of symbolic events, pageantry, dumb show, and sound effects. Correspondingly, A. P. Rossiter demonstrates in 'Angel with Horns: The Unity of *Richard III*' that Shakespeare's play is much more complex than the 'simple process of divine justice' exemplified by its chronicle-sources, chiefly because it embodies many paradoxes and ironies, seen especially in the 'grisly *comedy*' produced by Shakespeare's brilliant transformation of the Richard of earlier writers into an avenging angel with horns, a diabolical humorist who is the agent as well as the victim of divine nemesis. Similarly, Shakespeare's treatment of the reign of King John is profounder and more unified than that of any earlier writer because, as Professor William H. Matchett argues in his article on the play, it is focused on Faulconbridge's moral and intellectual development through the process of learning to estimate the value of hereditary right to a throne, native ability to rule, 'commodity', patriotism, and honour. In his analysis of 'The Structural Problem in Shakespeare's *Henry the Fourth*', Professor Harold Jenkins gives us cogent reasons for believing that although Shakespeare changed his mind in the course of writing *Part One* and did not necessarily plan *Part Two* before *Part One* was acted, the play is so audacious in its premises and so exquisite in its craftsmanship that it is possible to declare that 'The two parts are complementary, they are also independent and even incompatible'.

Other critics represented in this anthology have been especially concerned to rescue certain of Shakespeare's history plays from presumptions which run counter to an informed study of their texts. Thus Peter Ure, taking issue with those who have interpreted Richard II as essentially a self-deceiving, self-dramatizing poetizer, argues that his sufferings are tragic, not merely pathetic, and that they have this quality because he feels guilty of a heinous betrayal of the sacred office of kingship; as Richard himself puts it, 'I find myself a traitor with the rest'. Similarly, Professor A. R. Humphreys's assessment of Falstaff transcends the stiff censoriousness of some of the fat knight's critics and the over-indulgence of others by giving judicious attention to 'the controlling context' of the passages in which his faults and foibles are represented, and aptly concluding that 'One takes him in the tolerance of comedy when the results are comic; one condemns only when they threaten to be serious'. In his rehabilitation of Henry V, Mr M. M. Reese defends him efficiently against those critics who 'as pacifists, republicans, anti-clericals, little Englanders, moralists, even as arbiters of etiquette' have been prejudiced against him, and persuasively argues that the characterization of Henry 'gains its strength and conviction from all that has gone before, not from *Henry IV* only but from all the poet's earlier studies of kingship and society'. Defending *Henry VIII* against those critics who deny it unity, Professor Frank Kermode shows that its central concern is with the various falls of four great personages: Queen Katherine, Buckingham, Wolsey, and Cranmer.

Sir John Gielgud's essay on Richard II has been included in this anthology as a study of the role in terms of performance by one of its greatest interpreters. Significantly, Sir John's intuitions as an actor often harmonize with Peter Ure's deductions as a critic; he agrees with Ure that Richard is the sole protagonist of the play and that his character does not reveal its tragic depths until after his return from Ireland, when, far from being a poseur, he seems 'ever physically on his guard' against 'the dreaded impact of the unknown circumstances which, he feels, are always lying in wait to strike him down'. Professor A. C. Sprague's succinct stage history of the plays fittingly rounds off this anthology. Unlike other types of drama essayed by Shakespeare, the histories have never fallen into neglect; their great roles have fascinated actors, and their patriotic sentiments have attracted audiences in every period. On the whole, they have been fortunate in the manner of their presentation on the stage; the 'steadying ballast of known fact' in them has effectively curbed 'the fantastication of producers', and until well into the nineteenth century they were acted with fewer alterations of Shakespeare's words than either the tragedies or the comedies.

Quotations from *Richard III*, *Richard II*, *Henry IV, Part One*, *Henry V*, and *Henry VIII* are from the New Penguin Shakespeare editions of those plays. Quotations from the other history plays are from Peter Alexander's edition of the *Complete Works* (1951), with the exception of *King John*: in his article on this play, Professor William H. Matchett's references are to the new Arden edition (1954), edited by E. A. J. Honigmann, whose arrangement of the Act and scene divisions he prefers to any other.

1971   WILLIAM A. ARMSTRONG

SUGGESTIONS FOR FURTHER READING

THIS list is designed as a supplement to the works mentioned in the Introduction or anthologized in this volume.

General Studies

U. M. ELLIS-FERMOR: 'Shakespeare's Political Plays', in *The Frontiers of Drama* (1945). Shows how each of these plays contributes to an evolving image of the perfect ruler.

A. P. ROSSITER (ed.): *Woodstock: A Moral History* (1946). His preface demonstrates how the Morality play influenced the history play.

S. L. BETHELL: 'The Comic Element in Shakespeare's Histories', *Anglia* LXXI (1952). Shows how the comic scenes are organically connected with the main themes.

HAROLD JENKINS: 'Shakespeare's History Plays: 1900–1951', *Shakespeare Survey 6* (1953). A judicious survey of major developments in the recent criticism of the histories.

L. C. KNIGHTS: 'Shakespeare's Politics: With some Reflections on the Nature of Tradition', *Proceedings of the British Academy* LIV (1958). Relates Shakespeare's political thought to the tradition which bases society on an awareness of human beings as individuals.

G. BULLOUGH (ed.): *Narrative and Dramatic Sources of Shakespeare*, Volume III (1960), Volume IV (1962). An indispensable guide to the sources and Shakespeare's use of them.

A. P. ROSSITER: 'Ambivalence: The Dialectic of the Histories', in *Angel with Horns* (1961). Argues that Shakespeare found the Tudor conception of order and degree too doctrinaire and that he qualifies it in his histories with penetrating ironies and deliberate ambiguities.

L. C. KNIGHTS: *William Shakespeare: The Histories* (Writers and their Work, No. 151, 1961). Shows how Shakespeare's second tetralogy is linked with his tragedies as a deepening exploration of human nature.

CLIFFORD LEECH: *William Shakespeare: The Chronicles* (Writers and their Work, No. 146, 1962). Demonstrates how each play in the first tetralogy transcends its sources in literary skill and poetic insight.

KENNETH MUIR: 'Image and Symbol in Shakespeare's Histories', *Bulletin of the John Rylands Library* L (1968). Discusses the verbal imagery and stage imagery of the histories.

F. P. WILSON: 'The English History Play' in his *Shakespearian and Other Studies*, edited by Helen Gardner (1969). A discriminating survey, showing that Shakespeare's emphasis is on human agents rather than political doctrines.

'Henry VI'

HEREWARD T. PRICE: *Construction in Shakespeare* (1951). Contains detailed appreciation of the structure of *Henry VI, Part One*.

SIR BARRY JACKSON: 'On Producing *Henry VI*', *Shakespeare Survey 6* (1953). A man of the theatre's discussion of the problems of producing the three parts.

RONALD S. BERMAN: 'Fathers and Sons in the *Henry VI* Plays', *Shakespeare Quarterly* XIII (1962). Shows how unity is given to the three plays by the theme of the relationship between fathers and sons.

'Richard III'

R. B. HEILMAN: 'Satiety and Conscience: Aspects of Richard III', *Antioch Review* XXIV (1964). Argues that Richard is not a tragic character because deficient in feeling and self-knowledge.

NICHOLAS BROOKE: 'Reflecting Gems and Dead Bones: Tragedy versus History in *Richard III*', *Critical Quarterly* VII (1965). Finds a conflict between tragic and historical elements in the play, while admitting great virtuosity in their handling.

WOLFGANG CLEMEN: *A Commentary on Shakespeare's Richard III* (1968). A detailed scene-by-scene discussion, with valuable passages on the language and structure of the play.

'King John'

ADRIEN BONJOUR: 'The Road to Swinstead Abbey: A Study of the Sense and Structure of *King John*', *ELH* XVIII (1951). Discusses the structure in terms of a comparison between John and Faulconbridge.

E. C. PETTET: 'Hot Irons and Fever: A Note on some of the Imagery of *King John*', *Essays in Criticism* IV (1954). Relates the images of fire and heat to the proposed blinding of Prince Arthur and the fever of which John dies.

JAMES L. CALDERWOOD: 'Commodity and Honour in *King John*', *University of Toronto Quarterly* XXIX (1960). A cogent study of the play as an exploration of two contrasting principles, Commodity (i.e. scheming self-interest) and Honour (seen especially as loyalty to England).

'*Richard II*'

R. D. ALTICK: 'Symphonic Imagery in *Richard II*', *Publications of the Modern Language Association of America* XII (1947). Shows how certain image-motifs strengthen the structure of the play.

A. R. HUMPHREYS: *William Shakespeare: Richard II* (Arnold's Studies in English Literature, No. 31, 1967). A very discriminating study of the themes, characters, and structure of the play.

ROBERT RENTOUL READ: *Richard II: From Mask to Prophet* (1968). Examines Richard as a tragic hero who achieves self-knowledge.

'*Henry IV*'

MADELEINE DORAN: 'Imagery in *Richard II* and in *Henry IV*', *Modern Language Review* XXXVII (1942). Shows Shakespeare's developing powers as illustrated by his use of imagery.

CLIFFORD LEECH: 'The Unity of *2 Henry IV*', *Shakespeare Survey 6* (1953). Shows how the play combines 'morality intention' with 'a preoccupation with the effects of time, and a latent scepticism'.

C. L. BARBER: *Shakespeare's Festive Comedy* (1959). Discusses the festive conventions of the 'Lord of Misrule' at work in *Henry IV*.

R. J. BECK: *William Shakespeare: Henry IV* (Arnold's Studies in English Literature, No. 24, 1965). A well-balanced discussion of themes, characters, imagery, and style.

JOHN SHAW: 'The Staging of Parody and Parallels in *1 Henry IV*', *Shakespeare Survey 20* (1967). Discusses the parallel scenes and how Shakespeare's actors may have given them appropriate emphasis.

Falstaff

H. B. CHARLTON: 'Falstaff', in *Shakespearian Comedy* (1938). Argues that Shakespeare became dissatisfied with Falstaff as a comic creation because of his deficiency in the 'supreme values' of life.

J. I. M. STEWART: 'The Birth and Death of Falstaff', in *Character and Motive in Shakespeare* (1949). Reasserts Falstaff's 'indefeasible attractiveness' and argues that in the end he is a scapegoat, a 'dethroned and sacrificial king'.

WALTER KAISER: *Praisers of Folly* (1963). Relates Falstaff to traditional conceptions of the Fool, the Sot, the Vice, and the Tempter, and examines his relationship with other major characters in *Henry IV*.

H. E. TOLIVER: 'Falstaff, the Prince, and the History Play', *Shakespeare Quarterly* XVI (1965). Argues that the essential nature of the history play made it inevitable that Falstaff should be rejected.

'*Henry V*'

J. MIDDLETON MURRY: *Shakespeare* (1936). Chapter VIII is an eloquent vindication of Henry's character and conduct.

A. GILBERT: 'Patriotism and Satire in *Henry V*', in *Studies in Shakespeare*, edited by A. D. Matthews and C. M. Emery (1953). Shows the complexity of the play by demonstrating its use of satire and parody as well as epic themes.

Z. STŘIBRNÝ: '*Henry V* and History', in *Shakespeare in a Changing World*, edited by Arnold Kettle (1964). Interprets *Henry V* as a conspectus of Shakespeare's ideas of what history signifies.

CHARLES BARBER: 'Prince Hal, Henry V, and the Tudor Monarchy', in *The Morality of Art*, edited by D. W. Jefferson (1969). Praises Prince Hal as striking a happy mean between outdated chivalry (Hotspur) and the new cynicism of the 1590s (Falstaff), but regards Henry V as an uncritical glorification of the Tudor monarchy.

'*Henry VIII*'

G. WILSON KNIGHT: '*Henry VIII* and the Poetry of Conversion', in *The Crown of Life* (1947). Interprets the play as epic in structure, and Henry as 'kingliness personified'.

MURIEL ST CLARE BYRNE: 'A Stratford Production: *Henry VIII*', *Shakespeare Survey 3* (1950). A valuable record of Tyrone Guthrie's outstanding production.

HOWARD FELPERIN: 'Shakespeare's *Henry VIII*: History as Myth', *Studies in English Literature* VI (1966). Elaborates an interesting comparison between *Henry VIII* and Shakespeare's final romances.

Recordings

The Argo Company has made complete recordings of each of the ten history plays. The Caedmon Company has made complete recordings of all of them except *Henry VI, Parts One, Two*, and *Three*, and *Henry VIII*. Extracts from one or more of all ten plays have been recorded by the following companies: Argo, Caedmon, H.M.V., Spoken Arts, and R.C.A.-Victor. For full details, see *The Gramophone: Spoken Word and Miscellaneous Catalogue*.

ONE

History and Drama in the Age of Shakespeare*

Irving Ribner

THE type of history play which flourished in the age of Shakespeare was particularly an expression of the English Renaissance. Although its roots are deep in the medieval drama, it reached its full development in the last years of the reign of Elizabeth, and when John Ford wrote his *Perkin Warbeck*, it was with the awareness that he was reviving a dramatic type which had been dead for some decades. It is significant that later attempts to revive the history play often have been with an eye towards the Elizabethan era. Nicholas Rowe turned to his *Jane Shore* fresh from his edition of Shakespeare and full of the inspiration of Shakespeare's histories. In our own time Maxwell Anderson, in such plays as *Elizabeth the Queen* and *Anne of the Thousand Days*, has attempted to re-create Elizabethan verse drama, and it is significant that he has chosen his subjects from the very age he has sought to emulate.

To define the Renaissance history play as a distinct dramatic genre, however, has not been easy, although many attempts have been made. It is now, more than ever, necessary to so define it, for in the half century that has gone by since the appearance of Professor Felix E. Schelling's pioneer study,[1] our knowledge both of Elizabethan drama and of Renaissance historiography has increased vastly, and the time has come for a re-examination of the entire field of Elizabethan historical drama. But before we can begin to write of the English history play, we must decide by what specific standards we may distinguish history plays from other

*From *The English History Play in the Age of Shakespeare* (Princeton University Press, 1957; Methuen & Co. Ltd, 1965), pages 1–29. Copyright © Princeton University Press, 1957. Reprinted by kind permission of the author and Methuen & Co. Ltd, London.

plays of the Elizabethan era. The special use of the term 'histories' in the Shakespeare Folio of 1623 is, as we shall see, of little help in this respect. We must further bear in mind that those plays whose theme is the presently authenticated history of England do not comprise the whole of the dramatic genre we may call the history play.

This study will be concerned with but one part of the historical drama of the age of Shakespeare. It must of force limit itself to those plays which deal with the history of England. The emergence of this specific type of history play may perhaps best be studied as part of the general growth of the idea of history as a dramatic subject in the Elizabethan age. But once plays on English history began to be written, such plays inevitably acquired characteristics which could never be shared by plays drawn from the annals of either classical times or continental Europe. There is thus some justification for studying the English history play as an independent phenomenon.

The great age of the history play comes as perhaps the final distinctive manifestation of a new birth of historical writing in England. It may thus be well for us to have clearly in mind the particular historical works which served as the sources of Elizabethan and Jacobean history plays, and which, together with the historical drama and the widely current historical non-dramatic poetry, make up the historical literature of the age of Shakespeare. The Middle Ages had produced its great chroniclers: Matthew Paris, Thomas of Walsingham, Ranulph Higden, and others; but the coming of Henry VII to the English throne in 1485 gave a new impetus to historical writing, for among other things the right of the Tudors to the throne had to be demonstrated. The new English historical writings carried on much of the tradition of the medieval chronicles, but, as we shall see, they were profoundly influenced also by the new historical schools of Renaissance Italy. They were predominantly secular works, intensely nationalistic in their dedication to the greater glory of England, and deliberately propagandistic in their use of history to support the right of the Tudors to the throne and to preach political doctrine particularly dear to the Tudors. Although medieval chroniclers like Geoffrey of Monmouth were also sometimes drawn upon by the historical dramatists of the age of Shakespeare, it was chiefly the writings of these Renaissance English historians which furnished the sources of the history plays with which we shall be concerned.

The new Renaissance history had its birth in England when Duke Humphrey of Gloucester commissioned Tito Livio of Ferrara to write the history of Henry V. But the new historiography begins in earnest with the arrival in England of Polydore Vergil in about 1501. Vergil was commissioned by Henry VII to write a history of England which would, among other things, establish the right of the Tudors to the throne. The *Anglica Historia* was not published, however, until 1534, and in attacking the authenticity of Arthurian legend it did not accomplish the ends Henry VII had envisioned.[2] In 1516, in the meantime, had been published Robert Fabyan's *The New Chronicles of England and France*, essentially a medieval work, but one to be used by Elizabethan writers of history plays. It was to go through three more editions by 1559.

In 1543 appeared Richard Grafton's edition of a verse chronicle of England by John Hardyng, who had recorded English events down to 1436. Grafton continued Hardyng's chronicle down to his own time, and in his book he included also the *Historie of Kyng Rycharde the Thirde*, usually attributed to Sir Thomas More, there printed for the first time. In 1548 Grafton printed posthumously the important work of Edward Hall, a barrister at Gray's Inn. This was *The Union of the two Noble and Illustre Famelies of Lancastre and Yorke*, which, as we shall see, did so much to shape the philosophy of history in the plays of Shakespeare. Hall had based his work upon Polydore Vergil, and by writing in English he gave wide currency to Vergil's particular propagandistic view of English history. Hall's was probably the most influential of all Elizabethan accounts of the period from Richard II to the coming of Henry VII. In 1562 Grafton further brought out *An Abridgement of the Chronicles of England* which went through five editions by 1572.

In 1563 John Foxe produced his *Actes and Monuments* or *The Book of Martyrs*, as it was commonly called, which gave to the history he recorded the strong imprint of his own Reformation prejudices.[3] This work was to be a source for historical plays dealing with the Tudor period, and particularly the biographical plays. In 1565 John Stow published *A Summarie of Englyshe Chronicles*, which went through ten editions by 1611 and was probably the most important short history of England of its age.

But the most important work of all, in so far as the history play is concerned, appeared in 1577, when Raphael Holinshed published his monumental *Chronicles of England, Scotlande and Irelande*. This work was prefaced by a *Description of England*, written by William Harrison, and the history of Ireland was written by Richard Stanyhurst, who used materials collected earlier by the Jesuit, Edmund Campion. Holinshed had little imagination and little historical insight but he was a careful compiler of all that was available to him, and, what is particularly important for the period from Richard II to Henry VII, he used the earlier work of Edward Hall. It was probably through Holinshed that Hall's view of history received its widest currency. A second edition of Holinshed, greatly altered, appeared in 1587, and it was to this edition that Shakespeare and his contemporaries went for the greater part of the Elizabethan and Jacobean historical drama.[4] Holinshed himself had died around 1580, and the additions and expansions in the 1587 volume are the work of John Hooker, Francis Thynne, John Stow, William Harrison, and Abraham Fleming under whose editorial direction the others seem to have worked.[5]

Drama was, of course, not the only literary art in the Elizabethan age which went to the chronicles of England for its inspiration. There is also a long and vital tradition of historical non-dramatic poetry,[6] of which the most significant exemplar, for its influence upon the history play, is *A Mirror for Magistrates* – begun by William Baldwin as a continuation of John Lydgate's *Fall of Princes* – first printed in 1559 after having been suppressed by Queen Mary and enlarged and re-edited six more times by 1587. The *Mirror*, moreover, was widely imitated.[7] Other poetic histories of England include William Warner's *Albion's England*, four books of which were published in 1586 and two more in 1589; Samuel Daniel's *First Foure Bookes of the Civile Wars between the Two Houses of Lancaster and Yorke*, published in 1595, with a fifth book to follow in 1596, a sixth in 1601, and the complete work in 1609. Michael Drayton was the author of several historical poems. His *Piers Gaveston* was printed in 1593, and his *Matilda* followed in 1594. These were both reprinted in 1596, along with *The Tragical Legend of Robert Duke of Normandy*. In that year also Drayton published his *Mortimeriados*, which he was later to re-write and republish in 1603 as *The Barons Warres*. A related work, although not entirely historical, is Drayton's *Poly-Olbion*, a long topographical poem inspired by Camden's *Britannia*. This was first published in 1612 and then in an enlarged edition in 1622. The age was one of deep interest in history, manifest in prose, poetry, and the drama, and it was to the same preoccupations and tastes as the others that the historical drama catered.

Much confusion has resulted, I believe, from the use of the term 'chronicle play' to refer to the large body of extant plays which take as their subject matter the history of England. The term is always used with the unstated implication that a chronicle play somehow differs from a history play, although what a history is and just how a 'chronicle' may differ from it is never made clear. *Henry V* is labelled a 'chronicle play' and *Julius Caesar* a history, but the only generic difference between the two plays is that the one is drawn from English history and the other from Roman; and although Roman history could never have the same significance as English history to the Elizabethans, both are parts of the great sphere of history, and it is ridiculous to make generic distinctions on the basis of the national origin of subject matter. The term 'chronicle' is used, moreover, to refer to a kind of formless, episodic drama, and the implication is usually that this was the only kind of drama in which the history of England was ever treated. The inadequacy of this notion I shall attempt to demonstrate below. Since a meaningful distinction between 'chronicle' and history is impossible, we had best abandon the term 'chronicle' entirely. Plays which deal with the history of any country are history plays, and no other critical term is needed.

The Elizabethans themselves have left us little of value in so far as a definition of the history play is concerned. The famous induction to *A Warning for Fair Women* (1599), in which History appears upon the stage with Tragedy and Comedy, tells us something about tragedy but does nothing to define the history play. The editors of the Shakespeare Folio of 1623 divided his plays into tragedies, comedies, and histories; but it is not likely that Heminges and Condell approached their task with fine critical distinctions, as we know, for instance, from their inclusion of *Cymbeline* among the tragedies. Under histories, they included only Shakespeare's plays on recent British history, but certainly no Elizabethan would have questioned the historicity of such plays as *Julius Caesar* and *Antony and Cleopatra*, to say nothing of *King Lear* and *Macbeth*. It seems likely that the editors of the Folio were most interested in presenting Shakespeare's plays on recent English history in chronological order. This they did, labelling the group histories. All other plays they grouped as either comedies or tragedies – except for *Troilus and Cressida*, about which there was apparently some confusion – ignoring whether they were histories as well. The designations on the title-pages of quartos are equally useless, for the term 'history' was applied to almost anything.

Schelling called the history play a distinctively English product which sprang suddenly into being with the great tide of British nationalism and patriotism that accompanied the defeat of the Spanish Armada in 1588, and he held that it was more closely related to non-dramatic literature than to other forms of the drama.[8] Schelling made little attempt to fix the limits of the history play as a genre, and in separating it from the general course of Elizabethan drama he was, if anything, misleading. William Dinsmore Briggs, on the other hand, defined the history play in a more arbitrary manner:

Let us define the chronicle history as a dramatic composition purporting to draw its materials from the chronicles (or from an equivalent source), treating these materials in a way to bring out their accidental (particularly chronological) relations, recognizing as a rule no other principle of connection than that of personality, and having the general character of a survey of a more or less arbitrarily limited period.[9]

The limitations of such a definition are obvious. Even in so far as form alone is concerned, it will fit only the crudest specimens of the history play. Its inadequacy is implicit in that it cannot apply to such plays as *Woodstock*, *Edward II*, or *Richard II*, where we find well-knit dramatic structure and integrating forces far more important than the chronological. There is, moreover, in the greatest history plays a distinct political purpose which Briggs ignored. The history play cannot be defined on the basis of dramatic form, for the forms in which we find it are many. Far more important than form is the dramatist's artistic intention. Schelling and Briggs merely perpetuated what A. P. Rossiter has termed 'an academic myth raised by last century aversion to morals and politics, with the resulting failure to estimate aright the shaping influence of the Morality in particular and allegory in general' on the mature Elizabethan history play.[10] This is the critical myth, still widely accepted, which would define the Tudor history play as an episodic, disintegrated, non-didactic pageant.

A more realistic distinction has been drawn by Professor Alfred B. Harbage in his separation of Shakespeare's plays into history and fable.[11] Among the histories he would include the ten English and three Roman history plays and *Troilus and Cressida*; all others he would call fables. The primary distinction between the two groups, he holds, is that in fable 'the relationship among the characters is mainly personal and domestic, not political; and vice and virtue operate on individuals directly, not through the intermediary of national programs or party platforms' (page 124); in histories, on the other hand, moral choices are determined by national and political, rather than personal, concerns. The matter of fable, he holds, could be altered freely to suit the dramatist's purposes, whereas the authors of history plays were more closely restricted to their sources.

Professor Harbage is correct in pointing to the political motivation of history, and his distinction is essentially a valid one, although one might question his categorization of Shakespeare's plays, particularly since it is based upon a rigid distinction between history and tragedy which would deny to plays like *Coriolanus* and *Antony and Cleopatra* the status of tragedy. But as a means of defining the history play, Harbage's distinction does not go far enough. One wonders whether, in actual analysis of a play, the line between private and political conduct can be clearly drawn. The political and the personal are often inseparable,[12] and it is perhaps inevitably so in a dramatist such as Shakespeare who saw the problems of state in terms of the personality of the ruler and who conceived of society as a dynamic organism in which the goodness of individual men and women was indispensable to the health of the political whole.

The freedom with which a dramatist treats his sources depends largely upon personal attitudes and purposes. Robert Greene in his *Alphonsus of Aragon* could take a widely celebrated historical figure out of Bartolommeo Fazio's history of Naples and involve him in a mosaic of imaginary battles and romance situations, without any concern for historical truth whatsoever. When Shakespeare used Plutarch, he followed his sources much more faithfully than he did when he used Holinshed. To assume that there was in England before the middle of the seventeenth century any great concern for historical accuracy as an end in itself is unwarranted. The purpose of a history, as I shall explain below, was not to present truth about the past for its own sake; it was to use the past for didactic purposes, and writers of history, both non-dramatic and dramatic, altered their material freely in order better to achieve their didactic aims.[13] The King John story furnishes an excellent example. The chronicles through Polydore Vergil had all treated John harshly and from a Catholic point of view, but Reformation writers, from John Bale through Shakespeare, freely adapted the account to serve their own Protestant purposes.

Harbage's distinction, although useful and pertinent, will thus not give us all that we need in order to isolate the history play as a distinct dramatic genre. Another significant contribution to a definition of the history play has been that of Professor Lily B. Campbell. She has recognized that the historical dramatist attempted to fulfil the purposes of the historian as he and his contemporaries saw those purposes. But the actual criteria Miss Campbell offers are too narrow to be meaningful. The historical dramatist, she holds, deals with politics as opposed to ethics, with the public rather than the private virtues:

... it is to this distinction between private and public morals that we must look for the distinction between tragedy and history. Tragedy is concerned with the doings of men which in philosophy are discussed under *ethics*; history with the doings of men which in philosophy are discussed under *politics*.[14]

Like Harbage's distinction, to which it is closely allied, this is of course true. But as a definition of the history play it is too narrow, for all works which concentrate on the public virtues are not histories. And, as Miss Campbell recognizes (page 16), the public and private virtues are so completely interwoven in general Renaissance concepts of kingship that it is almost impossible for a dramatist to deal with the one to the exclusion of the other. No definition which places history and tragedy in mutually exclusive categories will stand the test of close examination. Miss Campbell has recognized, however, serious historical purpose as the distinguishing feature of the history play, and she has also recognized the political bases of Shakespeare's histories.

This historical purpose has also been recognized by E. M. W. Tillyard, who regards Shakespeare's history plays as designed to express a providential view of history in terms of the official Tudor interpretation of earlier events, particularly as expounded by Edward Hall. Tillyard feels that Shakespeare, in his use of Hall, asserts order, degree, and divine providence in the world. He sees Hall's 'Tudor myth' as presenting 'a scheme fundamentally religious, by which events evolve under a law of justice and under the ruling of God's Providence, and of which Elizabeth's England was the acknowledged outcome'.[15] And what he interprets as Shakespeare's conception of history, Tillyard calls the general Elizabethan conception and the doctrine which all of the best history plays embody.

What Tillyard says of Shakespeare is largely true, but by limiting the goals of the serious history play within the narrow framework of Hall's particular view, he compresses the wide range of Elizabethan historical drama into entirely too narrow a compass. There were other schools of historiography in Elizabethan England. The providential history of Hall, in fact, represents a tradition which, when Shakespeare was writing, was already in decline.[16] To dismiss, for instance, as Tillyard does (page 21), Machiavelli and all that he brought to historical method as lying 'outside the main sixteenth-century interests' is clearly short-sighted. In historiography, as in other intellectual areas, the Elizabethan age was one of flux and uncertainty, with new and heretical notions competing in men's minds against old established ideas which could no longer be accepted without doubt and questioning. Both the old and the new notions of history may be found reflected in Tudor history plays. There is room for Marlowe as well as Shakespeare. We cannot consider the history play outside the scope of Elizabethan historiography, as both Tillyard and Miss Campbell have wisely perceived, but we must have a more adequate conception of Elizabethan historical purpose and method than Tillyard has offered.

To understand the history play, we must return to an Elizabethan point of view with regard to subject matter. We cannot limit our analysis to plays on known British history, as is usually done. For instance, how much of the story of King Brute and his descendants, which we today relegate to the realm of myth, was considered actual history by Shakespeare and his contemporaries? And what of that vast body of romantic and apocryphal legend which attaches to every great historical figure and to every historical era, and which was so perpetuated in folk legendry that to Elizabethan chroniclers it was usually indistinguishable from actual historical fact? The body of plays drawn from such matter is a vast one. To what extent must they be included in any concept of the history play as a distinct dramatic genre? We must attempt to see the limits of history as the Elizabethans saw them; yet we cannot fall into the morass which Tucker Brooke so clearly saw when he warned that any discussion of the subject is in danger of 'losing itself hopelessly in the attempt to follow such quasi-historical will-o'-the-wisps as *George a Greene* and *James IV*'.[17] Tucker Brooke saw clearly the need for a definition of the history play, but he could find none which fitted all he chose to call histories. He finally contented himself with grouping all Elizabethan plays dealing with historical or pseudo-historical subjects into five general categories. The relations between these categories are often very vague; what makes all of them history plays is not clear.

The problem is a complex one, and there will always be some plays which defy classification. I believe, however, that we can establish certain general principles which will aid us in definition. We must recognize, to begin with, that any definition of a literary genre is essentially an abstract ideal, and that no conceivable definition will apply equally well to every play we choose to call a history play. Our definition must describe an ideal to which only some history plays will conform fully; the others fall within the genre by virtue of their striving for this ideal, whether or not they achieve it to any appreciable degree. Our concept of the history play is necessarily a twentieth-century construct which we impose upon a relatively homogeneous body of drama which the Elizabethans themselves made no attempt to define but which by its very homogeneity constitutes a separate dramatic genre, whether or not the Elizabethans so conceived of it.

As our principal distinguishing feature, we may assume with Lily B. Campbell that a history play was one which fulfilled what Elizabethans considered the purposes of history. This does not mean that the historical intention was necessarily more important than the dramatic one; a dramatist's primary concern is always to create drama. It implies merely that when a dramatist went to history for his subject matter he could do so with an understanding of the meaning and implications of the historical genre, and the purposes of history would thus naturally become the purposes of his play. To determine whether he first decided to write history or first decided to write a play is like asking whether the chicken preceded the egg, or vice versa. In the history play the dramatic and the historical intentions are inseparable. The dramatist's first objective is to entertain a group of people in a theatre. When he goes to history for his subject matter, however, he assumes the functions of the historian as well.[18]

With this in mind, we must determine, if necessarily only in broad and general terms, what to an Elizabethan was a purpose of history and what was not. We must remember that Elizabethan historical purposes were many and that, as the Renaissance reached maturity in England, particularly in the early seventeenth century, historical purposes were modified and changed. The legendary British history of *Gorboduc* and the Roman history of *Sejanus* are both history plays, although the truth of the events related and the purpose of each play may be far apart. It was not until the seventeenth century that anything approaching a modern conception of history began to evolve in England. We must further try to determine what, to people of the historical era with which we are dealing, was historical subject matter and what was not. This also is difficult, for the age of the English Renaissance is a long one and it embraced many cultural and historical events and points of view. Gorboduc was a real king for John Caius, but a mythical one for Edmund Bolton.

What then was a historical purpose in Renaissance England? Wallace K. Ferguson has written that an Italian humanist historian would have offered three reasons for the writing of history:

that it is a form of literature, highly regarded by the ancients and presenting attractive opportunities for the exercise of style; that it has great practical value since it teaches moral, ethical, and political lessons; and finally, that his history celebrated the past and present glories of his native land or of the state to which it was dedicated.[19]

Some Elizabethan historians might have offered much the same justification for their craft, for the Italian humanist history of Leonardo Bruni and his followers had begun its inroads into England in the middle of the fifteenth century. Duke Humphrey of Gloucester had corresponded with Bruni himself, and he had invited to England one of Bruni's most important disciples, Poggio Bracciolini.[20] It was upon the invitation of Duke Humphrey that the first English life of his brother Henry V was written, as we have noted, by Tito Livio of Ferrara, a humanist disciple of Pier Candido Decembrio.[21] The great work of humanist historiography in England was to be Sir Thomas More's *History of Richard III* which, as Edward Fueter has pointed out, followed closely the principles of Bruni and his school.[22] Polydore Vergil, who was brought to England by Henry VII and given the Archdeaconry of Wells, drew fully upon Italian humanist principles in writing his great *Anglica Historia*, and Vergil was closely imitated by the English chroniclers upon whom Shakespeare and his fellows drew directly for their history plays. The later Florentine historical school of Machiavelli and Guicciardini also left its mark in England, for it was in this tradition that Francis Bacon wrote his *History of Henry VII*.[23]

Principles of humanist historiography made their way into England through France as well as directly from Italy. Bernard André of Toulouse was brought to England to serve as tutor to Prince Arthur, and he incorporated humanist principles in his

History of Henry VII. The humanist influence upon French historiography had received great impetus in 1499, when Louis XII had commissioned Paulus Aemilius of Verona to write the work which became *De Rebus gestis Francorum libri X*, and in which were incorporated the historical principles of Leonardo Bruni. Paulus Aemilius was succeeded by Du Haillan, by Jean de Serres, whose work in Edward Grimestone's translation was to be the source of Chapman's *Byron* plays, and, perhaps most important, by Jacques-Auguste de Thou, whose *Historia sui Temporis*, begun in 1593 and still unfinished at his death in 1607, carried on the tradition of journalistic contemporary history, best exemplified in the Italian work of Paolo Giovio.[24] French humanist historians, and particularly Huguenots like Serres, were widely read and translated in England.

The Italian humanist historians began with an intention to draw a distinction between truth and legend, an intention they proclaimed in their prefaces and held up as their credo. Wherever possible they abandoned the ancient myths about the founding of their cities and instead examined the earliest archaeological records so as to write a true account. Flavio Biondo of Forli, one of the most diligent of humanist researchers, showed this critical tendency when he wrote of Geoffrey of Monmouth: 'Although I have read with care all the accounts I could find anywhere, I have never found anything so full of trivialities and of lies; to such an extent that the contents of this book outdo all the dreams of the drunken or feverish.'[25] It must be remembered, however, that the protest of historical truth was rarely more than a pose when matters of contemporary concern were involved, for the humanists never let truth stand in their way when they wished to glorify their native cities or to present political doctrine of immediate concern. These two latter purposes were far more vital to them.

The glorification by the humanists of history as a form of rhetoric need not concern us in so far as the historical purposes of Elizabethan dramatists are concerned, although it does remind us that the writing of history was always conceived of as a literary endeavour. Some of the other humanist ideals, however, are very important. Among these is the strong nationalist bias which we find in humanist history. Bruni and his followers sought to glorify their native lands. They abandoned the universal history of the Middle Ages, and they wrote national history instead. Giovanni Villani, one of the greatest of the prehumanist Italian historians, although a Florentine himself, had devoted to Florence only a small part of his history of the world; Bruni and his followers wrote of their native cities, whose glories they hoped to eternize. One of the most obvious purposes of Tudor historical dramatists carries on this humanistic tradition; it is the patriotic purpose, a nationalistic glorification of England.

Later humanist history differed both from medieval history and from its own antecedents in Petrarch, Boccaccio, and even Bruni in a concern with the political events of its own day. It came to serve a politico-journalistic function.[26] Since the Italian humanist historians were themselves politicians and men of affairs, they wrote of the contemporary politics they knew so well, to praise and to condemn the statesmen of their own times. Of this tendency Paolo Giovio is probably the best example, with his *Historiarum sui temporis libri XIV* and his many biographies of great Italian contemporaries. The humanist heritage in Elizabethan historiography came to include a place for contemporary history. While the Tudors lived, censorship made it impossible for dramatists to treat contemporary English history. The accession of James I, however, was followed by a wave of history plays on the reign of Elizabeth. Elizabethan dramatists did turn freely to contemporary continental history in such plays as Marlowe's *Massacre at Paris* and Chapman's *Byron* plays and *Chabot, Admiral of France*. The histories of foreign countries were very popular in Tudor England, as we know from the great vogue both of those written by Englishmen – such as William Thomas's *Historie of Italie* (1549) and Richard Knolles' *Generall Historie of the Turkes* (1603) – and of the numerous translations into English of foreign histories, among the most notable of which were Guicciardini's *Wars of Italy*, Machiavelli's *History of Florence*, and Contarini's *History of Venice*. These plays on contemporary foreign history lie outside the scope of this volume, but they constitute a species of Elizabethan drama which might well reward further study.

But the most important feature of Italian humanist history, and the one which perhaps most strongly affected Elizabethan historical drama, was its particular moral and didactic purpose. Humanist history, of course, was not unique in its didacticism. In this it was merely following the model of Greek and Roman history; medieval history had been fully as didactic, although its didacticism had been of a different sort. Bruni regarded history, as B. L. Ullman points out,[27] as the 'guide of life', one of the surest means of solving contemporary problems. One of the greatest of French humanists, Isaac Casaubon, called history, 'nothing else but a kind of philosophy using examples'.[28] The events of the past were to be studied for the light which they might throw upon the problems of the present and thus serve as a guide to political behaviour. There was in this an important Renaissance assumption: that man had some measure of control over his own destiny, that by his reason and strength he might determine political success or failure. This had been a basic principle of Greco-Roman historiography, but it had been obscured during the Christian Middle Ages with their *de contemptu mundi* emphasis upon the insignificance of human affairs and their doctrine of the helplessness of man in the face of God's will and the power of divine providence as the governing force of the universe. 'At the Renaissance,' writes Reese (page 11), 'classical didacticism, never wholly extinguished in the Middle Ages and newly invigorated as the control of the Church weakened, joined hands with the medieval belief in providence to produce a highly specialized and tendentious form of historical writing that has no exact parallels in any other century.'

This didactic purpose of the humanist historians is in the greatest of Elizabethan history plays. As Lily B. Campbell has pointed out in her study of Shakespeare, historical eras were chosen for dramatization particularly because they offered direct parallels with the events of the dramatists' own times. It was in part for this reason, as well as because it was perhaps the most recent period which censorship permitted dramatists freely to treat, that the period from Richard II to Henry VII was so popular with Shakespeare and his contemporaries.

In the sixteenth century Niccolò Machiavelli and Francesco Guicciardini, the direct descendants of the fifteenth-century humanists, extended this didactic function of history into a new area. The age was full of speculation about the nature of government. The expulsion of the Medici from Florence, the establishment of the republic and then its collapse and the return of the Medici, had led to a concern with types of government, problems of sovereignty, and abstract questions of political theory. The sixteenth-century Florentine historians became political theorists, and history was the device with which they supported their political theories. Francesco Guicciardini, in this respect, was much more of a scientific historian than was Machiavelli. Although he had his own strong prejudices, and although he was concerned with problems less universal than Machiavelli's, he may ultimately be more important as a scientific analyst of history. Guicciardini examined the history of his native city, and he attempted to find in it the causes of political events and thus derive theories of political causation which would be universally applicable. He did not generally warp history to support his preconceived theories.

When Machiavelli came to write his *History of Florence*, however, his political doctrines were already well formulated; he had expressed them in the *Prince* and the *Discorsi*. Rather than derive his political theory from the facts of history as he found them, Machiavelli selected from history what would prove his preconceived notions, and when necessary he deliberately warped history to serve his purposes. This is particularly evident in his *Life of Castruccio Castracani*, in which he transformed the rather contemptible petty tyrant of Lucca into a great statesman such as could unify Italy and repel her foreign invaders. Actually, he drew most of his material from Diodorus Siculus's portrait of Agathocles, the tyrant of Syracuse, using merely the name of Castruccio and such events from his life as suited his doctrinaire purposes. Historical truth for Machiavelli became a matter of relatively small importance. The importance of history was for the support it might lend to political theory. Thus the warping of history so that it may more effectively support political doctrine, such as we find in English history plays from *Kynge Johan* through *Woodstock* and Shakespeare's *Henry IV* plays, had its precedent in the work of one of the most influential historical thinkers of Renaissance Europe.

A word must be said here about the general influence of Machiavelli in Elizabethan England, a subject about which much has been written,[29] but about which there is still widespread confusion. The important intellectual current represented by Machiavelli was not foreign to Elizabethan thought, as so many writers have argued, and as I have sought to disprove in a series of studies.[30] That Machiavelli was misunderstood by many Elizabethans is certain, but it is equally certain that there were many – and, for our purposes, most significantly Christopher Marlowe – who understood him well. We must remember that the popular stage 'Machiavel', the villain who delights in his own villainy and gloats over his successes in lengthy soliloquies, is more surely descended from the Senecan villain-hero and the Morality play Vice than from anything in Machiavelli's writings, and that the 'Machiavel' was a stage device used primarily for dramatic rather than political purposes. The idea of the 'Machiavel' has a life and history of its own, related only obliquely to the history of Machiavelli's actual ideas in England. The 'Machiavel' was subjected to ridicule in *The Jew of Malta* by such a writer as Christopher Marlowe, who we know could also display a true awareness of Machiavelli's actual ideas in *Tamburlaine* and who shared many of Machiavelli's most fundamental premises. Machiavelli's doctrine came from the same classical sources as much of serious Elizabethan political thought, and it was shaped by many of the same Renaissance forces, both historical and intellectual. His philosophy of history is paralleled in Elizabethan historiography, where we may find the same altering of history for political purposes.[31]

The use of history as documentation for political theory was systematized and popularized by Jean Bodin in his widely influential *Methodus ad facilem historiarum cognitionum*, first published in 1566 and circulated throughout Europe. By 1650 it had appeared in thirteen Latin editions. In 1608 Thomas Heywood, one of the most influential of Elizabethan popularizers of history, translated the fourth chapter of Bodin's treatise and published it in the introduction to an English translation of Sallust.[32] Bodin held that from the objective study of history could be learned universal laws which govern political institutions, and that kings by understanding these laws could rule wisely and well.[33] Machiavelli, Guicciardini, and Bodin furthered a purpose in history

which became a part of the general Renaissance cultural heritage
and which made itself felt ultimately in the Elizabethan history
play. Thus the use of history for the exposition of political theory
has its roots distinctly in Italian humanism.

These, then, represent the more important aspects of the Italian
humanist influence in Elizabethan historical drama. The humanist
influence, however, was far from the only current in Elizabethan
historiography. There was an older current which we may find
extending from the earliest medieval chronicles well into the
seventeenth century. This was the tradition of Christian historiography which, as R. G. Collingwood has pointed out,[34] was
universal, providential, apocalyptic, and periodized. It was anti-
nationalist, emphasized world history, and began usually with the
creation of Adam. It treated history as above all the illustration
of the working out of God's judgement in human affairs, and thus
it tended to ascribe relatively little to the independent judgement
or to the will of humanity. And – of great importance – it saw in
history an intelligible and rational pattern which was inevitably
good and which always affirmed the justice of God.[35] It is just
such a pattern which both Lily B. Campbell and E. M. W. Tillyard
have found in Shakespeare's history plays. And finally, although
this has little significance for drama, Christian history divided the
experience of man on earth into certain distinct epochs, each of
which had peculiar characteristics of its own, and each of which
came to an end with a cataclysmic event, Noah's flood and the
birth of Christ being typical 'epoch-making' events.

This Christian philosophy of history persists throughout the
Elizabethan era, although Elizabethans generally conceded that
in addition to the will of God, the 'primary cause' of all human
events, there were 'secondary causes' which could be found in the
will of men. Chroniclers like Edward Hall learned much from the
new Italian historiography, but they did not abandon the religious
premises of the older Christian historiography. Hall differed from
his medieval predecessors in his strong political partisanship. He
interpreted the purposes of God to coincide with the purposes of
the Tudors; the Wars of the Roses were to him part of a divine
plan which would culminate in the accession of Henry VII. His
school of historiography made great improvements in historical

method, some directly due to Italian humanistic examples, and it was marked by peculiarly sixteenth-century English political prejudices, but the medieval Christian current in it is nevertheless very strong.

In Thomas Blundeville's treatise on history,[36] which is typically Elizabethan in its mingling of humanist and medieval notions, we find as the first reason for reading history 'that we may learn thereby to acknowledge the providence of God, whereby all things are governed and directed ... that nothing is done by chance, but all things by his foresight, counsel, and divine providence.'[37] Charles H. Firth has written that 'the Elizabethans in general held this belief that Providence intervened in the government of the world, and most of them held that it was the business of the historian as a teacher of morality to point it out when he related the events.'[38] Firth has indicated this notion at the basis of Raleigh's *History of the World*, one of the most ambitious and influential historical works of its age. In 1622 the idea appears in Edmund Bolton's *Hypercritica, or Rule of Judgement for Writing or Reading our Histories*, a highly influential work which incorporated also many of the ideals of the humanists. Of the four duties of the historian, Bolton lists as first: 'As a Christian cosmopolite to discover God's assistance, disappointments, and overrulings in human affairs'.[39]

Its providential scheme is the most important aspect of medieval historiography which we find in the Elizabethan history play. Neither its universalist bias nor its concept of periodization is particularly significant in this respect. Neither was, in any case, applicable to the requirements of drama. The rational pattern which Christian historians found in human events, however, fitted perfectly the needs of drama, and this aspect of Christian history came to have a large part in the history play. One of the most important historical purposes of many Tudor dramatists was to show the logic and reason in God's control of political affairs.

We thus can isolate two distinct trends which exerted an influence upon Elizabethan historiography: a humanist trend essentially classical in origin, and a medieval trend based upon the premises of Christian belief. We cannot suppose, however, that in the minds of Elizabethans there was any clear distinction between these two lines of influence. Writers like Blundeville and Bolton fuse the two traditions without apparent awareness of any inherent contradiction. Both historical traditions found expression in the drama, and in the greatest history plays of the era we find an easy mingling of the two.[40] In *Richard II*, *King John*, and the *Henry IV* plays, Shakespeare uses history both to glorify England and to support temporal political doctrine, and at the same time he uses it to assert divine providence in the universe and to illustrate a rational plan in human events. The English Renaissance, in most intellectual areas, shows an easy merging of the medieval and humanist.

There were other currents in Elizabethan historiography, such, for instance, as the antiquarian school of Bale, Leland, and Camden. Only one other historical influence is of any real significance for the drama, however, and that is the historical tradition of classical antiquity, which is embodied most clearly in the Roman histories of Jonson and Chapman. The Italian humanist historians, had, of course, modelled their work upon the classics. Bruni, as Ullman points out,[41] had drawn his philosophy of history largely from Cicero, and Livy was the ideal which all of the humanists hoped to equal. In the later Italian Renaissance, the work of Polybius was an influence of particular importance, and we may find its marks clearly in Machiavelli and his school.

Most of the purposes of Italian humanist history are thus also the purposes of classical history. There are, however, certain differences between the two. One is the substantialist metaphysics underlying classical history.[42] Another is the strong Stoical trend in classical history, a trend perhaps most notably present in Polybius. The great value of history was for the lessons which the past might teach the present, and of these lessons the most important for Polybius was that of how to bear political misfortune:

> But all historians, one may say without exception, and in no half-hearted manner, but making this the beginning and end of their labour, have impressed on us that the soundest education and training for a life of active politics is the study of history, and that the surest and indeed the only method of learning how to bear bravely the vicissitudes of fortune is to recall the calamities of others.[43]

History for Polybius would not necessarily teach a ruler to avoid the disasters of others; it could, however, teach him to bear them with fortitude and thus to attain a victory over self which Polybius considered more important than victory over circumstances. The use of history for the exposition of Stoical philosophy as an answer to political problems became, particularly in the Jacobean drama, an important dramatic purpose. We may find it most notably in George Chapman's *Tragedy of Caesar and Pompey*.

Although medieval chroniclers had sometimes recorded the insignificant private affairs of individuals, and something of this practice is carried over in the work of uncritical compilers like Holinshed, the subject matter of Renaissance history was the life of the state. To borrow Fulke Greville's words written in another context, it was 'the growth, state, and declination of princes, change of government, and laws, vicissitudes of sedition, faction, succession, confederacies, plantations, with all other errors or alterations in public affairs'.[44] We may summarize the purposes for which these matters were treated under two general headings. Those stemming from classical and humanist philosophies of history include (1) a nationalistic glorification of England; (2) an analysis of contemporary affairs, both national and foreign, so as to make clear the virtues and the failings of contemporary statesmen; (3) a use of past events as a guide to political behaviour in the present; (4) a use of history as documentation for political theory; and (5) a study of past political disaster as an aid to Stoical fortitude in the present. Those stemming from medieval Christian philosophy of history include (6) illustration of the providence of God as the ruling force in human – and primarily political – affairs, and (7) exposition of a rational plan in human events which must affirm the wisdom and justice of God.

We may then define history plays as those which use, for any combination of these purposes, material drawn from national chronicles and assumed by the dramatist to be true, whether in the light of our modern knowledge they be true or not. The changing of this material by the dramatist so that it might better serve either his doctrinal or his dramatic purposes did not alter its essential historicity in so far as his Elizabethan or Jacobean audience was concerned. Source thus is an important consideration, but it is secondary to purpose. Plays based upon factual matter which nevertheless do not serve ends which Elizabethans considered to be legitimate purposes of history are thus not history plays.[45] John Webster's *White Devil* and *Duchess of Malfi* might be included among examples of such plays. Whether a dramatist considered certain matter mythical or factual is often impossible now to determine. Ultimately each play must be judged individually with all our modern knowledge brought to bear upon it, and still there will be plays about which we can never be entirely certain. But if a play appears to fulfil what we know the Elizabethans considered to be the legitimate purposes of history, and if it is drawn from a chronicle source which we know that at least a large part of the contemporary audience accepted as factual, we may call it a history play

But what of that great body of the world's legendry which, if traced far back enough, has its roots in factual sources? A legend based upon actual fact may, through a passage of time, pass out of history and become folk-lore. This may occur when it is taken out of its historical context and told, modified, and retold as popular literature, with no attempt to fulfil the functions of history. This is true of the *Hamlet* story. Plays based upon such legends, although they may have serious political undertones, as does *Hamlet*, cannot be called history plays, for their political implications are secondary to the dominant purposes of the plays.

We must also remember that there is inherent in history a romantic quality which in every age has had a wide popular appeal, but which seems to have delighted the Elizabethans particularly. This romance is a part of all history plays, but we may find it also in plays which are not history. Dramatists with no historical purpose and little historical sense often used the outer trappings of history in their plays, and thus created a type of historical romance which must not be confused with the true history play. Such a dramatist was Robert Greene, all of whose plays draw upon the romance of history, but accomplish none of the accepted purposes of history. The usual device of the writer of historical romance was to take an Italian novella and to place it in a pseudo-historical setting – as Greene does in his *James IV*, where a tale from Giraldi Cinthio's *Hecatommithi* is placed in the setting of the Scottish court. We may distinguish such plays by an examination of their sources and by the fact that in them the historical setting is used entirely to set off romantic themes which have no relation to the serious purposes of history.

We know that Elizabethans generally distinguished between tragedy and comedy and that they admitted a third form, tragicomedy, although an early writer like Richard Edwards felt the need to justify it in his preface to *Damon and Pythias*. That they made any distinction between tragedy and history as dramatic forms, however, appears very doubtful, although the author of *A Warning for Fair Women* seems to have had some distinction in mind. Francis Meres in his *Palladis Tamia* listed *Richard II*, *Richard III*, *King John*, and *Henry IV* as among 'our best for Tragedy'. History was one of the classes of serious matter suitable for treatment in tragedy. Indeed, as the sixteenth century progressed, history came to be regarded as the most suitable matter for tragedy. Ben Jonson, in a preface to the 1605 edition of *Sejanus*, offers his 'truth of argument' as one of the evidences that he has 'discharged the other offices of a tragic writer', points to his indebtedness to Tacitus, Suetonius, and Seneca, and indicates his specific use of these historians in marginal notes throughout the text of his play.[46]

Although modern critics often have attempted to distinguish between the history play and tragedy as mutually exclusive dramatic genres, it is impossible to do so. History and tragedy, in fact, are closely allied to one another, and, what is more, we find them so linked almost as far back as we can follow Western civilization. Aeschylus in his *Persians* tells the same story of Xerxes' invasion of Greece which we find in Herodotus. We have little reason to doubt that the great story cycles which furnished the plots of Aeschylus, Sophocles, and Euripides were regarded by the Greeks as historically true. F. M. Cornford has argued that Thucydides used as his models for history works of the Greek tragedians, and chiefly those of Aeschylus. In doing so, says Cornford, he was interested chiefly in applying the form of drama to history.[47] J. B. Bury has suggested that the later books of Herodotus may have been influenced by the tragedies of Aeschylus and Phrynicus.[48] It is clear that in classical times there was a relation and interdependence between history and tragedy,[49] that history was a fitting subject for tragedy, just as it was in neo-classic critical theory of the seventeenth century. Evanthius, whose distinction between comedy and tragedy was perhaps the most widely known in the Middle Ages, since his treatise on drama was prefixed to medieval editions of Terence, had written, 'postremo quod omnis comoedia de fictis est argumentis, tragoedia saepe de historia fide petitur'.[50]

Aristotle, who would have reduced history to a strict science, felt the need for a distinction between history and poetry, or tragedy.[51] But his distinctions, as Ullman points out, were ignored by later Greek and Roman historians. Following the lead of Isocrates, they more and more introduced the devices of rhetoric and poetry into their histories, until in the age of Cicero we find a distinction between two types of history: the continuous or general history, and the monograph or particular history. 'The former', writes Ullman (page 44), 'follows the chronological order and serves *veritas* and *utilitas*; the latter is more artistic, more akin to poetry, and aims at *delectatio*'. Cicero himself compared this latter type of history to a play. Sallust's monographs on Jugurtha and Catiline are perfect examples of such 'particular history', and a German scholar has, in fact, analysed them as drama.[52]

The close inter-relation between history and tragedy has continued through the ages. Not all history plays are tragedies, of course, nor are all tragedies histories, but some of the greatest plays of the Elizabethan era are both: *Edward II*, *Richard II*, *Julius Caesar*, *Sejanus*, and others. A history play as we have defined it is, after all, an adaptation of drama to the purposes of history, and tragedy is merely one form of drama. Aristotle's very attempt to separate history and poetry left room for historical tragedy which is a fusion of both. For when he distinguished between the historian who tells what actually has happened and the poet who tells what might have happened, he added that the poet who puts into poetry what actually happened is still a poet, for what has happened might happen.[53] Here then is historical tragedy.

In so far as the form of the Tudor history play is concerned, we must remember that Elizabethan drama, as the last century of investigation has made clear, has its structural roots in two sources: primitive folk ritual and the medieval religious drama. To these were added in the middle sixteenth century the regularizing influences of classical models, but the classical influence never replaced native English dramatic traditions. We have come to recognize, moreover, that of the two native sources of Elizabethan drama, primitive folk pageantry was by far the less important, and that in so far as the religious drama is concerned, we must distinguish between the influence of the Miracle play and that of the Morality play. From them came two separate streams of influence which we can trace throughout the later drama, although, as is inevitable, the two streams coalesce and complement one another. Perhaps nowhere may we see this more clearly than in the history play, for it is almost possible to divide extant history plays into two groups, the one embodying a dramatic structure stemming from the Miracle play and the other one stemming from the Morality.

The Miracle play was episodic in structure. It was virtually plotless in its simple presentation of incidents as the author found them in his biblical or apocryphal sources. There was little attempt to relate one incident to the next; the method was factual, entirely devoid of symbolism or allegory. This episodic structure Briggs called the distinctive form of the Elizabethan history play,[54] but it is obvious that such an unintegrated dramatic form was incapable of fulfilling many of the functions which Elizabethans considered historical. This form does not characterize the Elizabethan history play as a whole, although it continued to be a feature of some history plays throughout the life of the genre. Far more important than this Miracle play influence, however, is that of the Morality play. The history play in its highest form emerged from the Morality, as we shall see from our study of *Kynge Johan* and *Gorboduc*. The Morality play structure was a perfect vehicle for executing the true historical function, for the Morality was didactic and symbolic, designed to communicate idea rather than fact, built upon a plot formula in which every event was related to the others so as to create a meaningful whole. This is so in spite of the extraneous horseplay which came to characterize the later interludes. It was these qualities which the history play had to embody before it could reach its ultimate development. Of the two streams of dramatic influence that of the Morality play is by far the more significant. In so far as dramatic form is concerned, we must,

unlike Schelling, relate the history play to the general development of Elizabethan drama. We see then that it is not only an
entirely representative part of that development, but one which
serves to illuminate aspects of it which otherwise might not easily
be perceived.

NOTES

1. *The English Chronicle Play* (New York, 1902).
2. See Denys Hay, *Polydore Vergil: Renaissance Historian and Man
   of Letters* (Oxford, 1952).
3. See Helen C. White, *Tudor Books of Saints and Martyrs* (Madison,
   Wisconsin, 1963), pages 169–95.
4. For perhaps the best accounts of the Tudor chroniclers see Lily
   B. Campbell, *Shakespeare's 'Histories': Mirrors of Elizabethan
   Policy* (San Marino, California, 1947), pages 55–84; Louis B.
   Wright, *Middle-Class Culture in Elizabethan England* (Chapel Hill,
   1935), pages 297–388; and M. M. Reese, *The Cease of Majesty: A
   Study of Shakespeare's History Plays* (1961), pages 42–65. See also
   W. R. Trimble, 'Early Tudor Historiography 1485–1548', *Journal
   of the History of Ideas* XI (1950), 30–41.
5. See R. Mark Benbow, 'The Providential Theory of Historical
   Causation in Holinshed's Chronicles: 1577 and 1587', University of
   Texas *Studies in Literature and Language* I (1959), 264–76.
6. See Louis R. Zocca, *Elizabethan Narrative Poetry* (New Brunswick,
   N.J., 1950), particularly pages 3–93.
7. Willard Farnham, 'The Progeny of *A Mirror for Magistrates*',
   Modern Philology XXIX (1932), 395–410.
8. pages 2–3. The relation of the history play to the defeat of the
   Armada is a very dubious one, as E. M. W. Tillyard has shown,
   Shakespeare's History Plays (1944), page 101.
9. *Marlowe's Edward II* (1914), pages xxi–xxii.
10. *Woodstock, A Moral History* (1946), pages 8–9.
11. *As They Liked It. An Essay on Shakespeare and Morality* (New
    York, 1947), pages 123–5.
12. The unity of public and private concerns in *Julius Caesar* and
    Coriolanus has been argued by L. C. Knights, 'Shakespeare and
    Political Wisdom', *Sewanee Review* LXI (1953), 43–55.
13. Beatrice R. Reynolds, 'Latin Historiography: A Survey 1400–

1600', *Studies in the Renaissance* II (1955), 7–58, has discussed the slow growth of the ideal of scientific truth as an end in itself in Humanist historiography. She concludes that 'Between the theoretical concept, however, and the actual compositions, scientific objectivity was abandoned. The break-up of the Western empire, realized long after the event, induced a defensive attitude which manifested itself in an early nationalism among the authors of histories. While their prefaces expatiated upon the search for sources and claimed objectivity, the text betrays two areas which were above the law – their nation and their religion' (page 58). Even in the Tudor historians most influenced by the Italian humanists – such as Polydore Vergil and Sir Thomas More – there is never more than the same pretence of objectivity, which is thoroughly belied by the contents of the histories themselves.

14. *Shakespeare's 'Histories'*, page 17.

15. *Shakespeare's History Plays*, pages 320–21.

16. See Leonard F. Dean, 'Tudor Theories of History Writing', *University of Michigan Contributions in Modern Philology* No. 1 (1941), pages 1–24. Dean indicates that although Elizabethan historians generally professed the theories of providential history, they found it difficult to follow them in their actual writings, and he offers Raleigh's *History of the World* as an example. Benbow (op. cit.) has noted, however, that Abraham Fleming in preparing the 1587 edition of Holinshed made alterations which emphasize a theory of history as the working out of God's providential scheme for mankind even more strongly than the notion is stressed either in the 1577 Holinshed or in Hall, and it is significant that this 1587 volume served as the major source for Elizabethan history plays.

17. *The Tudor Drama* (Boston, 1911), page 297.

18. The relation of history to drama has been well summed up by Reese, pages 65–6: 'The matter of Renaissance historiography was the life of the state, and its methods penetrated alike into epic poetry and poetic drama. Reacting to the vitality and urgency of the subject, the dramatists appropriated the themes of history and chose their materials in the same way as the professional historians. The process was largely intuitive. Vergil, More and Hall had shown that events could be recorded in dramatic form, the historical "plot" being shaped to have a beginning, middle and end. But they had done more than that. Their moralising on cause and effect, which amounted to a concern with personal responsibility, had directed attention to the purely human drama that governed

great events. Treated in one way, this drama would be the material of tragedy; but wherever the serious political issue was allowed to dominate, it was the material of the history play, the play that was properly so called because it served the recognised purposes of history. Playwright and historian were equally conscious of their duty as moralists to hold up a mirror to the times, and in this *genre* the didactic functions of history and drama were congenially allied.'

19. *The Renaissance in Historical Thought* (Boston, 1948), page 5.

20. See Lewis Einstein, *The Italian Renaissance in England* (New York, 1902), pages 5, 14, and particularly 307–15.

21. See C. L. Kingsford, *The First English Life of King Henry the Fifth* (Oxford, 1911).

22. *Histoire de l'historiographie moderne* (Paris, 1914), page 199.

23. Fueter, pages 205–8. See also Leonard F. Dean, 'Sir Francis Bacon's Theory of Civil History Writing', *ELH* VIII (1941), 161–83; Thomas B. Wheeler, 'The Purpose of Bacon's *History of Henry the Seventh*', *Studies in Philology* LIV (1957), 1–13.

24. Fueter, pages 178–81.

25. Cited by Reynolds, op. cit., page 11.

26. See Fueter, page 9.

27. 'Leonardo Bruni and Humanistic Historiography', *Medievalia et Humanistica* IV (1946), 45–61.

28. Cited by J. W. H. Atkins, *English Literary Criticism: The Renascence* (1947), page 277.

29. Among the more influential studies have been Edward Meyer, 'Machiavelli and the Elizabethan Drama', *Litterarhistorische Forschungen* I (1897), 1–180; Mario Praz, 'Machiavelli and the Elizabethans', *Proceedings of the British Academy* XIV (1928), 49–97; Napoleone Orsini, *Bacon e Machiavelli* (Genoa, 1936).

30. 'The Significance of Gentillet's *Contre-Machiavel*', *Modern Language Quarterly* X (1949), 153–7; 'Machiavelli and Sidney's *Discourse to the Queenes Majesty*', *Italica* XXVI (1949), 177–87; 'Machiavelli and Sidney: The *Arcadia* of 1590', *Studies in Philology* XLVII (1950), 152–72; 'Sidney's *Arcadia* and the Machiavelli Legend', *Italica* XXVII (1950), 225–35; 'Marlowe and Machiavelli', *Comparative Literature* VI (1954), 349–56.

31. See George L. Mosse, 'The Acceptance of Machiavelli in England', *The Holy Pretence* (Oxford, 1957), pages 14–33.

32. Leonard F. Dean, 'Bodin's *Methodus* in England before 1625', *Studies in Philology* XXXIX (1942), 160–66.

33. See Beatrice Reynolds (ed. and trans.), *Method for the Easy Comprehension of History* by Jean Bodin (New York, 1945); Henrie Sée, 'La Philosophie de l'Histoire de Jean Bodin', *La Revue Historique* CLXXV (1935), 497–505.

34. *The Idea of History* (Oxford, 1946), pages 49–50.

35. For an excellent survey of Christian historiography from its Hebrew origins to its last great appearance in Milton's *Paradise Lost*, see C. A. Patrides, *The Phoenix and the Ladder: The Rise and Decline of the Christian View of History* (Berkeley, California, 1964).

36. *The True Order and Methode of Wryting and Reading Hystories, according to the precepts of Francisco Patricio and Accontio Tridentino, two Italian Writers* (London, 1564), edited by Hugh G. Dick, *Huntington Library Quarterly* III (1940), 149–70.

37. page 165. In this passage Blundeville is translating Accontio. When he follows Patricio we find a somewhat different attitude. Patricio distinguishes between the outward and the inward causes of action, the inward being those over which man himself has control, and the outward being the forces in the world over which he has no control; these logically would include the purposes of God. But history, for Patricio, would concern itself only with inward causes. He writes, in Blundeville's translation, 'the mind is the fountain and father of all actions', and he emphasizes that actions stem from man's environment, his education, family, country, etc., all of which combine to make him do what he does (page 161). Patricio is presenting the attitude of the Italian humanists; Accontio is presenting a medieval Christian idea. It is interesting that Blundeville should have combined the two without realizing the inconsistencies involved. But this was typical of the Renaissance fusion of cultures.

38. 'Sir Walter Raleigh's History of the World', *Proceedings of the British Academy* VIII (1918), 434–5.

39. Cited by Firth, page 435.

40. The Renaissance fusion of Christian and classical ideas of history has been well summed up by Reese (pages 15–16): 'The sixteenth century blended these two conceptions of history by teaching that while God ordains human affairs after a pattern that is rational and inevitably good, secondary causes may be found in the behaviour of men. As moralists, historians had a duty to reveal the logic and benevolence of God's plan and to explain and justify His interventions. ... But the humanist belief in the dignity and

self-determination of man would not permit him to be merely the plaything of fate, even if it were God who directed it. There was a sense in which man's independent choice might fulfil the will of God. This is not as intellectually absurd as it sounds. In finite terms God's omniscience and God's omnipotence are self-cancelling, but finite terms are not appropriate in matters of this kind. Man's own acts were felt to have a positive value. Although enclosed within a foreordained scheme, sixteenth-century history was not determinist.'

41. *Medievalia et Humanistica* IV (1946), 50–52.

42. A metaphysics whose chief category is substance implies that only the unchanging is knowable, since substance, by definition, is fixed in form and cannot change. Since the subject matter of history is not the unchangeable and eternal, but transitory events, a dichotomy thus arose in classical times between history, which was regarded as transitory and unknowable, and the agents of history, which were considered substantial, unchanging in form, and thus knowable. Collingwood thus explains it: 'A distinction is now taken for granted between act and agent, regarded as a special case of substance and accident. It is taken for granted that the historian's proper business is with acts, which come into being in time, develop in time through their phases and terminate in time. The agent from which they flow, being a substance, is eternal and unchanging and consequently stands outside history. In order that acts may flow from it, the agent itself must exist unchanged throughout the series of its acts: for it has to exist before this series begins and nothing that happens as the series goes on can add anything to it or take away anything from it. History cannot explain how any agent came into being or underwent any change of nature; for it is metaphysically axiomatic that an agent, being a substance, can never have come into being and can never undergo any change of nature' (page 43). I have discussed the impact of this substantialist view of history on Marlowe's *Tamburlaine* in 'The Idea of History in Marlowe's *Tamburlaine*', *ELH* XX (1953), 251–66.

43. *Histories*, translated by W. R. Paton (Loeb Classical Library, 1922), I, 3.

44. *The Life of Sir Philip Sidney*, edited by Nowell Smith (Oxford, 1907), page 15.

45. That a truthful tragedy is not necessarily a history is shown in the final lines of the anonymous *A Warning for Fair Women* (sig. K 3ᵛ):

Bear with this true and home-borne Tragedy,
Yielding so slender argument and scope,
To build a matter of importance on,
And in such form as haply you expected.
What now hath failed, tomorrow you shall see,
Performed by History or Comedy.

46. See Joseph Allen Bryant, Jr, 'The Significance of Ben Jonson's First Requirement for Tragedy: "Truth of Argument"', *Studies in Philology* XLIX (1952), 195–213.

47. *Thucydides Mythistoricus* (London, 1907), pages 137–9.

48. *The Ancient Greek Historians* (New York, 1909), pages 33, 69.

49. See B. L. Ullman, 'History and Tragedy', *Transactions of the American Philological Association* LXXXIII (1942), 25–53.

50. Cited by J. W. Cunliffe, *Early English Classical Tragedies* (Oxford, 1912), page xi. ('Finally, although the argument of comedy is all of falsehood, tragedy often is faithfully derived from history.')

51. His distinction, as Ullman (page 26) summarizes it: 'Tragedy imitates the actions of men, history states facts; the purpose of tragedy is to arouse fear and pity, especially through the unexpected and through change of fortune; tragedy deals with a complete action, having a beginning, middle, and end, history does not necessarily do so'.

52. R. Reitzenstein, *Hellenistische Wundererzählungen* (Leipzig, 1906), pages 84 ff.

53. *The Basic Works of Aristotle*, edited by Richard McKeon (New York, 1941), pages 1463–4.

54. *Marlowe's Edward II*, pages ix–xxii.

TWO

The Substance of Shakespeare's 'Histories'*

S. C. Sen Gupta

I

IT may be asked whether historical plays can form a separate class in dramatic literature. All literature is fiction, and the historical playwright takes so much liberty with his materials – the exigencies of the theatre compel him to be even more drastic than the historical novelist – that the mere fact that some of the incidents and characters had their counterparts in reality does not affect their basic fictional quality. On the other hand, if a historical drama – or a historical novel – is a faithful transcript of the past, it will be more history than literature. Secondly, historical literature which represents particular individuals living in particular epochs cannot have the universal significance we demand of the creations of the imagination. The distinction drawn by Aristotle between poetry and history – the statements of poetry are of the nature of universals and those of history are singulars – may be extended to fictional literature which follows history in its outlines even if it departs from facts in details, for such literature, too, is about particular persons who lived at a particular time and in a particular place.

Did Shakespeare himself want to make a separate genre of his historical plays? The titles of *Richard II* (Quarto) and *Richard III* (Quarto and Folio) describe them as tragedies. *Henry V* is, indeed, called a chronicle history and *Henry VIII* a history, but the Quarto (the first issue of it as well as the second) of *Troilus and Cressida* is also called a history, though it is less historical than *Timon of Athens* and much less so than either *Julius Caesar* or *Antony and Cleopatra*. Heminges and Condell, however, who could

* From *Shakespeare's Historical Plays* (1964), pages 1–29. Copyright © Oxford University Press, 1964. Reprinted by kind permission of the publishers, the Clarendon Press, Oxford.

not have been unaware of all this, called the ten plays dealing with English kings 'histories' and placed the Roman plays, and also *King Lear*, *Macbeth*, and *Cymbeline*, which, like the English historical plays, were derived from Holinshed, among the tragedies. The principle of classification adopted in the first Folio is not without its point, and Heminges and Condell may have had the support of Shakespeare himself, for after the Armada writing plays on themes derived from English history became a craze, and Shakespeare either followed a popular fashion or was in the van of it. We know, further, that Tudor monarchs tried to inculcate a particular view of history, and Shakespeare, it is sometimes said, only dramatized what the historians propounded in their chronicles. In a sense these plays were even more historical than the chronicles, many of which failed to draw a distinction between legend and history. In the ten plays classified as 'histories', the incidents do not concern remote and legendary figures such as Lear and Cymbeline[1] but English kings and barons whose actions formed part of authentic history. And although Shakespeare modifies historical data in his English history plays, here he does not take such liberties as in *King Lear* or *Macbeth*. Referring to Shakespeare's modification of his sources in *Macbeth*, a critic has remarked that Macbeth in history was a good man, and Shakespeare's play shows what genius can make of history! One could not say the same of Richard III, an incredible monster, but no invention of Shakespeare who only transferred him from chronicle to drama. Even in *King John*, although Shakespeare makes large modifications, he does not manipulate history in the manner of John Bale, who makes a Protestant martyr of a cowardly villain.

From yet another point of view, these ten plays may be said to form a separate category which is best named 'history', for even if we do not accept the thesis that here Shakespeare wants to mirror the political problems of his own time or the Tudor interpretation of history, there is no doubt that these plays reflect certain definite periods of English history, which sets them apart from other plays in the canon. *Hamlet* could have been written only by a dramatist of the English Renaissance, but the incidents might have happened at any time and Elsinore might be any place in the world. The same thing may be said of the comedies, and also of *King Lear* and *Macbeth*. In *Othello*, the only assumption we have to make is that the heroine is a white woman in love with a man of a coloured race – black or brown – and beyond that it is not necessary to know who are the men of royal siege from whom Othello fetched his life and being or to inquire into the moving accidents by flood and field, which he passed through before coming to Venice. The plots of *Julius Caesar*, *Coriolanus*, and *Antony and Cleopatra* seem to be firmly rooted in history, but except partly in *Coriolanus* the historical background has little to do with the significance of these dramas. Indeed, these Roman plays are not derived from any historian but from Plutarch, who, although he might have given 'essential history', was a literary artist with a didactic purpose rather than a historian. The very scheme of his biographies, his drawing parallel portraits of people far removed from each other, shows that he was interested more in universal moral significance than in local colour. Shakespeare was more concerned about problems of character than about morals, but in the Roman plays he too uses the historical background only to draw out meanings that are independent of history. Even in *Coriolanus* he wants primarily to reveal the tortured workings of impulses and not to transcribe a slice of Roman history.

This is not the impression produced by the historical plays. The two tetralogies cover a definite period – from 1398 to 1485 – and the story is continued after a brief interval in *Henry VIII*, which reproduces events not far off from Shakespeare's own time. *King John* relates to a more remote period, and it is less historical than the other plays in this genre. Nevertheless the story of King John, who attempted a breach with Rome, had a special appeal for Elizabethan England, and in spite of a highly wayward treatment of the sources this drama in spirit and substance produces an impression of historicity. Of the ten plays, nine are about medieval England, and although they are not devoid of universal significance, that significance is rooted in the particular periods which they represent. One prominent feature of all these histories is their largeness. There are generally more speaking parts in a 'history' than in a comedy or a tragedy and the characters are drawn from all shades of life. What is more, the historical plays – *King John* and the two tetralogies – give us the spirit and atmosphere of medieval England as visualized by an Elizabethan dramatist. The interposition of a particular point of view involves the risk of over-simplification, and it may be questioned if a dramatist who omits the Magna Carta from the story of King John and who gives a caricature of Lollardry in Sir John Falstaff can be said to have portrayed the Middle Ages in all their richness and complexity. Indeed, Bernard Shaw goes to the opposite extreme when he says:

Now there is not a breath of medieval atmosphere in Shakespeare's histories. His John of Gaunt is like a study of the old age of Drake. Although he was a Catholic by family tradition, his figures are all intensely Protestant, individualist, sceptical, self-centred in everything but their love affairs, and completely personal and selfish even in them. His kings are no statesmen: his cardinals have no religion: a novice can read his plays from one end to the other without learning that the world is finally governed by forces expressing themselves in religions and laws which make epochs rather than by vulgarly ambitious individuals who make rows.

(Preface to *Saint Joan*)

This is an exaggerated statement, and like all exaggerations it is misleading. Shakespeare's account of John of Gaunt in *Richard II* is indeed too sympathetic and takes no notice of Gaunt's errors and failures. But it is very similar to and may have been derived from Froissart's account, and since Froissart lived for some time in the court of Edward III and Richard II it will not be true to say that such a portrait, although imbued in Shakespeare's drama with Tudor patriotism, is unmedieval in spirit. One is free to hold that not one of Shakespeare's kings, not even Henry V, is a statesman, but they may all the same be true representatives of the medieval idea of kingship. The charge of lack of religion is subtler and has to be examined in greater detail. Shakespeare portrays a number of cardinals – Pandulph, Beaufort, Bourchier, and Wolsey, who, of course, belongs to the Renaissance rather than to the Middle Ages – and the archbishop whom Henry V consults is the highest dignitary of the English church. These princes of the church, it must be admitted, are politicians rather than pious men. Shakespeare does not portray the mysticism or the humble piety of medieval Christianity, neither does Shaw.

But it does not follow that Shakespeare fails to represent other aspects of the religion of the Middle Ages. Although the medieval religious outlook was other-worldly, the medieval church made tall claims of suzerainty over all temporal authority and Pope Innocent III was as much a representative of the Middle Ages as St Thomas Aquinas or St Francis of Assisi. It is this aspect of medieval Catholicism which is portrayed in its successive phases in Shakespeare's plays. Cardinal Pandulph is a legate of Pope Innocent III who raised the papacy to the height of political power, and as a faithful servant of this masterful Pope he treats the secular authority of kings as subservient to the church; he first excommunicates John and then, after extorting abject submission, proceeds to disarm the opposition arrayed against the royal scapegrace. From the days of John to those of Henry IV and Henry V there is a gap of more than two centuries, and we find that from the position of a dictator the priests have descended to that of advisers who comfort, warn, and occasionally rebel. In *Richard II*, the Bishop of Carlisle gives a stern warning to Bolingbroke when Richard is deposed, but his argument is based not on the supremacy of the church but on the inviolability of the king's authority:

> Would God that any in this noble presence
> Were enough noble to be upright judge
> Of noble Richard. Then true noblesse would
> Learn him forbearance from so foul a wrong.
> What subject can give sentence on his king? –
> And who sits here that is not Richard's subject?

IV.1.117–22

At this stage the Pope's authority is not challenged, but he is regarded as an alien power who might prove a source of danger to the English crown. When Winchester is made a cardinal, the Duke of Exeter reminds us in an aside that:

> Henry the Fifth did sometime prophesy:
> 'If once he come to be a cardinal,
> He'll make his cap co-equal with the crown'.

Henry VI, Part One, V.1.31–3

In *Richard III*, Cardinal Bourchier and the bishops play a very ignoble part; they are pawns in Richard's nefarious game and only show how subservient the church has become when a power-ful and unscrupulous king is on the throne. We have travelled a long way since the days of King John and even of King Henry V. In *Henry VIII*, Cardinal Wolsey figures as the last great ecclesiastic who fixes his ambition on Rome and is crushed by the king whom he wanted to serve and control. Here we are in Renaissance England and on the threshold of the English Reformation. If we trace the progress of Shakespeare's cardinals from Pandulph to Wolsey and of English kings from John to Henry VIII, we get a glimpse of the emergence of English nationalism and a vivid picture of a very significant aspect of the transition from the medieval world to the modern. Here, indeed, we can visualize the forces which, lying behind the rows made by vulgarly ambitious men, effect a change from one epoch to another. That is the true function of historical drama as distinct from chronicles or chronicle plays.

2

There are critics who think that the distinction between the 'history play' written by Shakespeare and the top people, and the 'chronicle play' of journeymen is unnecessary. 'It is more useful', says Reese, 'to regard as a history play any that, however partially or inexpertly, handled past events in a serious political spirit.' For such critics the distinction between other men's political plays and those written by Shakespeare 'is rather one of quality than of kind'.[2] But whether of quality or of kind, there is, indeed, a vast difference between the chronicle play and Shakespeare's 'histories'. We need not enter here into the controversy whether Shakespeare found writing historical plays a fashion and followed it or whether he himself set the fashion and others took it up. Even F. P. Wilson admits that *The Famous Victories of Henry the Fifth* is anterior to Shakespeare's work in this branch of drama,[3] and we may make the same assumption about the priority of *The True Tragedie of Richard the third*. An examination of these two plays will be enough to show the difference between the chronicle play and the new genre evolved by Shakespeare. The anonymous playwrights who recorded the careers of Henry V and Richard III were anxious above everything else to report as many episodes as could be compressed within two hours' traffic of the stage. Not that there is no emphasis on the main characters, however crudely these might be drawn. Henry V is a heroic figure; and Richard III is a villain built on the grand scale, a monster without scruples but with a conscience which makes him very human. Yet the dramatists are not primarily concerned to reveal the deeper and subtler shades of their characters; they hurry on from incident to incident, condensing in *The Famous Victories* episodes which supplied Shakespeare with plots for three whole plays and amassing in *The True Tragedie* materials only a fraction of which Shakespeare could make use of in *Richard III*. The similarity between *The True Tragedie* and *Richard III* is so striking that some critics look upon the former as a vamped version of the latter. But the anonymous play, which must have been one of Shakespeare's source-books, elaborates the episode of Mistress Jane Shore who is only mentioned in *Richard III*, and gives elsewhere a large slice of English history from the death of Clarence to the defeat of Richard III at Bosworth Field, relying on such characters as Page, Boy, and Report. Shakespeare does include certain incidents not mentioned in *The True Tragedie* and also elaborates others which are passed over in the older play. But it is not by comparing details here and there that we can find the basic difference between them. What is important is that in Shakespeare's *Richard III*, although it is an early play, incidents, numerous as they are, have no importance of their own but are subordinated to the portraiture of character and the organization of the play as an aesthetic structure. In *The True Tragedie*, although Richard III is powerfully portrayed and the Jane Shore episode is made the basis of a moral homily, the total impression is of a string of incidents loosely connected through character and idea.

The present study proceeds on the assumption that the greatness of Shakespeare consists chiefly in his ability to create men and women, who, if not imitations of reality, have the vividness of living characters. In the historical plays Shakespeare succeeds in endowing the dead skeletons of history with flesh and blood, and also in creating, with or without suggestions from history, new characters that are more real than living men. This aspect of Shakespeare's genius will be dealt with in greater detail later on. What is relevant in the present context is an inquiry into the central idea – moral, political, or dramatic – which may be said to emerge from the whirl of incidents and the crowd of characters. By the time Shakespeare came to handle historical materials, histories and historical poems – and plays – were being written with the definite purpose of inculcating what has been called the Tudor historical myth. It is often thought that Shakespeare's historical plays are also essentially homiletic, that they are an elaborate discourse on the duties of kingship and the dangers of civil dissension. Tillyard, for example, says that Shakespeare was among the select few who saw a dramatic and philosophical pattern in the period covering the Wars of the Roses, and he is thus to be distinguished from those who saw it as a welter of misery and a rich repertory of lessons on the fickleness of fortune and the chastisement of peccant individuals.[4] Many other critics think that Shakespeare's histories were a mirror of the politics of his own day. Lily B. Campbell points out that there is, indeed, a dividing line between ethics and politics, and

... it is to this distinction between private and public morals that we must look for the distinction between tragedy and history. Tragedy is concerned with the doings of men which in philosophy are discussed under *ethics*; history with the doings of men which are discussed under *politics*.[5]

Although most people think – and rightly think – that the historical plays deal primarily with the fortunes of princes, the art of government, and the doings of men which are discussed under politics, yet there are others who seem to hold that the dividing line between politics and ethics mentioned above is not easy to draw and that patterns of the old Morality play with its emphasis on private morals survive in all the historical plays, most notably in the two parts of *Henry IV*. It is contended that, much as Elizabethan drama owes to foreign influences and the original genius of the dramatists, it is largely a continuation of native English drama beginning with the cycle plays, and some have gone so far as to hold that the Morality structure is deeply embedded in Shakespearian tragedy and comedy. In Dover Wilson's view, '*Henry IV* was certainly intended to convey a moral. It is in fact

Shakespeare's greatest morality play'.[6] The essence of the Morality play is that man is confronted with a choice between good and evil, he is tempted by the forces of Evil and then is saved from imminent disaster by his own virtues or by the mediation of some super-human power. According to Dover Wilson, Shakespeare symbol-izes Vanity in Falstaff, anarchic old-world Chivalry in Hotspur, and the Rule of Law and the new ideal of service to the state in the Lord Chief Justice. The technical centre of the play is thus not the fat knight but the lean Prince, who links the revelry of East-cheap with the serious affairs at Westminster, and who finally abandons vanity for government. It has been suggested that Richard III is lineally descended from the medieval Vice who was both a clown and a villain.[7]

The limitations of the above theory will be effectively demon-strated if, leaving out *Richard III* for the moment, we consider its applicability to *Henry IV* alone. First, even if the Lord Chief Justice, who is not even named, is taken as a representation of the rule of law, Hotspur is too subtly drawn to be looked upon as a mere symbol of anarchic chivalry. What is more damaging to this moralistic interpretation of *Henry IV* is that it gives a completely misleading picture of Falstaff. He is indeed a drunkard and a lecher, but to label him a personification of Vanity is no more adequate as an explanation of his character than yellow is as a definition of gold. He is a much more intricate and a much more sympathetic character than the Sir John Paunch imagined by Quiller-Couch and Dover Wilson,[8] and that is why the Rejection at the end produces an impression of discomfort which Shakespeare himself seems to have anticipated, and tried to counter by holding forth the assurance which he did not honour that he would continue the story of the old knight in his account of the reign of Henry V. Falstaff is a roisterer and a reveller but he is also the exponent of an attitude to life which is revealed in its different facets in ten long Acts, and of which, in spite of the Rejection at the end of *Henry IV, Part Two*, we have no reason to think Shakespeare totally disapproved. When Falstaff ridicules Puritanism by describ-ing his sins in scriptural phraseology, he does it with so much grace and with such inverted appropriateness that we feel that here, if anywhere, we hear the voice of Shakespeare himself, inveighing against the cramping effect of religion and morals. Even if we leave Shakespeare the man out of account, he must have been a poor dramatic moralist if he intended to present such an enchanting parodist of the scriptures as a symbol of the loathsomeness of irreligion.

An equally serious objection – and one that is admitted by the sponsors of this theory – is that in this play there are really no alternatives to choose between, even though a tension between two opposing forces is of the essence of a Morality play. Arguing along the lines laid down by realistic critics, we may say that Prince Hal's soliloquy at the end of the first tavern scene (*Henry IV, Part One*, I.2) only follows a theatrical convention of giving information to the audience. But the speech also reflects character, for it correctly describes the Prince's attitude throughout the whole course of the story. All through the play he looks upon his boon companions as base contagious clouds that seem to strangle him but cannot. He does not take part in the Gadshill robbery; he only robs the robbers, and in trying to outwit Falstaff is over-whelmed by Falstaff's lying like truth. Although a 'good angel' to Falstaff, he sees that the money robbed is 'paid back again' – a procedure which Falstaff disapproves of as 'double labour'. Indeed, Shakespeare's purpose here seems to be to show that the youthful riotousness alleged by chroniclers against Henry V was only a cloak behind which his greatness lay unbedimmed. It is his father and others who are deceived by appearances; he himself is never the victim of temptation or self-deception. When the call of duty comes he responds to it spontaneously – and without a twinge; he is friends with his father and goes forth to battle, not recklessly like Hotspur, but with courage and a full awareness of the risks involved:

> The land is burning, Percy stands on high,
> And either we or they must lower lie.
> *Henry IV, Part One*, III.3.200–201

Where is the temptation and where is the choice? Falstaff does, indeed, ask him, now that he is friends with his father, to rob the royal exchequer, but the Prince takes no notice of the sugges-tion. Nor is he a lecher or a lady-killer, and it is noteworthy that even in the midst of riotous merry-making his dealings with women are impeccable. He is never guilty of any impropriety towards Mistress Quickly and is not even acquainted with Doll Tearsheet. In spite of what the Lord Chief Justice says about separating him from Falstaff, he does return to his low companions and mixes freely with them, but now, too, he maintains his old aloofness. When Poins broaches the subject of his father's illness, his answer is characteristic:

> By this hand, thou thinkest me as far in the devil's book as thou and Falstaff for obduracy and persistency: let the end try the man. But I tell thee my heart bleeds inwardly that my father is so sick; and keeping such vile company as thou art hath in reason taken from me all ostentation of sorrow.
>
> *Henry IV, Part Two*, II.2.43–7

The only effect vile company has on him is that it has taken away all ostentation of sorrow. Whether his heart bleeds inwardly is another matter, one with which we are not concerned here. This dialogue shows, further, that although a good mixer, he is not for a moment forgetful of the difference in rank and character between himself and the vile company he keeps. When Poins proposes that he and the Prince disguise themselves as drawers, his reaction is characteristic:

> From a god to a bull? A heavy descension! It was Jove's case. From a prince to a prentice? A low transformation! That shall be mine; for in everything the purpose must weigh with the folly.
>
> *Henry IV, Part Two*, II.2.167–70

His purpose weighs with the folly when it is no more than making a fool of Falstaff, but when weightier matters are before him he casts off his folly without a moment's thought. It is only once that he has occasion to reproach himself for neglect of serious duties; when he is busy eavesdropping on Falstaff in his amours and twitting the old rogue, news comes of a tempest of commotion, and he blames himself for idly profaning his precious time when the country is torn with civil dissension. But the quick and curt farewell he gives to Falstaff – 'Falstaff, good night' – and the alacrity with which he hurries to the post of duty show that he was not 'engraffed to Falstaff', never tempted or deluded as the protagonist of a Morality play should be. However painful the final Rejection might be, it was not sudden; neither was it the result of a deliberate choice made at a particular moment, and it was not also due to the intercession of any heavenly power. Even the harried Lord Chief Justice, now exalted to unlooked-for honours and authority, is as much taken by surprise as Falstaff. 'I know thee not, old man', says Henry V on ascending the throne, but he never knew the old man in any intimate sense of the term. He kept the rogue's company partly for a brief holiday, and largely for astounding the world by the denouement of the Rejection, when by dismissing the fat knight the lean prig would be able to shine like the sun emerging from the clouds. There is nothing of the Morality pattern in this game of the sun and clouds.

3

The theory that Shakespeare's historical plays embody the Tudor view of history has received wide currency and should be examined in some detail. The Tudor myth effectively propagated in the time of Henry VII and encouraged in that of his successors has to be related to the medieval concept of life. Although medieval writers were interested in the progress of mundane affairs and some medieval chroniclers like Froissart had a shrewd sense of history, the medieval outlook on life – if the generalization may be permitted – was singularly unhistorical. The mind of medieval Europe was dominated by theology and the principal tenet of medieval Catholicism was the omnipresence of God for whom all things exist simultaneously and in whose knowledge there can be no discursiveness. 'In our knowledge', says St Thomas Aquinas,

there is a double process; one of succession only, when from actually understanding one object we turn our attention to another; the other of causality, as when we arrive at conclusions through principles. The first process cannot apply to God, for the multiple objects we understand successively when they are taken in themselves can be understood all at once when they are seen in one principle. God sees everything in one, namely, in himself alone. Nor does the second process apply; first, because it entails succession, for in working from principles to conclusions, we do not simultaneously consider them both; secondly, because it is a process from the known to the unknown.[9]

The predominant idea in this theological view of life – according to St Thomas, wisdom is equivalent to theology – is of order and unity. All life emanates from God who is one, and although there are contingent occurrences, all mutable things go back to a first immutable. So long as the church retained its supremacy and theology was relied on to govern other sciences and set them in proportion, history was free to explore contingent occurrences and to satisfy men's curiosity about past happenings, because there was the implicit conviction that there was nothing ultimate in such happenings; and when two sciences – say theology and history – are engaged, their respective conclusions need not be taken as counterbalancing each other for the lower should be subsumed under the higher. 'Man', says St Thomas Aquinas, 'is directed to his ultimate end by the notion of the first cause, and to his proximate end by the notion of subordinate movers, as the soldier is directed to victory by the high command, and to his tactical dispositions by the regimental commander.'[10] Looked at from this point of view, all events, even those which seem to be fortuitous, may be properly orientated, and then comprehended in the order of divine providence. The Thomist view of the universe finds adequate expression in Dante's *Divina Commedia*, in which even capricious Fortune is looked upon as a part of the divine order:

> Her permutations never know truce nor pause;
> Necessity lends her speed, so swift in fame
> Men come and go, and cause succeeds to cause.
> *Inferno*, VII.88–90 (translated by D. Sayers)

Dante does not ascribe the course of history to blind chance; for him in spite of fortuitous happenings the universe is like a book in which accidents are bound up with substances as leaves in one volume.

Other medieval writers had not the same assurance, but when confronted by the topsyturvydom of mundane affairs they too tried to explain it by means of their other-worldly philosophy. Medieval theology was anxious to inculcate the virtue of laying up one's treasures in heaven, and one of the surest methods of this propaganda would be to expatiate on the disaster that was to overtake human aspirations after worldly power or wealth. It was shown that vice was sure to bring its own punishment, and if a moralist failed to connect a person's unhappy ending with any known vice, he would try to invent one. Dido, as Virgil presents her, is a spotless heroine whose misfortune is undeserved. But Lydgate argues that it was wrong of Dido to remain unprovided with lovers, and noble matrons should not imitate her example.[11] There are occasions, however, when even such excuses cannot be found, and the accepted medieval view is that tragedy is only the story of misfortune, of decline from prosperity:

> Tragedie is to seyn a certeyn storie,
> As olde bokes maken us memorie,
> Of him that stood in greet prosperitee
> And is y-fallen out of heigh degree
> Into miserie, and endeth wrecchedly.
>
> *The Monk's Tale*, Prologue, 85–9

It is immaterial whether this fall from prosperity is deserved or undeserved, and Chaucer's Monk, who gives the above definition, does not mention any hamartia. Tragedy, however, represents only one aspect of life. Comedy gives us the other side of it, for it exchanges a sad beginning for a happy ending: *Est autem comœdia poesis, exordium triste, laeto fine commutans.* 'This is', says Nevill Coghill, 'comedy as Dante, Chaucer, and Lydgate knew and understood it.'[12] Vincent de Beauvais, the author of this definition, does not say that the happiness at the end is deserved.

What is more relevant is that happiness is not likely to remain permanent. The most popular symbol of medieval times is that of the Wheel of Fortune, which in its ceaseless rotation takes a man as surely from prosperity to adversity as from adversity to prosperity. Following Boccaccio, Lydgate portrays Fortune as a 'double fals goddesse' with a hundred hands, who lifts men to high estate and then casts them down to adversity. She is partly an engine of retribution, punishing princes for such vices as pride and covetousness, but she is essentially changeable and does not require any excuse for plunging them down from 'al ther great richesse'. This is all due to Adam's fall from Paradise, and now man is doomed. Reference may be made to the fate of Arsinoe whose sons were for no fault murdered by Cereaunus or of the Scipios who laboured for the community but died in ignominy.[13] The only way to fight Fortune is to cultivate the virtue of fortitude or Glad Poverty, which defies changes in material conditions and sets its trust wholly in Jesus, who 'may best in myscheeff helpe'.

Tudor historiography had its roots in medieval thought and could not get rid of its medieval heritage, but its outlook was essentially humanist and largely free from the domination of theology. It tried to explain human affairs in a human way, laying emphasis on secondary and contingent causes, and although not denying the first cause, keeping it as far as possible in the background. The activities of the 'stormy queen' Fortune were regarded as caprices of chance, and Sidney, a typical Renaissance critic who found history an incomplete discipline, tried to remedy its defects not by cultivating the spirit of *de contemptu mundi* but by escaping into the golden world delivered by poetry.[14] Secondly, Tudor historians were fervent nationalists, far different in their outlook from the medieval chronicler who saw history from a universal point of view, 'not as a mere play of human purposes, in which he took the side of his own friends, but as a process, having an objective necessity of its own'.[15] Although nationalism was not unknown in the Middle Ages, its impact was not felt in medieval historiography. In Tudor historical writing there is, in spite of moralization on the inevitability of retribution and the instability of Fortune in the medieval manner, a noticeable change both in content and in attitude. The themes are taken largely from English history and only occasionally from legends; the moralization is generally political and the tone pronouncedly nationalist. Indeed, even where the subject is feudal warfare, there is a recognition of the force of nationalism which ran counter to feudal claims. Tudor historians glorify Henry V, whose title to the French throne would appear to be absurd by modern standards. But Hall admits that the English king was in France 'a straunge Potestat', 'a forein prince', and Henry himself, in the course of one of his orations, said that his enemies, the people of France, formed 'one nacion of one language and one country'.[16] Hall's book was designed as a moral discourse on the evils of civil dissension, and his principal illustration was the loss of French possessions as a result of warring factions in the government of England. Yet both Hall and Polydore Vergil admit that the English were driven out of France largely on account of the readiness of the French – they, of course, call it 'perfidy' – to throw off the foreign yoke.

Another remarkable pointer to the change in outlook – from the theological to the political – is furnished by the *Mirror for Magistrates*, which was intended as a continuation of Boccaccio's *De Casibus Virorum Illustrium* and Lydgate's *Falls of Princes*. The *Mirror* moralizes on vice bringing its own punishment and also on the capriciousness of Fortune, but its moralization is not 'universalistic' as in Boccaccio or Lydgate. Not only are the protagonists all English (or Scottish), but the monologues in which the unfortunate men recount the stories of their life on earth try, however haltingly, to build a working political theory that would help magistrates, who are the king's deputies, in the work of government. The period especially chosen by the authors of this miscellany as well as by some other writers is the stretch of about a hundred years between Richard II and Richard III, and all the calamities which happened between the accession of Henry IV (1399) and that of Henry VII (1485) were traced to the original sin of the deposition and murder of Richard II. Bolingbroke had an unquiet time as king, and if the curse was suspended for some years after his death it was due to the exceptional prowess and piety of his son. But it fell with redoubled force on his grandson, and an appropriate prophecy as well as an appropriate precedent was found for this delayed retribution. This disingenuous explanation was no answer to the political-ethical problem which lay behind the horrors of the Wars of the Roses. If Bolingbroke were a usurper, it should be no sin to dethrone him or people lineally descended from him, and in this way the rising of the Percies on behalf of Mortimer and the subsequent Yorkist intrigues would be the assertion of right against might. But Hall slurs over the problem and looks upon all rebellion against the reigning monarch as sinful. Much as he blames Bolingbroke, the Oxford conspiracy to restore Richard II is for him a mischief set forth by the Devil, and when the Percies rise in arms against

Henry IV, the King's cause is right and his quarrel just. King-maker Warwick is a mighty figure in Shakespeare's *Henry VI, Part Two* and *Part Three*, but his attitude to the basic problem is comically self-contradictory. In the earlier stages of the Wars of the Roses, he stands up for the 'right' of the Duke of York, but later on he regrets that for the house of York he 'put Henry from his native right'.

In the *Mirror*, the Duke of York has no doubt that he has a better title to the throne than Henry VI, but he is cruelly killed and humiliated by the Lancastrians. The conclusion he arrives at is unconnected with the political problem raised by him:

> Wherefore warne princes not to wade in warre,
> For any cause, except the realmes defence:
> Their troublous titles are unwurthy farre,
> The blud, the lyfe, the spoyle of innocence.
> *Richard, Duke of York*, 162–5

Henry VI, his opposite number, lives 'so cleare a life', and yet he too had 'cruell lucke'. The moral lesson preached by him is equally tame; it could have been drawn by any medieval moralist, for it has nothing specifically Tudor about it. Misfortunes are caused by divine will which 'appoynteth payne for good mens exercise' and by sin which 'God doth highly hate' and which deserves due punishment. The valiant Earl of Salisbury, who was slain at Orleans, probes the question deeper, but he too fails to come to a very satisfactory conclusion. His father John, Lord Montacute, was beheaded by Henry IV for taking part in the Oxford conspiracy 'to restore Kyng Richard to the rose'. The cause was right, but

> How many agayn through helpe of fortune blind,
> For yll attemptes atchieved, with honour blest?
> Sucess is wurst ofttimes whan cause is best,
> Therefore say I: God send them sory happes,
> That judge the causes by their after clappes.
> *Thomas, Earl of Salisbury*, 24–8

But what should the righteous man do? Should he suffer wrongs in silence and allow things to drift from bad to worse? That is the tame ending to the Earl's rigmarole:

Who furdereth right is not thereby excused,
If through the same he do sum other wrong:
To every vice due guerdon doth belong.
Thomas, Earl of Salisbury, 75–7

Tudor political philosophy was indecisive, ambiguous, and confused, because there was a basic contradiction in the Tudor postulate about history and politics. At the time that the Battle of Bosworth Field was fought, there was little doubt that Richard III was established on the throne and he had possibly then the best title to it, certainly a better title than could be claimed by the Earl of Richmond, who had only a distant connexion with the house of Lancaster. But the question cannot be disposed of so simply. The Lancastrian family was in possession when the Duke of York disturbed the existing arrangement, although he had an arguably better case than the Lancastrians. So from the politico-moral point of view the Wars of the Roses seemed to have no end, for here one right was contending against another, and factions were irreconcilable and almost equally balanced. Even when Richard III is firmly entrenched, he cannot trust Buckingham, his 'other self' and 'counsel's consistory', for that deep-revolving Duke is, after all, a Lancastrian.[17] Only Richmond could deliver the people out of the shambles to which England had been reduced, because although not a direct descendant – in *Richard III*, Queen Margaret never mentions him – he is connected with the house of Lancaster, and in his favour Buckingham waives his own claim. And Elizabeth is the indubitable heir of Edward IV. By marrying her Richmond would unite the two Roses and put an end to civil dissension. This was a working arrangement, and it worked well. But it would be unsafe to deduce any political philosophy or moral maxim from such a compromise. It is reasonable to think that Shakespeare, who presents Bolingbroke as a saviour in *Richard II* and as a usurper with a stricken conscience in *Henry IV, Part Two*, who does not mention the Mortimer claim in *Henry V* but dilates on it in *Henry IV* and *Henry VI*, interpreted history aesthetically rather than philosophically and presented every point of view for its dramatic significance rather than for its doctrinal value. Having stated the central paradox in the Tudor position, we may proceed to a closer examination of the dominant ideas in Tudor historiography and see how Shakespeare presents them in his historical plays.

4

Such ideas may be reduced to three: (1) English nationalism, (2) absolute obedience to the reigning monarch, and (3) order and unity. These ideas have been so powerfully expressed in Shakespeare's historical dramas that many critics think that they were intended by him as political Moralities and that it is from that point of view that their dramatic significance ought to be judged. There are minor differences between one writer and another, and there are some critics who think that Shakespeare expressed the opposition point of view rather than the one officially encouraged, but it is generally held that the histories differ from the comedies and tragedies largely because of their politico-ethical emphasis.

If, however, the plays are considered *as* plays, it will appear very doubtful whether Shakespeare was primarily interested in propagating any particular political or moral idea. Rather it will seem that Elizabethan notions of history were part of the raw materials he transformed, and only remotely connected with the ultimate dramatic effect of his plays. Not that Shakespeare was unpatriotic or did not seriously mean what he said so eloquently through John of Gaunt in *Richard II* and the Bastard in *King John*; but although these passionate outbursts have an appeal of their own, it is in the dramatic context that their appropriateness can be properly realized. John of Gaunt's poetical glorification of This other Eden, this demi-paradise, must be seen as a part of his indictment of Richard who is ruining the beautiful land; and it lends support to those who would afterwards save England from the reckless tyrant. The theme of the play is the deposition of an anointed but unworthy king, and this speech has to be set against the Bishop of Carlisle's plea later on that no subject has the right to judge or depose God's deputy on earth. Indeed, immediately after delivering that eloquent oration on the beauty and glory of England, Gaunt says that Richard's actions are tantamount to suicide – 'Thou diest' – and then points out that although he may be God's anointed, he deserves to be deposed:

> O, had thy grandsire with a prophet's eye
> Seen how his son's son should destroy his sons,
> From forth thy reach he would have laid thy shame,
> Deposing thee before thou wert possessed,
> Which art possessed now to depose thyself.
>
> *Richard II*, II.1.104–8

It is the tension between these two ideas – the necessity or desirability of deposing a bad king and the inviolability of his position and person – that is one of the strands of the complex web of this drama.

As king, John was possibly worse than Richard II. Richard's alleged murder of his uncle is only reported and not represented on the stage, but the atrocity which was intended against Arthur is a part of the action of *King John*. Moreover, John – in Shakespeare's drama – is admittedly a usurper, occupying the throne more by strong possession than by rightful title. It may be that Shakespeare deliberately chose this subject as suitable for the inculcation of militant nationalism, because he would be able to show that the country is greater than the king. Behind John looms the mighty figure of the Bastard, who professes to follow Commodity but really stands for national unity and unflinching loyalty to the country:

> Now these her princes are come home again,
> Come the three corners of the world in arms,
> And we shall shock them. Nought shall make us rue,
> If England to itself do rest but true.
>
> *King John*, V.7.115–18

Although patriotism or united resistance to a foreign invader may be looked upon as the leitmotive of *King John*, it is an idea that emerges living and vibrant and not a moral lesson that is expounded. For if the argument is carried to its logical conclusion, the play might be interpreted, as indeed it has been, as a satire on kingship, and then its ideological significance runs counter to a favourite Tudor doctrine – the unquestionable supremacy of the king. Tudor history would never tolerate the separation of king and country, and Shakespeare, unlike Bale, refuses to make a hero of John, while he also omits the long didactic speeches in which the author of *The Troublesome Raigne* inculcates endurance of tyranny. It would be absurd, therefore, to claim that Shakespeare was preaching English nationalism independently of English 'royalism', though that is the idea which emanates from the play.

If Shakespeare's historical plays are interpreted as political Moralities, there would be confusion and contradiction at every step. *Henry V*, for example, would present a thesis that would clash with the lesson conveyed in *King John*. Henry V lays claim to the throne of France through a woman, and that is exactly the French Dauphin's title to the throne of England. Lewis, as Holinshed tells us, 'defended the cause that moved him to take upon him this journey into England, disproving not onelie the right which King John had to the crowne, but also alledging his owne interest, not onelie by his new election of the barons, but also in the title of his wife, whose mother the queene of Castile remained onelie alive of all brethren and sisters of Henrie the second late King of England'.[18] It is not reasonable to suppose that Shakespeare would be blind to the implications of his own theme. If preaching nationalism had been his dominant purpose, would he have written two such plays as *King John* and *Henry V*, inspiring national resistance against a foreign foe in one of them and inciting foreign aggression in the other? In an earlier play – *Henry VI, Part One* – the patriotic note, strangely enough, is struck not so much by the English lords, who for all their prowess look like freebooters in a country not their own, but by England's enemies – the Pucelle and the Duke of Burgundy. Joan looks upon herself as a person divinely assigned to be the English scourge in order to free her country from alien domination, and she is the only person in the whole trilogy to speak of 'country' and 'countrymen'. Although she makes a cruel comment on Burgundy's turning and turning again as only a Frenchman may be expected to do, even this joke stems from a passionate love of her country, and she converts the slippery Duke by a fervent appeal to his patriotic sentiments:

> Behold the wounds, the most unnatural wounds,
> Which thou thyself hast given her woeful breast.
> O, turn thy edged sword another way;
> Strike those that hurt, and hurt not those that help!

> One drop of blood drawn from thy country's bosom
> Should grieve thee more than streams of foreign gore.
> Return thee therefore with a flood of tears,
> And wash away thy country's stained spots.
>
> *Henry VI, Part One*, III.3.50–57

If Shakespeare meant England to be the protagonist of his historical plays, he would not have made Joan of Arc, who was 'devil or devil's dam' to the English, the mouthpiece of patriotic resistance to foreign aggression; and he would not have extolled in *Henry V* what he cries down in *King John*. Although to an Elizabethan chauvinist – let us imagine that Shakespeare wanted to represent such sentiment – English aggression on France would be different from a French invasion of England, as a moralist Shakespeare must have realized that the difference between the two was as between tweedledum and tweedledee. And there is the further consideration that although Shakespeare boosts Henry V's victories and seems to present him as an epic hero, he also makes the Chorus warn the audience at the end of the play that the English success is only a temporary adventure and that all that Henry has gained will be lost by his son.

Shakespeare's treatment of the second dominant idea in Tudor historical writing – that of absolute royal supremacy – has already been touched on above; here, too, the crucial play is *Richard II*, where a king is deposed by a usurper who unleashes the forces of retribution that are stayed during his son's reign but devastate England in the third generation. When Bolingbroke ascends the throne, the Bishop of Carlisle sounds a stern note of warning:

> My Lord of Hereford here, whom you call king,
> Is a foul traitor to proud Hereford's King;
> And if you crown him, let me prophesy
> The blood of English shall manure the ground,
> And future ages groan for this foul act.
> Peace shall go sleep with Turks and infidels,
> And in this seat of peace tumultuous wars
> Shall kin with kin, and kind with kind, confound.
> Disorder, horror, fear, and mutiny
> Shall here inhabit, and this land be called
> The field of Golgotha and dead men's skulls.
>
> *Richard II*, IV.1.134–44

Not only does he prove a true prophet, but even in his own life-time, the usurper acknowledges the honourableness of his conduct and, indirectly, the justness of his argument. When exiling him, Bolingbroke says:

> So as thou livest in peace, die free from strife;
> For though mine enemy thou hast ever been,
> High sparks of honour in thee have I seen.

> V.6.27–9

Richard himself thinks that he is God's anointed, and therefore inviolable. Shakespeare draws such a vivid picture of the reluctant pangs of abdicating royalty that we are tempted to think that he himself regarded the deposition as a sacrilege. But even in Shakespeare's lifetime the followers of the Earl of Essex staged this play on the eve of the Earl's rebellion, and Queen Elizabeth herself said that she was likened to the deposed King.[19] The sponsors of the rebellion would not have staged *Richard II* if they thought that it condemned the seizure of the crown by Boling-broke. Indeed, in Shakespeare's play – if not exactly in the chron-icles – Richard surrenders the crown more than Bolingbroke snatches it from him. If in the base court (III.3), when Bolingbroke said, in terms of his promise, 'My gracious lord, I come but for mine own', Richard had taken him at his word, and, following Aumerle's advice, had fought with gentle words till time lent friends and friends their swords, one cannot say whether Boling-broke would have seized the throne or not. But instead of doing so Richard says that he is Bolingbroke's and all, calls the latter his heir, and proceeds to surrender the crown which even then he might have tried to retain. No one in *Richard II* accuses Boling-broke of being false to his oath. The indictment on the usurpation is uttered by Bolingbroke's enemies – the Bishop of Carlisle in *Richard II*, and Hotspur and Worcester in *Henry IV, Part One*, and alone of these men Worcester – rather late in the day – accuses the King of having forgotten the oath made to them at Doncaster (V.1.58). Shakespeare observes the same neutrality of tone with regard to the rebellion of the Percies. He holds no brief for the conspirators; Hotspur, for all his greatness, is a madcap, Worcester a malevolent and perfidious intriguer, Northumberland a backslider, Mortimer a nincompoop, and Glendower a braggart and a fool. But although victory comes deservedly to the King and his son, the arguments advanced by the conspirators remain unanswered, and the final act of perjury which puts an end to the rebellion only shows how ungodly God's deputies may be.

The third leading idea of Tudor historiography – love for order and hatred of dissension – is repeatedly and strongly expressed in some of the plays, but once again it will be wrong to hold that the significance of any of them centres on this idea. *King John* ends with a passionate appeal to Englishmen to close their ranks in face of foreign aggression. The opening scene of *Henry VI, Part One*, is conceived in the spirit of Hall, who wrote his history to show 'What mischiefe hath insurged in realmes by intestine devision, what depopulacion hath ensued in countries by civill discension, what detestable murder hath been committed in citees by separate faccions, and what calamities hath ensued in famous regions by domesticall discords and unnaturall controversy'.[20] The defeat of Talbot, later on in the play, is represented as due mostly to the rivalry of York and Somerset; the destruction caused by internecine strife during the Wars of the Roses is luridly described; and the advent of Henry VII, who unites the two Roses, is shown as providential. But this moral lesson about unity and order, although it acquires prominence towards the end of *King John*, occurs intermittently in the three parts of *Henry VI*, and is also enforced at the conclusion of *Richard III*, is no part of the substance of these dramas, and the other 'histories' have very little to do with it. In *King John*, the English lords do unite after Melun's disclosures, but the Dauphin is persuaded to sue for peace as much by this new alignment of forces as by the sinking of his supply ships and his ignorance of a similar disaster to the Bastard's army. Nor should we attach much importance – dramatically – to the political significance of the Earl of Richmond's victory in the last act of *Richard III*. It is like the conventional ending in Bernard Shaw's unconventional plays. Such a conclusion flattered Tudor political sentiment and, what is more important, it draws the long tetralogy – a story of violence and unnatural strife – to a peaceful end. There is no reason to believe that such a conclusion is an integral part of the tetralogy, or even of *Richard III*, which is a tragedy of Richard's downfall and not a comedy of Richmond's triumph. Richmond appears once in *Henry VI, Part Three* merely to give King Henry an opportunity for making a prophecy. This episode, although drawn from history, is irrelevant to the dramatic context, and Richmond appears only in the last Act of *Richard III*, where he just defeats Richard and wrests the crown from him. If it had been Shakespeare's intention to give primacy to the moral lesson to be derived from Richmond's triumph and his oration on unity and order, he would certainly have given him a more important place in the main body of the play. That would have made it more effective as a Morality but possibly weakened it as a drama.

The evil effects of civil strife are, indeed, forcefully presented in *Henry VI, Part One* and also in *Part Three*, II.5, where a Father has killed his Son and a Son his Father, and there are other references to this theme scattered in different parts of the trilogy. It will, however, be doing injustice to the multiple interest of these plays if this theme is given more prominence than others. Rather *Henry VI* is dramatically effective more because of the clash of rival personalities – Talbot against Joan, Gloucester against Winchester and Suffolk, York against Somerset and Margaret – than on account of the civil dissensions which throw these personal clashes into relief. But for the warring factions and the general turmoil, Richard, Earl of Warwick, or Richard, Duke of Gloucester, would not have come into prominence, but it is these and other flamboyant personalities who dominate the trilogy and give it its dramatic interest. Even in the episodes which are directly connected with the theme of civil faction, Shakespeare transcends the purely didactic significance of the incidents in order to bring out their dramatic appeal. Henry VI's marriage to Margaret helps to sharpen the animosities of the barons, but Shakespeare lays emphasis on the romance of Suffolk's wooing, the arrogance of the Duchess of Gloucester and the rivalry between her and the new Queen – episodes which are largely un-historical and only remotely political. Although Jack Cade's rebellion, which was engineered by the Duke of York, is a direct offshoot of the Wars of the Roses, the dramatic interest of the episode is nevertheless derived from the character of Jack Cade and not from the political implications of his misdeeds. Jack Cade disturbs order in civil society and Alexander Iden restores it by killing Cade. Iden delivers an elaborate sermon on the philosophy of order which Shakespeare is supposed to have embodied in his historical plays:

> Lord, who would live turmoiled in the court
> And may enjoy such quiet walks as these?
> This small inheritance my father left me
> Contenteth me, and worth a monarchy.
> I seek not to wax great by others' waning
> Or gather wealth I care not with what envy;
> Sufficeth that I have maintains my state,
> And sends the poor well pleased from my gate.
>
> *Henry VI, Part Two*, IV.10.16–23

This should be contrasted with Jack Cade's vision of violent disorder in the state:

> There shall be in England seven halfpenny loaves sold for a penny; the three-hooped pot shall have ten hoops; and I will make it felony to drink small beer. All the realm shall be in common, and in Cheapside shall my palfrey go to grass.
>
> *Henry VI, Part Two*, IV.2.63–6

Irving Ribner places these two passages side by side in order to bring out the political lesson implied by their contrast,[21] but he does not notice that the first passage, although written in verse, is prosaic and dull, but the second is dramatically vivid. Many readers would fail to recall Iden, but who can forget Jack Cade?

Unlike his son, Henry V was a very powerful king who had no reason to be afraid of civil disorder. He would not scruple to 'awake [his] sleeping sword of war' if political necessity or a just title demanded it. For him mere order is stagnation, a part of idle Ceremony:

> O ceremony, show me but thy worth!
> What is thy soul of adoration?
> Art thou aught else but place, degree, and form,
> Creating awe and fear in other men?
>
> *Henry V*, IV.1.237–40

Ulysses, in *Troilus and Cressida*, praises 'degree' only to explain the temporary eclipse of the Greek army in Troy and to wean away Achilles from indolent retirement. But Henry V, arrayed like Mars, disturbs 'place, degree, and form', because he knows that he can restore order, and impose his will even in a foreign country. Emphasis is laid in the three parts of *Henry VI* on the necessity for unity, and in the later portions of the trilogy there is expressed a longing for peace and order, but that is because the country has been ravaged by civil strife. There is faction in *Henry VIII*, too, where the barons and the prelates are eager to rush at one another's throats. Mighty Buckingham is thought to be guilty of treason as was the Duke of York, Wolsey is as ambitious of power as King-maker Warwick, soft-hearted Katharine is as much opposed to Wolsey as Margaret, She-wolf of France, was to Humphrey, and Cranmer is drawn into a net by the Lord Chancellor and Bishop Gardiner as Humphrey was by Suffolk and Cardinal Beaufort. But in this play there is no moralizing on 'degree' or order or on the evils of dissension, because when the necessity arises the King is powerful enough to set everybody in his proper place.

The idea that Shakespeare in his historical plays tried to express the Tudor view of history is somewhat 'naive', and some critics not without justification have gone to the opposite extreme of suggesting 'that there was a political current in Shakespeare's mind, which in the days of Elizabeth led him into opposition'.[22] On this view, Shakespeare was obliged to use words which might be plausibly explained, but under a veneer of conformity he concealed scathing criticism of the established order. As pointed out already, Henry V makes out an elaborate plea about the justness of his title to the French throne but Queen Elinor depends more on strong possession than on right. In *Richard II*, 'the depreciation of the people and the exaggeration of the royal prerogative are put into the mouths of favourites and evil counsellors'. If *Henry IV*, *Henry V*, and *Henry VI* are viewed as a single dramatic unit, it will be seen that 'the constant prominence of the law which fatally conducts traitors to punishment is . . . modified by a large-hearted sympathy with their grievances and temptations'.[23] In fact, Shakespeare has no definite answer to give to the problems of political right or political justice, nor does he seem to be interested in them. He shows that Henry IV might be a usurper but Richard II did not deserve to rule. He never suggests a clear answer to the basic questions which lay behind the carnage of the Wars of the Roses: Who had the better right to the throne – Henry VI or the Duke of York? Does Henry VI suffer for his grandfather's sin? Or does he deserve to be cashiered on account of his own incompetence? And do not these two concepts contradict each other? 'In *Henry VI*', says Brockbank, 'the sacrificial idea, which makes catastrophe a consequence of sin, is sharply challenged by the "machiavellian" idea that makes it a consequence of weakness.'[24] Those who believe that Shakespeare was primarily interested in dramatizing the political assumptions of Tudor monarchy think that he gave in his political plays his concept of the ideal king, the type of sovereign that should succeed Elizabeth. 'The central and continuous image in these plays, more specific than a mood, more comprehensive than a character, is, I believe,' says Ellis-Fermor, 'a composite figure – that of the statesman-king, the leader and public man, which Shakespeare builds up gradually through the series of political plays from *Henry VI* to *Henry V*.'[25] But other critics have found in these plays a point of view or a bias of an opposite character. For Walter Pater the ruling conception under which Shakespeare arranged the lights and shadows of the story of the English kings is the 'irony of kingship – average human nature, flung with a wonderfully pathetic effect into the vortex of great events'.[26] John Bailey goes a step further and says that though Shakespeare's histories are more royal than national, more personal than political, that is a long way from being all they are. No republican can demand a better text for a sermon against personal monarchy than he can find in scene after scene of Shakespeare's 'histories'.[27]

The historical plays are neither moral homilies nor political treatises. Shakespeare borrowed his incidents from the chronicles and other sources and he sometimes retold them with little change. But it would be rash to conclude that he merely gave a verse-paraphrase of what he found in his source-books. The changes he made – both in general concept and in details – and even the slight shifts in emphasis when he did not make any large modifications show that he transformed his sources rather than re-produced them. Yet in spite of modifications and shifts of emphasis, these plays are not 'mythical', and the Duke of Marlborough had some justification for saying that he was content to know no more English history than what he found in Shakespeare. The difference between history and drama is pithily expressed by Aristotle when he says that dramatic imitators have to represent a story as though they were actually doing the things described.[28] That is to say, the dramatic poet is to identify himself with his characters and to show them as actually doing what history merely reports them as doing. Dramatic poetry has also to follow, like all other forms of art, the law of harmony, and the crowd of incidents and characters must round themselves off into what Carlyle calls 'a kind of rhythmic coherence'.[29] It is for these reasons that the dramatist has to telescope time and space, and not only shorten the sprawling historical narrative but also occasionally add to it.

The causes of action, Aristotle points out, are two: character, which makes us ascribe certain moral qualities to the agents, and thought, which is shown in the arguments advanced by them in support of a particular point or a general truth. But these two causes run into each other, for our intellectual arguments are coloured by our moral qualities and the intellect influences moral proclivities. Northumberland's advocacy of Bolingbroke's plea and the Bishop of Carlisle's denunciation of it emanate from their characters and their characters are partly moulded by their ways of thought. What it is necessary to emphasize here is that neither set of arguments – Northumberland in *Richard II* acts more than he argues and Carlisle argues more than he acts – is Shakespeare's; he only represents the men as though they were doing the things which historians report they did. In *King John*, the Bastard is shocked at the sight of Arthur's dead body, but he passes over the affair and proceeds to unite England against the aggressor without caring to find out how Arthur met his death; he is too shrewd not to have understood who was at the root of it. In *Richard III*, however, the murder of the Princes in the Tower is the climax to a long series of crimes; as soon as the suggestion is made Buckingham deserts Richard, and after this murder everything goes wrong for the murderer. Are we to conclude that Shakespeare connives at a murder by a reigning sovereign in *King John* and condemns it in *Richard III*? It is in such contradictions that we shall be landed if we pursue political and ethical interpretation to the logical end. Shakespeare, in fact, took all sorts of ideas and arguments, political and moral, and he appropriated for his own use images and expressions he found ready to hand just as he lifted his stories from Hall, Holinshed, and other sources. But he transmuted them all; it would, therefore, be equally wrong to emphasize either his medieval heritage of the Morality tradition or his political background of Tudor monarchy. He was not a writer of homilies or of political history, though his vision of life included both history and politics.

A dramatist is a creative artist, and not a mere medium like a platinum wire, and he surveys life from a point of view. This means that the poet, too, has his ideas, and since these ideas are aesthetic they are different from the political or moral ideas of his time or of the characters in his work. This ideology, which is an emanation from his plot and characters, is subtler than anything expressed by any one amongst the *dramatis personae*, but it comprehends all that is said by them. The ideas projected by Shakespeare's 'histories' may be said to be moral, but only in the sense that all thinking about life, or all application of ideas to life, is moral. But the principal characteristic of such ideology is that it cannot be detached from the life portrayed in the dramas, from the movement of plot and evolution of character.

NOTES

1. Wilson Knight (possibly alone of all critics) looks upon *Cymbeline* 'mainly as an historical play' (*The Crown of Life*, 1947, page 129), on the ground that it delves into the historic origins of the English nation.
2. M. M. Reese, *The Cease of Majesty: A Study of Shakespeare's History Plays* (London, 1961), page 88.
3. F. P. Wilson, *Marlowe and Early Shakespeare* (Oxford, 1955), page 106.
4. E. M. W. Tillyard, *Shakespeare's History Plays* (London, 1944), page 59.

5. *Shakespeare's 'Histories': Mirrors of Elizabethan Policy* (San Marino, California, 1947), page 17.

6. J. Dover Wilson, *The Fortunes of Falstaff* (Cambridge, 1944), page 14.

7. Bernard Spivack, *Shakespeare and the Allegory of Evil* (Columbia, 1958), pages 170, 386–407.

8. A. Quiller-Couch, *Shakespeare's Workmanship* (Cambridge, 1919), pages 135 ff. Dover Wilson, *The Fortunes of Falstaff.*

9. *The Works of St Thomas Aquinas: Philosophical Texts,* edited by T. Gilby (London, 1956), page 101.

10. op. cit., page 66.

11. John Lydgate, *Fall of Princes,* edited by Henry Bergen (Washington, 1923–7), page 261.

12. *Shakespeare Survey 8* (1955), page 17.

13. *Fall of Princes,* pages 551, 633.

14. *An Apologie for Poetrie,* edited by J. Churton Collins (Oxford, 1907), pages 8, 14–24.

15. R. G. Collingwood, *The Idea of History* (Oxford, 1946), page 53.

16. Hall's *Chronicle, Containing the History of England during the Reign of Henry the Fourth and the Succeeding Monarchs to the End of the Reign of Henry the Eighth,* reprint of 1809, page 85.

17. It should be pointed out, however, that Shakespeare never mentions Buckingham as a possible claimant to the throne.

18. Raphael Holinshed, *Chronicles of England, Scotland, and Ireland,* reprint of 1807–8, page 330.

19. Although all critics do not agree that this was the play staged by Shakespeare's company on the day before the Essex rising, the balance of evidence is in favour of such a supposition. (See *Publications of the Modern Language Association of America* XLII (1927), 686–720; XLVI (1931), 694–719.)

20. Hall's *Chronicle,* page 1.

21. *The English History Play in the Age of Shakespeare* (Princeton, 1957, pages 107–8; London, 1965, pages 103–4).

22. R. Simpson, 'The Politics of Shakspere's Historical Plays', *Transactions of the New Shakspere Society* (1874), page 440.

23. op. cit., pages 409, 415.

24. *Early Shakespeare* (Stratford-upon-Avon Studies 3, 1961), page 83. [See page 103 below.]

25. Una Ellis-Fermor, *The Frontiers of Drama* (London, 1948), page 21.

NOTES

26. *Appreciations* (London, 1889), page 193.
27. John Bailey, *The Continuity of Letters* (Oxford, 1923), page 62.
28. *On the Art of Poetry* (translated by Ingram Bywater, Oxford, 1948), page 27.
29. *Heroes and Hero-Worship*, 'The Hero as Poet'.

THREE

The Frame of Disorder – *Henry VI**

J. P. Brockbank

THE four plays about the Wars of the Roses were staged fully and in sequence, probably for the first time, in 1953. The experience was arresting and moving, testifying to the continuity of our own preoccupations with those of Tudor England; here, it seemed, was yet another historical instance of anarchy owed to innocence and order won by atrocity. The three parts of *Henry VI* express the plight of individuals caught up in a cataclysmic movement of events for which responsibility is communal and historical, not personal and immediate, and they reveal the genesis out of prolonged violence of two figures representing the ultimate predicament of man as a political animal – Henry and Richard, martyr and machiavel. But one would not wish to over-stress whatever analogues there may be between the fifteenth century and the twentieth, since these might be proved quite as striking for ages other than our own. If we are now more sympathetically disposed towards Shakespeare's history plays than were the readers and audiences of seventy years ago, it is largely because we have more flexible ideas about the many possible forms that history might take. We are less dominated by the Positivist view that the truth is co-extensive with, and not merely consistent with, the facts. Contemporaries of Boswell-Stone were reluctant to take seriously a vision of the past that made free with the data for purposes they took to be simply dramatic. Following the lead of Richard Simpson, critics began to read Shakespeare's histories as documents of Tudor England, addressed primarily to contemporary problems

*From *Early Shakespeare* (Stratford-upon-Avon Studies No. 3), edited by J. R. Brown and Bernard Harris (1961), pages 73–99. Copyright © Edward Arnold (Publishers) Ltd, 1961. Reprinted by kind permission of the author and the publishers, Edward Arnold Ltd, London.

and not fundamentally curious about the pastness of the past.[1] Now we are better placed to see them from the point of view represented, for instance, by R. G. Collingwood's *The Idea of History* and Herbert Butterfield's *Christianity and History*, putting a less exclusive stress on facts, and looking harder at the myths and hypotheses used to interpret them – at ideas of providence, historical process, personal responsibility and the role of the hero. These are precisely the ideas that the playwright is fitted to explore and clarify, and Shakespeare's treatment of them is the most searching our literature has to offer. For Shakespeare was peculiarly sensitive to the subtle analogues between the world and the stage, between the shape of events and the shape of a play, between the relationship of historical process to individuals and that of the playwright to his characters. He tried from the beginning to meet the urgent and practical problem of finding dramatic forms and conventions that would express whatever coherence and order could be found in the 'plots' of chronicle history. Where narrative and play are incompatible, it may be the record and it may be the art that is defective as an image of human life, and in the plays framed from English and Roman history it is possible to trace subtle modulations of spectacle, structure, and dialogue as they seek to express and elucidate the full potential of the source material. A full account would take in *The Tempest*, which is the last of Shakespeare's plays to be made out of historical documents and which has much to do with the rule of providence over the political activities of man. But from these early plays alone there is much to be learned about the vision and technique of historical drama, and these are the plays that are submitted most rigorously to the test of allegiance to historical record.

Part One *and the Pageantry of Dissension*

We might begin by taking a famous passage of Nashe as the earliest surviving critical comment on *Part One*[2]:

How would it have joyed brave *Talbot* (the terror of the French) to think that after he had lyne two hundred yeares in his Tombe, hee should triumphe againe on the Stage, and have his bones new embalmed with the teares of ten thousand spectators at least, (at severall times) who, in the Tragedian that represents his person, imagine they behold him fresh bleeding.

This, primarily, is the ritual experience Shakespeare sought and won. He transposed the past of the tombs, the 'rusty brass' and the 'worm-eaten books' into living spectacle. Whatever else must be said about all three plays, they keep this quality of epic mime and with it an elementary power to move large audiences. There is, too, something in Nashe's glance at those early performances that chimes with Coleridge's observation that 'in order that a drama may be properly historical, it is necessary that it should be the history of the people to whom it is addressed'.[3] Shakespeare's early histories are addressed primarily to the audience's heroic sense of community, to its readiness to belong to an England represented by its court and its army, to its eagerness to enjoy a public show celebrating the continuing history of its prestige and power. This does not mean, however, that we must surrender these early plays to Joyce's remark that Shakespeare's 'pageants, the histories, sail full-bellied on a tide of Mafeking enthusiasm'. In the more mature plays of *Henry IV* the heroic sense of community will be challenged by the unheroic – by that range of allegiances which binds us less to authority and the king than to each other and to Falstaff; and the death of Hotspur is a more complicated theatrical experience than that of Talbot in Nashe's description. But the early histories too express stresses and ironies, complexities and intricate perspectives beyond the reach of the condescensions usually allowed them.

Even *Part One* has its share. If this is a play more moving to watch than to read it is because it makes the historical facts eloquent through the language of pageantry. In a way that Nashe does not sufficiently suggest, Shakespeare exploits the poignant contrast between the past nostalgically apprehended through its monuments, and the past keenly re-enacted in the present – between the pasts 'entombed' 'and fresh-bleeding'. The effect, which testifies to the continuity of stage techniques with those of the Tournament and the civic pageant, is felt immediately in the first scene (where the mood of a cathedral entombment is mocked by the energies of the brawl), in the scene of Bedford's death (III.2), and, most distinctly, in the death of Talbot (IV.7). These are among the several episodes of *Henry VI* that are presented both as 'events' – as if they actually happened, the figures caught up in them alive and free – and as 'occasions' – happenings that have some symbolic significance, or are (in retrospect) 'inevitable' turning-points in the history. Thus the scene of Talbot's and Lisle's death would, if perfectly executed, present the chronicled event with convincing documentary detail, in a style befitting the occasion – the fire of English chivalry glowing brightest before it expires. The context ensures that Talbot stands at his death for the martial glory of England, and Bordeaux for the dominion of France. When the English and French nobles meet over his corpse (IV.7), the retrospective, reflective mood and the instant, practical mood are sustained side by side; the first calling to mind the image of a memorial tomb seen in the remote perspective of a later time, and the second recalling us to the hard realities of the battlefield. Talbot is discovered dead with his son 'inhearsed in [his] arms' (IV.7.45), resembling a figure on a monument. Lucy's long intonement of Talbot's titles was taken at first or second hand from the inscription on Talbot's actual tomb at Rouen, and it retains its lapidary formality.[4] Joan's lines,

> Him that thou magnifi'st with all these titles,
> Stinking and fly-blown lies here at our feet

> IV.7.75–6

have been mocked for their documentary impropriety (fly-blown in two minutes!) but they serve to accent the recollection in the spectacle of a Tudor tomb. Beneath the effigy of the complete man in, as it were, painted marble finery, lies the image of the rotten corpse. Joan's jeer mediates between the mutability threnody and the return to the exigencies of battle; the action gets under way again – there is a body to dispose of.

While there are other opportunities to arrest the flux of events, they are not all of this kind. The changes in pace and shifts of perspective owe as much to the chronicle as to the techniques of pageantry. The essential events and the processes and energies that shape and direct them are transmitted into the spectacle with a high sense of responsibility to the chronicle vision.

The three parts of *Henry VI* coincide with three distinct phases of the history and show that Shakespeare did what he could to tease a form for each of the plays out of the given material. The first phase of Holinshed's version[5] reports about four hundred incidents in the French campaign, some perfunctorily and some with full solemnity. The siege of Orleans is the most conspicuous in both chronicle and play. Holinshed finds occasion to deploy his epic clichés, with the 'Englishmen' behaving themselves 'right valiantlie under the conduct of their couragious capteine' to keep and enlarge 'that which Henrie the fift had by his magnanimite & puissance atchived'.[6] But the accent changes to sombre historical prophecy, marking the ineluctable, impersonal historical law:

> But all helped not. For who can hold that which will awaie: In so much that some cities by fraudulent practises, othersome by martial prowesse were recovered by the French, to the great discouragement of the English and the appalling of their spirits; whose hope was now dashed partlie by their great losses and discomfitures (as after you shall heare) but cheeflie by the death of the late deceassed Henrie their victorious king.

These opening pages license a chauvinistic battle-play framing a historical Morality about the evil consequences of civil dissension. Here is Holinshed on the loss of a group of towns in 1451:

> Everie daie was looking for aid, but none came. And whie? Even bicause the divelish division that reigned in England, so incombred the heads of the noble men there, that the honor of the realme was cleerelie forgotten.

> (Holinshed, page 228)

The chronicled sources of disaster are more nakedly sprung in the play: the loss of the puissant and magnanimous Henry V, the hostile stars, the hard fortunes of war, the perverse skill of the French, the steady eclipse of English chivalry with the deaths of its ageing heroes, and the corrosive quarrels and dynastic rivalries of the nobles at home. All this is manifest in the mere pantomime of *Part One* — its force would be felt by the stone-deaf, and the routine of the play's rhetoric does much to accent and little to qualify, explore or challenge the basic simplicities of the history.

The originality of Shakespeare's accomplishment is in the shedding of all literary artifice except that which serves to express the temper and structure of the history. The first scene, for instance, establishes at once that double perspective which controls the mood of the chronicle – the sense of being close to the event together with a sense of knowing its consequences. The messenger's long review of the calamities of thirty future years, spoken in the memorial presence of the dead Henry V, is a precise dramatic expression of the narrative's parenthesis, 'as after you shall heare', of which many repetitions catch the effect of a remorseless historical law expounded by an omniscient commentator.

The symmetrical sallies and counter-sallies of the next hour of the pantomime express the fickle movement of Mars, so often moralized by Holinshed: 'thus did things waver in doubtful balance betwixt the two nations English and French'; 'thus oftentimes varied the chance of doubtful war'; 'thus flowed the victory, sometimes on the one party, and sometimes on the other' (Holinshed, pages 172, 180, 192). So speaks the dramatic Dauphin:

> Mars his true moving, even as in the heavens
> So in the earth, to this day is not known.
> Late did he shine upon the English side;
> Now we are victors, upon us he smiles.

> I.2.1–4

The literary commonplace carries the chronicle moral in a naïve rhetoric transparent enough to let the raw facts tell.

It is French cunning that most often conspires with Mars to confound the English. The sniping of Salisbury at Orleans exemplifies it in an arresting stage effect ready-made in Holinshed for upper stage (tarras) performance. But as Holinshed's data is otherwise scanty and undramatic, Shakespeare amplifies it by making the French instead of the English employ 'counterfeit husbandmen' to capture Rouen.[7] He betrays the chronicle detail in order to enforce one of its generalizations, for while on one occasion defending the use of fraud in lawful war, Holinshed habitually prefers honest violence – an impression strengthened in the play by the rival characterizations of Joan and Talbot. Talbot's stratagem at Auvergne (II.3) is not subtle-witted but represents the triumph of soldierly resourcefulness over French and female craft.

While 'martiall feates, and daily skirmishes' continue in France, the play returns in four scenes to England and conveys the essential Holinshed by keeping the civil causes coincident with the military effects. Thus the dramatic concurrence of the siege of Orleans and the brawl outside the Tower of London (I.3) directly expresses the chronicle point, 'Through dissention at home, all lost abroad' (Holinshed, page 228). The Gloucester–Winchester feud is elaborately chronicled and patience and some skill go into Shakespeare's abbreviation of it. More important than his management of the intricate detail, however, is the strategic liberty taken with the facts in order to reduce the formal reconciliation elaborately mounted in the chronicle to a repetition of the earlier squabble, but this time concluded with a reluctant, casual handshake; the Mayor, the muttered asides, and the servants off to the surgeon's and the tavern, demote the dignity of the event (Holinshed, page 146).[8] That quarrel thus becomes representative of those which Holinshed ascribes to 'privie malice and inward grudge', while the dynastic rivalry assumes by contrast a status appropriate to its remoter origin and more terrible consequence.

It is in his presentation of the struggle between Lancaster and York that Shakespeare does most to transcend the temper and enrich the data of the chronicle. For in the early pages of Holinshed the struggle is nowhere clearly epitomized. There are only allusions to things that will 'hereafter more manifestlie appeare'; Henry, for instance, creates Plantagenet Duke of York, 'not foreseeing that this preferment should be his destruction, nor that his seed should of his generation be the extreame end and finall conclusion' (Holinshed, page 155; Stone, page 223). Hence Shakespeare's invention of four scenes which, through the heraldic formality of their language, reveal the hidden keenness and permanence of the dynastic conflict. The only distinguished one – the Temple scene – is much in the manner of *Richard II*; there is the same tension between ceremony and spleen:

> And that I'll prove on better men than Somerset,
> Were growing time once ripened to my will.

> II.4.98–9

But the note is caught again in the scene of Mortimer's death:

> Here dies the dusky torch of Mortimer,
> Chok'd with ambition of the meaner sort.

> II.5.122–3

The two scenes between Vernon and Basset (III.4 and IV.1) extend the Roses dispute from the masters to the 'servants'; but unlike those other servants who enter *'with bloody pates'* (III.1.85 stage direction) in pursuit of Winchester's and Gloucester's causes, these conduct their quarrel according to 'the law of arms'. Ceremony and savagery are equally characteristic of chronicle taste, and in *Part One* a full range of types of dissension is displayed by the mutations of the spectacle.

The laboured and repetitious data of the chronicle are clarified without undue simplification, with the audience required to dwell at leisure on episodes of momentous and lasting significance to the course of history. The rhythm between pattern and process is maintained; the play like the history must be both reflected upon and lived through, its moral shape apprehended but its clamour and hurly-burly wracking the nerves. But not all the chronicle material is adroitly and happily assimilated. Shakespeare's embarrassment as heir to the facts and judgements of Holinshed is disconcertingly evident in his treatment of Joan. Holinshed presents two versions; a 'French' one, stated at length but unsympathetically, 'that this Jone (forsooth) was a damsell divine' (Holinshed, page 171; Stone, pages 210–12); and an 'English' one, owed to Monstrelet, that she was 'a damnable sorcerer suborned by Satan' (Holinshed, page 172). Shakespeare pursues the chronicle by making her a manifestly evil angel of light, and as the trick of turning devil into seeming angel was a Morality-play commonplace, a technique of presentation lay to hand.[9] But the figure was much easier to accept under the old allegoric conventions of the Morality play that Shakespeare had all but discarded than under the new historical documentary ones he was forging. In the early scenes the nice and nasty views about Joan are credibly distributed between the French and English,[10] but after allowing her to voice an authentic French patriotism (winning Burgundy back to her cause) Shakespeare capitulates and throws his French Daniel to the English lions, 'Done like a Frenchman — turn and turn again' (III.3.85). Shakespeare — as an examination of the detail would show — does nothing to mask and much to stress the tension between the rival images of 'Puzel' and 'Pussel', the 'high-minded strumpet' and the 'holy prophetess'. Late in the play she is made to speak a searching indictment of English hypocrisy (V.4.36 ff.) whose barbs are not removed by the spectacle of her converse with evil spirits.

The play ends with the patching of a false peace which holds no promise of a renewed civil order, and whose terms, born out of a silly flirtation, prefigure the final loss of France. None of the many reconciliations have any quality of goodwill, Shakespeare taking his tone again from Holinshed:

> But what cause soever hindered their accord and unitie . . . certeine it is, that the onelie and principal cause was, for that the God of peace and love was not among them, without whom no discord is quenched, no knot of concord fastened, no bond of peace confirmed, no distracted minds reconciled, no true freendship mainteined.
>
> (Holinshed, page 183)

Suffolk's courtship of Margaret (V.3) prefaces a false peace with a false love. To parody the absurdities of political romance Shakespeare allows Suffolk the style of a professional philanderer (one thinks of de Simier's wooing of Elizabeth for Alençon) and compiles for him 'a volume of enticing lines' more felicitous than Lacy's in *Friar Bacon and Friar Bungay*; but in Greene's play the courtship is an engaging frolic merely, while here the treacheries exercised in the politics of flirtation are as sinister as they are amusing — the betrayal of trust must have evil consequences in the harsh chronicle setting.

Holinshed grieves that 'the God of peace and love' was not among the jarring nobles; but in a sense he was — in the unfortunate person of King Henry — and Shakespeare is well aware of the irony. Henry is 'too virtuous to rule the realm of England', like Elidure, the comically naïve king in the early chronicle-morality *Nobody and Somebody*,[11] but Shakespeare makes the point unsmilingly. In the *Henry VI* plays, virtue, through varying degrees of culpable innocence, connives in its own destruction. Had they been performed in the reign of Henry VII, when the canonization of 'Holy Harry' was still a point of debate and his martyrdom a theme for civic spectacle, those who thought the King an innocent might have appealed to the first two plays, and those who took him for a saint, to the last. For as the plays advance, the paradoxical plight of moral man under the rule of historical and political processes grows more disturbing until it reaches something like a tragic solution.

Part Two: *the Sacrifice of Gloucester and the Dissolution of Law*

There is much in *Part Two* to remind us that we are witnessing the education of a tragic playwright. Shakespeare assimilates and puts to the test theological, political, and moral outlooks which, however ugly and pitiless, seem to meet with unsentimental honesty the recorded facts of human experience. *Part One* could not end in the manner of a heroic tragedy, for the history confronted Shakespeare with the fact that society somehow survives the deaths of its heroes and the conditions for its survival must go on being renewed – a point that tells again in *Julius Caesar*. *Part One* concludes by establishing the minimal and provisional terms of survival – the death of Joan and the marriage bargain, but the historical facts allow no revival in *Part Two* of the austere, soldierly virtues that supply the moral positives of the first part – Talbot will be displaced by Gloucester.

From one point of view the second and third plays share the same structural frame, supplied by Holinshed in passages such as this:

But most of all it would seeme, that God was displeased with this marriage: for after the confirmation thereof, the kings freends fell from him, both in England and in France, the lords of his realme fell at division, and the commons rebelled in such sort, that finallie after manie fields foughten, and manie thousands of men slaine, the king at length was deposed, and his sonne killed, and this queene sent home againe, with as much miserie and sorrow as she was received with pompe and triumphe: such is the instabilitie of worldlie felicitie, and so wavering is false flattering fortune. Which mutation and change of the better for the worse could not but nettle and sting hir with pensiveness, yea and any other person whatsoever, that having beene in good estate, falleth into the contrarie.

(Holinshed, page 208)

In their unabashed drift from God's displeasure to the waverings of fortune Holinshed's pieties are characteristic of chronicle theology. The subtler medieval distinctions between the will of God and the waywardness of Fortune are lost, but the dominant ideas remain, and they are crucial to an understanding of Shakespeare's tetralogy, and, more particularly, of the role of Queen Margaret. The chronicle is enlisting Old Testament theology to rationalize the processes of history: when the land is sinful, God's judgement recoils upon it, and evil must be atoned by blood sacrifice. Shakespeare makes fullest use of Margaret to exemplify this moral order; through the span of the plays she is in turn its agent, victim, and oracle. It is in *Richard III* that Shakespeare's ironic questioning of the chronicle providence is most telling, when Margaret, disengaged from the action but brought to the court in the teeth of historical fact, is made the malignant prophetess of God's displeasure, and Clarence is allowed to protest with humane eloquence against the theology of his murderers (I.4.178–270). In the *Henry VI* plays the chronicle theology is exposed to a different kind of test – that of the chronicle's own political ideology.

The chronicles were more ready to accept the tragic-religious solution of social disorder as a past and finished process than as an omnipresent law. They wrote in a tradition which had quietly assimilated the mundane, realistic attitudes for which Machiavelli was to become the most persuasive apologist; and whenever they write with an eye on the prospect of Tudor security, they show themselves sympathetic to the 'machiavellian' solution – stability imposed by strong authority. Hence their strictures on the 'overmuch mildness' of a Henry found 'too soft for governor of a kingdom', and hence the coolness with which they recognize the peace and prosperity of the later part of Edward IV's reign,[12] which owed more to the King's military ability and popularity (however limited) with nobility and commons than to his integrity as Rightful King and Servant of God. Shakespeare's most decisive criticism of the chronicle is his virtual suppression of the temporary recovery under Edward, thus making his moral of peace at the end of *Richard III* distinctly less 'machiavellian' than it appears in Holinshed – peace returns by God's ordinance only when the forces of evil are quite expended. The kind of dramatic thinking about history that makes Shakespeare's plays does not prove hospitable to the kind of uncritical good sense that allows the chroniclers to shift from one scale of values to another. In *Henry VI* the sacrificial idea, which makes catastrophe a consequence of sin, is sharply challenged by the 'machiavellian' idea that makes it a consequence of weakness.

While this range of problems is entertained in *Part Two* about the plight of the King himself, the unique form of the play is yielded by the martyrdom of Gloucester. The play climbs to one crisis – a central point in the third Act where the killing of Gloucester calls out the strongest statement of the moral-political positives; and it falls to a second – where the battle of St Albans occasions the most powerful poetry of negation.

It opens with a '*Flourish of trumpets; then hautboys*' announcing Margaret with chronicled 'pompe and triumph', but almost at once, as he lets the paper fall and addresses his 'peroration with such circumstance' to the assembled peers, it is Gloucester who dominates the theatre, assuming his representative and symbolic role. Like Gaunt in *Richard II*, he recollects the chivalry of the past and epitomizes a political wisdom alienated in the dramatic 'present'. But there is none of the spiritual and physical malaise that complicates the figure of Gaunt, no sterility or decay. Gaunt's prophecy is the 'ague's privilege' – his approaching death calls out his honesty; but Gloucester is vigorous and defiant, and his honesty brings about his death. If the Gaunt study is the more penetrating exploration of the relation of moral strength to political impotence, this version of Gloucester is the shrewder study of heroic virtue.

Holinshed says that Gloucester's praise should be undertaken by writers of 'large discourse', and notes (as he takes over the Tudor legend) the 'ornaments of his mind', his 'feats of chivalry', 'gravity in counsell' and 'soundness of policy' (Holinshed, page 211; Stone, pages 250, 265). Together with his magnanimity Holinshed finds a love of the commons and a devotion to the public good. With so strong a lead from the chronicle Shakespeare makes Gloucester's qualities both personal and symbolic. In the first two Acts he comes to stand for the rule of law and for the integrity of nobility and commons – the conditions of social order that cease to prevail the moment he is murdered. Holinshed is outspoken about the destruction of the rule of law: 'while the one partie sought to destroie the other, all care of the common-wealth was set aside, and justice and equitie clearelie exiled' (Holinshed, page 237). But his moral is untied to any single incident, and Shakespeare gives it greater dramatic force by linking it specifically with the destiny of Gloucester. The chronicle supplied hint enough:

> Suerlie the duke, verie well learned in the law civill, detesting malefactors, and punishing offenses in severitie of justice, gat him hatred of such as feared condigne reward for their wicked dooings. And although the duke sufficientlie answered to all things against him objected; yet, because his death was determined, his wisedome and innocencie nothing availed.

> (Holinshed, page 211; Stone, pages 250, 265)

In the chronicle Gloucester's learning in civil law takes the form of a wearisome passion for litigation. In the play he is first the severe executor of Justice and then its patient, vicarious victim. As Protector he prescribes the judicial combat between Horner and his prentice, and replaces York by Somerset in France: 'This is the law, and this Duke Humphrey's doom' (I.3.208). When Eleanor is banished he again speaks the formal language of his office: 'the law, thou seest, hath judged thee. | I cannot justify whom the law condemns' (II.3.15–16). Too much in this manner would have been wearing, but Shakespeare traces in Gloucester the humane impulses from which and for which the Law should speak. His practical genius for improvising justice is exemplified in the mock-miracle of St Albans (II.1); it delights the dramatic townsmen as much as the theatre audience, making Humphrey the shrewd, popular hero respected and 'beloved of the commons'. The King's piety gives place to laughter, displaying his curiously mixed qualities of ingenuousness and insight; and the scene concludes with an elegant exchange of sarcasms, a timely reminder that Suffolk and Beaufort are jealous of Gloucester's public virtues.

Shakespeare makes less use in *Part Two* of the heraldic and pageant devices which accent the pattern of *Part One*, and fuller use of the specifically dramatic techniques of the Morality play and English Seneca. Borrowing as much of the chronicle language as he can, he illuminates the historical event by casting it into a Morality perspective:

> Ah, gracious lord, these days are dangerous!
> Virtue is chok'd with foul ambition,
> And charity chas'd hence by rancour's hand;
> Foul subornation is predominant,
> And equity exil'd your Highness' land.
>
> III.1.142–6

'Justice and equitie clearelie exiled,' says Holinshed (page 237). But the Morality abstractions are in their turn tempered by the immediate interest in people that Shakespeare learned from his attempts to make historical facts dramatically convincing.

The private man is never for long masked by the public figure. Gloucester speaks of his condemned Duchess in tones admirably poised between personal feeling and the decorum of his office (II.1.185 ff.), and he speaks from his office unequivocally when she is led from the court (II.3.16). But as soon as she is gone, his eyes 'full of tears', he asks the King's permission to leave, and for the first time we learn that Shakespeare's Gloucester (not the chroniclers') is an old man; the personal pathos is heightened and we are reminded that honour is the prerogative of a fading generation. When he next appears, as looker-on at Eleanor's penance, the scene enlarges into a mutability threnody, including the conventional *Mirror for Magistrates* image of summer giving place to barren winter, and the chronicle sentiment about the irony of personal misfortune – 'To think upon my pomp shall be my hell' (II.4.41). But it remains an event in the London streets. The picture of Eleanor's humiliation (however deserved) confesses the cruelty of

> The abject people gazing on thy face,
> With envious looks, laughing at thy shame.
>
> II.4.11–12

The intensely passive philosophy of Gloucester meeting the frustrated malice of his Duchess foreshadows the second scene of *Richard II*, but Gaunt puts jaded faith in the principle of non-resistance to an anointed king, while Gloucester's more naïve faith is in the integrity of the law: 'I must offend before I be attainted' (II.4.59). His trial scene (III.1) takes on a symbolic quality. Henry's reaction to it, undescribed in the chronicles, is used in the play to disclose the natural sympathy between the King's impotent saintliness and Gloucester's political and personal integrity:

> Ah, uncle Humphrey, in thy face I see
> The map of honour, truth, and loyalty! ...
> And as the butcher takes away the calf,
> And binds the wretch, and beats it when it strays,
> Bearing it to the bloody slaughter-house,
> Even so, remorseless, have they borne him hence.
>
> III.1.202–3, 210–13

Gloucester's murder is a piece of politic butchery at the centre of the 'plotted tragedy' of the conspirators who are credited with a perverse skill in making an unnatural offence taste of expediency and practical wisdom: 'But yet we want a colour for his death', and ''Tis meet he be condemn'd by course of law' (III.1.236–7).

We are not made witnesses to the actual murder, but Gloucester's strangled body is exhibited in a sort of verbal close-up, a remarkable passage, which throws an unusual stress on physical horror (III.2.160 ff.). By this device a frightening spectacular force is given to the dominant historical and tragic idea of the play. By a staged metaphor now, 'Virtue is chok'd with foul ambition', and the play's mime displays the historical cause-and-effect, by which the murder of Gloucester issues in the Cade rebellion. The strangled body lies on the stage while the commons 'like an angry hive of bees' beat upon the doors.

But his death, as Gloucester says himself, is but the prologue to the plotted tragedy. Shakespeare is exposing a period of English history when atrocities became part of the routine of public life and stayed so for some twenty years. Hence his knowledge, if not experience, of the arts of English Seneca becomes relevant to his own art as dramatic historian. It is perhaps no accident that at this point of the narrative Holinshed refers us to 'maister Foxe's book of acts and monuments' (Holinshed, page 212). No reader of Foxe could be easily startled by the *Thyestes*, the *Troades*, or *Titus Andronicus*. And in the central Acts of *Part Two* we can observe the confluence of the Senecal dramatic tradition, with its ruthless retributive morality, and the Christian (or Hebraic) cult of *Vindicta Dei*. These acts present not only what Foxe calls 'the cruel death or martyrdom of the Good Duke of Glocester' but also 'the judgement of God upon them which persecuted the Duke'.[13] But Shakespeare is not uncritical of the myth behind the grim theocratic drama that features the deaths of Suffolk and Winchester. Although he allows some of his characters to enjoy a complacent relish in witnessing or executing the interventions of the wrath of God, the audience is not allowed to share it. All the acts of retribution in this play and the next are invested in an atmosphere of evil – the images sickening and grotesque:

> And thou that smil'dst at good Duke Humphrey's death
> Against the senseless winds shalt grin in vain.
>
> IV.1.76–7

Suffolk's death is an act of lynch law, and one of several similar happenings which are at once a satisfying act of retribution, and therefore a recognition of the chronicle 'Providence'; and a 'barbarous and bloody spectacle' (IV.1.144) and therefore a moral and aesthetic challenge to the validity of that Providence. In his presentation of the Cardinal's death (III.3), however, and in his insinuations of the causal chain of prophecy, omen, curse, imprecation, and dream, Shakespeare does stage the pitiless pageant of Holinshed and Foxe – *Vindicta Dei* works through revenge figures, through the worm of conscience (as plastic as a tapeworm) and through 'chance' contingencies. But so much (were it not for the tightness of the organization) might have been within the range of Peele or Greene. Shakespeare's play is distinguished by its understanding of the tragic rhythm of political history.

At first glance it might seem that Shakespeare's treatment of the Cade rebels is less sympathetic than Holinshed's. The chronicle Cade is 'of goodlie stature and right pregnant wit'; his 'fair promises of reformation' and his 'Complaint of the Commons of

Kent' are responsible and sensible (Holinshed, page 222); and his tactics at the start are admirably humane. Why then the comic but bloody spectacle of the fourth Act of *Part Two*? Brents Stirling[14] suggests that Shakespeare was aligning himself with those who most severely judged the rioting Brownists and Anabaptists of his own day, and claims a specific parallel between the dramatic Cade and Hacket, a riot leader convicted in 1591. But Hacket was a far grosser fanatic than the Cade of the play (out of spiritual zeal he bit off a man's nose and swallowed it), and in any case there is evidence that Shakespeare deliberately avoided giving any religious savour to the rebellion; it might have been quite otherwise had he delayed the Cardinal's death for a scene or two. It has been said too that Shakespeare coarsened his stage mobs from personal antipathy, and no doubt he had an eye for outrages in the London streets, a nose for the sour breath of the plebeians and an ear for riotous chop-logic; but at no point in any play do they pervert Shakespeare's objectivity of judgement or his rich human sympathies.

To understand the Cade scenes we must recognize that Shakespeare distorts Holinshed's account of the rebellion itself merely in order to emphasize its place in a larger and more significant movement of historical cause and effect. The rebellion is offered as an evil consequence of misrule, specifically of the misrule of Suffolk. The fuse is touched early, when Suffolk tears the petitions of the innocent, conscientious citizens (I.3.37). But the petitioners, voicing their bewildered, nervous protests, the apprentices of the Peter Thump scenes, and the crowd at St Albans, while they make up the 'populace' are not yet the 'mob'. The mob emerges at the moment of Gloucester's death, when the people are compelled, through lack of a law-giver, through the total breakdown of the constitutional rule of order, to take the law into their own hands. The 'populace' with a just grievance is by the exercise of violence transformed into the 'mob', executors of lynch law. At first they are free from a 'stubborn opposite intent' (III.2.251), but finally, 'thirsting after prey' (IV.4.51), they are capable of a full range of atrocities.

The violence is not merely self-generated; all that York stands for in the way of destructive political purpose is right behind the reprisals of Smithfield. Nor are the reprisals quite arbitrary. Since Gloucester is the dramatic symbol of regular administration of the law, and unquestioning faith in its authority, it is no accident that Shakespeare focused the iconoclasm of the rioters upon the agents and monuments of the civil law. To do so he turned back in the chronicle to the Tyler rebellion in the reign of Richard II and borrowed just those touches which furthered his purpose – the killing of the lawyers, the destruction of the Savoy and the Inns of Court, and the burning of the records of the realm.[15] It is significant too that Lord Say, the 'treasurer of England' in 1450, is merged with the Lord Chief Justice beheaded by Tyler in 1381; his stage martyrdom (IV.7) is that of a humane judge – thus obliquely repeating the point about Gloucester.

Holinshed tells how the rising was subdued by Canterbury and Winchester bringing to Southwark a pardon from the King (Holinshed, page 226; Stone, page 280). In the play the bishops figure only momentarily, in a soft-hearted plan of Henry's (IV.4.9), and Shakespeare abstains from giving to Lord Say the role he allows Sir Thomas in comparable circumstances in *Sir Thomas More*, quietening the people by authoritative eloquence (II.4.62–177). Although Lord Say has a comparable dignity,

> The trust I have is in mine innocence,
> And therefore am I bold and resolute
>
> IV.4.59–60

he shares the vulnerability of Gloucester as well as his integrity, and his head soon dances on a pole. Stafford tries abuse (IV.2.117), but that fails too, and it is left to Buckingham and Clifford to restore their version of 'order' (IV.8). In place of the leisured approach of two prelates, gathering exhausted citizens about them, Shakespeare offers the murderous rabblement, their full cry silenced by a trumpet and by the appearance of two leading soldiers with their body-guards. The pardon, garbled by Buckingham (IV.8.8), is not made a factor in the peace. Clifford steps in with a sharply different appeal, invocating, as Shakespeare puts it elsewhere, the ghost of Henry V. Cade brutally reminds the people that they have still to recover their 'ancient freedom', but his brand of demagoguery is surpassed by the fine irrelevance of Clifford's patriotic exhortation – as from soldier to soldiers, from one English-man to another. The oratory is not endorsed by the situation in the play (no French invasion threatens) but its effect is to canalize destructive energy along a track less threatening to the Nobles of England – profitable indeed, and, as Shakespeare shows in *Henry V*, even glorious in its own way. But *Henry V* touches the heroic through its setting of a tiny group of English against terrible odds; here the mob yell of 'A Clifford! a Clifford! We'll follow the King and Clifford' (IV.8.52–3) is ironically close in spirit to the 'Kill and knock down' of the scene's opening. The true interpretation of these events is voiced by the only figure on the stage who is not implicated any longer, in Cade's: 'Was ever feather so lightly blown to and fro as this multitude? The name of Henry the Fifth hales them to an hundred mischiefs, and makes them leave me desolate' (IV.8.54–6). Cade is seen for what he is, but when he is chased off stage by his followers, there is a strong impression that he is victimized. The blood-lust of the mob has been diverted but not sublimated.

In accents reminiscent of his apostrophe on Horner's death (II.3.98–102), Henry acknowledges the gruesome gift of Cade's head: 'The head of Cade! Great God, how just art Thou!' (V.1.68). There is this recognition that God's spirit showed itself in the dispersal of the rebels, not in the tide of rebellion; in the killing of Cade, not in his subornation. But Henry's outlook is of a piece with his isolation and impotence. Cade's death is not much more than a marginal note (IV.10); it occurs when he is alone and starv-ing and cannot have the central significance that Henry's piety attributes to it. Iden, the yeoman in the garden and Cade's killer, is (as E. M. W. Tillyard puts it) a 'symbol of degree', one who 'seek[s] not to wax great by others' waning'; but he is a formal symbol, mechanically put together out of the chronicle, and can only appear as a 'representative figure' to King Henry himself in a scene which Shakespeare is careful not to put last. As it is, the silence of the stage garden is not allowed to still the audience's memory of the clamour of Southwark; the internecine violence of the rebellion is carried through, across the recessed interludes, to the battlefield of St Albans, where Clifford himself speaks the most terrible of Shakespeare's pronouncements about war (V.2.31 ff.).

Thus the moral of the last part of the play is not the simple-minded one of the *Mirror for Magistrates* which tells 'How Jack Cade traitorously rebelling against his King, was for his treasons and cruel doings worthily punished'.[16] It is assimilated into a firm comprehensive structure, a version of political and historical tragedy that will serve later as the ground of *Julius Caesar* — another play which moves through the plotting and execution of an assassination, through the generation of lynch-law in the streets, to the deflection of that violence into civil war.

Part Three *and the Shape of Anarchy*

The tragic alignments of *Part Three* are declared on the St Albans battlefield. Henry pre-figures the sacrificial victim, suspended between action and inaction — he will 'nor fight nor fly' (V.2.74). Richard of York is the agent of that political realism that is born in *Part Two* to flourish in the later plays; he is the calculating joker and killer who despises the law of arms, rejoicing in the superstitious prophecy by which he slaughters Somerset underneath 'an ale-house' paltry sign', and he states the harsh moral assumption that makes for anarchy in *Part Three*:

> Sword, hold thy temper; heart, be wrathful still:
> Priests pray for enemies, but princes kill.
>
> V.2.70–71

Clifford, Richard's antagonist in fact and symbol, is not a 'machiavel' but a nihilist, recognizing the virtues of chivalry and order but dedicated to the defilement of both. Some disturbances of the text and inconsistency of fact suggest that his key speech (V.2.31–65), provoked by York's killing of the elder Clifford, was written during or immediately after the composition of *Part Three*, and set back into *Part Two* to offer intimations of the violence to come.[17] Its opening lines are powerfully symbolic:

> Shame and confusion! All is on the rout;
> Fear frames disorder, and disorder wounds
> Where it should guard.
>
> V.2.31 ff.

They refer literally to the sort of confusion sometimes reported in the chronicles, where men are led to kill their friends instead of their enemies. But Shakespeare abstains from specifying the kind of disorder; by not limiting the connotation of 'disorder', 'frame', and 'confusion' he keeps the abstract force of the words and makes the image immense and the idea metaphysically reverberant. In the next lines war is both the son of hell and the minister of heaven, ideas from Holinshed transmuted into a searching and disturbing rhetoric.

> O war, thou son of hell,
> Whom angry heavens do make their minister,
> Throw in the frozen bosoms of our part
> Hot coals of vengeance!

But while the speech epitomizes scattered groups of chronicle ideas, it keeps the urgency of the battlefield and it charges its destructive generalizations about war with heroic resolution.

> Let no soldier fly.
> He that is truly dedicate to war
> Hath no self-love; nor he that loves himself
> Hath not essentially, but by circumstance,
> The name of valour.

The simple idea that the true soldier does not nurse his life is transformed with measured, emphatic finality, into an absolute acceptance of an ideal of nihilistic self-sacrifice. The nihilism that follows outreaches the St Albans situation and assumes cosmic scale.

> O, let the vile world end
> And the premised flames of the last day
> Knit earth and heaven together!
> Now let the general trumpet blow his blast,
> Particularities and petty sounds
> To cease!

The lines glance with magnificent assurance from the image of the last judgement to the dead figure of old Clifford, to age and wisdom in time of peace:

> Wast thou ordain'd, dear father,
> To lose thy youth in peace and to achieve
> The silver livery of advised age,
> And in thy reverence and thy chair-days thus
> To die in ruffian battle?

There is a suddenly gathering intimacy, and then, out of the personal pathos, a re-generation of the mood of total war.

> Even at this sight
> My heart is turn'd to stone; and while 'tis mine
> It shall be stony.

The rare accomplishment of Clifford's speech should not blind us to its organic function in the plays. It is simply the most lucid and telling expression of one range of anarchic impulses at large in the tetralogy. The other range, which does as much or more to precipitate anarchy, is represented in the emergence of the Richards of York and Gloucester. In the play as history, Richard of York is isolated from the rival barons by his greater political know-how. But, equally important, in the play as theatrical entertainment he is isolated by his privileged relationship with the audience. The politician is from the chronicle; the soliloquizer is from the dramatic conventions of the Morality play, and the key to Shakespeare's success is the intimate connexion that he found between the two. The main fact about the chronicle York is that he takes his opportunities skilfully because, unlike the unreflective opportunists among his peers, he anticipates, calculates, and prepares the ground. His 'attempt', says Holinshed, 'was politicly handled', 'secretly kept' and his purpose 'ready' before it was 'openly published' (Holinshed, page 212; Stone, page 255). If all that York stands for in history is to be properly conveyed in the play, his emergence when 'mischief breaks out' must take his enemies by surprise. But it must not take the audience by surprise; hence Shakespeare introduces short conspiratorial scenes to put fellow Yorkists *partly* 'in the know' (the colloquialism fits the mood), and adds a number of soliloquies to put the audience wholly in the know. The soliloquy given to York at *Part Two*, I.1.209, becomes the first experiment in the form to be turned to such advantage in *Richard III*; it enlists the audience's sympathy against the 'others', exploits its readiness to take a low view of human nature and be brutally realistic about politics. In this first soliloquy York voices the muscular chronicle judgement that critics have sometimes taken for Shakespeare's definitive verdict on Henry:

> And force perforce I'll make him yield the crown,
> Whose bookish rule hath pull'd fair England down.
>
> *Part Two*, I.1.253–4

But the rough verbal shoulder-shrugging of York is precisely expressive of the factious energy which does most to pull down fair England. A second soliloquy, in the same manner, sets York, 'the labouring spider', behind the inception of the Cade rebellion (*Part Two*, V.1.1 ff.).

In a passage of reflection on 'the tragicall state of this land under the rent regiment of King Henrie', Holinshed speaks of the 'sundrie practices' which 'imbecilled' the 'prerogative' of the King, and wonders at the pitched battles, which he divides into two groups, that were fought over and about him (Holinshed, pages 272–3). Shakespeare keeps the outline and emphasizes the distinction between the military and political sources of catastrophe. The first two Acts deal with the battles of 1460–61, when Henry had that 'naked name of king'; the third and fourth Acts are dominantly political, and about the chicanery of the nobles with their rival kings; and the last presents the campaigns of 1471, in which politics and war are indistinguishable. Once again one is struck in performance by the expressive force of the mere dumb-show and noise (witness the stage directions); kings and crowns are treated as stage properties to enforce the chronicle moral about contempt for sovereignty, and Warwick is made quite literally the setter-up and plucker-down of kings (e.g. IV.3). The panto-mime is as skilful in the political scenes. The scene in the French court (III.3), for instance, where Margaret has won the support of King Lewis, only to lose it to Warwick who comes as ambassa-dor from Edward, becomes a superb exercise in the acrobatics of diplomacy, when letters are at last brought from Edward about the Bona marriage.

For the greater part of the third play Shakespeare is content to follow Holinshed in making his characters public masks, without intimately felt life, and therefore hardly seeming responsible for what they do. He tightens the sequence of atrocities, telescopes time, and eliminates all rituals of government, until the stage action and reaction appear yet more savagely mechanical than in the chronicle. So long as the characterization is neutral the first tetralogy displays a barbarous providence ruling murderous automatons whose reactions are predictable in terms of certain quasi-Hobbesian assumptions about human nature: when argument fails men resort to force; when an oath is inconvenient they break it; their power challenged, they retort with violence; their power subdued, they resort to lies, murder, or suicide; their honour impugned, they look for revenge; their enemies at their mercy, they torture and kill them; and if a clash of loyalties occurs they resolve it in the interest of their own survival. Such might be the vision of the play's pantomime, but its dimensions are not confined to its pantomime and to its shallower rhetoric. The anarchic, egocentric impulses are not presented as the inescapable laws of human nature; they are at most manifestations of forces that automatically take over when the constraints of government are withheld. Law and order cease to prevail when men cease to believe in them, and the process by which this comes about is explored in the play's dominant characters.

The figures of Clifford and York who, in *Part Two*, personalize two kinds of anarchic scepticism — the soldier's nihilism and the politician's realism — are displaced in *Part Three* by the more significant contrast between Richard of Gloucester and King Henry. With obvious propriety these are chosen to characterize the moral tensions which give meaning to the deep chaos of the last phase of the reign. But the crimes of the Roses Wars are so multiple and their agents so numerous that Shakespeare could not attempt, even if at this early date it were within his power, the comprehensively intimate exploration of evil he undertakes in *Macbeth*, and he allows himself only that measure of intimate soliloquy and address which will accord with the conventions of historical pageant.

In the first two plays the chronicle myth of a King absurdly and irrelevantly virtuous can just about pass muster, and in the first scene of *Part Three* Henry's virtue is still associated with impotence; his war of 'frowns, words, and threats' is disarmed by his readiness to concede the Yorkist claims, by the wry defection of Exeter (unwarranted by the history), and by the Robin Hood trickery of Warwick; his conscience-stricken asides carry as little conviction as his military posturing, and one feels the *gaucherie* is the playwright's as well as the character's. In the next phase, however, Shakespeare's tragic art wins distinction from the ferocity of the material and Henry assumes a stature outside the chronicle compass.

Both the finer qualities of Henry's virtue and the intensity of Richard of Gloucester's virulence spring from Shakespeare's treatment of the Battle of Wakefield. Conventional heroic ideals cannot survive the battle which turns on two blasphemies of chivalry – the killing of the prince and the degradation of the mock-king. Clifford's slaughter of Rutland (I.3), in calculated contempt of the Priest and the law of arms, is a repudiation of the myth that expects from every 'gentleman' in battle the virtues of the lion. The values apt to a heroic battle-play are displaced by those prevailing in parts of English Seneca; in Heywood's *Thyestes*, for example, where 'ire thinks nought unlawful to be done', 'Babes be murdered ill', and 'bloodshed lies the land about' (I.1.79–89). Shakespeare gives the revenge motive a great political significance by relating it to the dynastic feud for which Clifford is not alone responsible.

Anarchism, Shakespeare had learned from the Cade scenes, is more dramatic when it is iconoclastic, and the next Wakefield outrage, the paper crowning (I.4), mutilates the idols of Knighthood, Kingship, Womanhood, and Fatherhood. In making a ritual of the atrocity Shakespeare imitates the history – the scene is a formal set-piece because it was so staged by its historical performers. Holinshed tells how the Lancastrians made obeisance and cried, 'Haile, king without rule' – 'as the Jewes did unto Christ' (Holinshed, page 269; Stone, page 299). Although Shakespeare suppresses the open blasphemy, he keeps the crucifixion parallel with the line, 'now looks he like a king' (I.4.96), and, more significantly, by combining the mockery reported in one of a choice of chronicle accounts with the paper-coronation in another (Holinshed, page 268; Stone, page 299). He takes little liberty with the chronicle, moreover, when he makes the stage-managed historical ceremony into an ordered, antiphonal combat of words, with Northumberland presiding, as it were, in the rhetorical lists. In spite of the controlling formality the language moves on several planes between gnomic generalization,

> 'Tis government that makes them seem divine;
> The want thereof makes thee abominable;
>
> I.4.132–3

stylized feeling,

> O tiger's heart wrapp'd in a woman's hide!
> How couldst thou drain the life-blood of the child;
>
> I.4.137–8

plain, personal pathos,

> This cloth thou dipp'dst in blood of my sweet boy;
>
> I.4.157

and colloquial venom,

> And where's that valiant crook-back prodigy,
> Dicky your boy, that with his grumbling voice
> Was wont to cheer his dad in mutinies?
>
> I.4.75–7

In the blinding scene of *King Lear* the same changes will be rung in a richer peal, but there is enough in the Wakefield scene's counterpoint of reflection and feeling to tax the resources of its actors.

Henry is not made witness to the event. He is allowed the dignity of total isolation, and when he comes to the stage molehill at Towton (II.5), it is to speak the most moving of Shakespeare's comments on the civil wars. Shakespeare is less fully engaged when he writes about the objectives of the battle as seen by the participants than by its futility as it appears to a suffering observer. Hall had felt a similar need to withdraw into reflection:

This conflict was in maner unnaturall, for in it the sonne fought agaynst the father, the brother agaynst the brother, the Nephew agaynst the Uncle, and the tenaunt agaynst hys Lorde, which slaughter did sore and much weaken the puyssance of this realme.[18]

In *Gorboduc* and in Daniel's *Civil Wars* the commonplace is retailed with a complacent omniscience damaging to living language.[19] But by attributing it to the King in the course of battle Shakespeare is able to quicken it with personal feeling; beneath the ceremonious surface we again sense the pulse and surge of events.

The hint for the opening lines is one of Hall's 'ebb and flow of battle' clichés (Stone, page 306), but Shakespeare insinuates rarer images of the peaceful, symmetrical rhythms of nature – 'the morning's war' and 'the shepherd, blowing of his nails', and after touching the conflicts inherent in nature, arrests the movement of battle in that of the sea – 'the equal poise of this fell war'. A glance at the humour and pathos of Henry's isolation (Margaret and Clifford have chid him from the battle), with a touch of wry exhaustion ('Would I were dead, if God's good will were so'), offers assurance of Shakespeare's gift for 're-living the past', and the sequent lines of exquisite pastoral seem to re-create the convention out of the kind of human experience which underlies it. An alarum returns us to the battle and to a glimpse of its victims in another statuesque mirror-scene in which blood and pallor are made heraldic (II.5.97 ff.). Once again the feeling for the past is the cathedral-pavement sort, not the chronicle sort; it is at once a refreshing and a potentially devitalizing mood, and after a hundred and twenty lines Shakespeare pulls us out of it and lets the pantomime get under way again.

The authority of Henry's commentary on Towton is sufficiently memorable to help vindicate the innocence of the speech he makes before the keepers arrest him:

> My pity hath been balm to heal their wounds,
> My mildness that allay'd their swelling griefs,
> My mercy dried their water-flowing tears.
>
> IV.8.41 ff.

From this and a few other passages in the plays it would be possible to present Henry as the centre of a moral parable whose lineaments are traced in Thomas Elyot's *The Governour*. The King, says Elyot, must be merciful, but too much *Clementia* is a sickness of mind; as soon as any offend him the King should 'immediately strike him with his most terrible dart of vengeance'. But the occasions when

Henry seems guilty of an excess of virtue are rare, and he is at his most impressive when he is martyred in his last scene of *Part Three*, not when he tries to throw his weight about in the first. The Wakefield battle once fought, moreover, 'the terrible dart of vengeance' is lost to the armoury of virtue. Henry's bemused and disappointed faith in the political efficacy of mercy, pity, peace, and love does not deserve the editorial mockery it has received – 'characteristically effeminate' and 'smug complacency'.[20] Henry's virtue may be defective but Shakespeare commands from his audience a full reverence for it when, at the moment of his extermination, the King confronts his ultimate antagonist, Richard of Gloucester.

Richard is introduced as York's heroic soldier son, but in his first characteristic speech of length (II.1.79 ff.) he becomes the bitter, unchivalrous avenger – a reaction to the Messenger's report of Wakefield which seems instinctive and inevitable. But Richard not only reacts to events (all the barons do that), he also becomes the conscious embodiment of all the drives – moral, intellectual, and physical – that elsewhere show themselves only in the puppetry. Translating into theatrical terms, we might say that when he takes the stage for his first exercise of the soliloquy-prerogative he inherits from York (at the end of III.2), his language shows him capable of playing the parts of York, Clifford, Edward, Margaret, or Warwick. All their energies are made articulate: the doggedness of York 'that reaches at the moon' and the same eye for the glitter of the Marlovian crown; the dedication to evil which characterizes Clifford; the prurience of Edward; the decorated and ruthless rhetoric of Margaret; and Warwick's gifts of king-maker, resolute 'to command, to check, to o'erbear'. Shakespeare has him use the fantastic lore about his birth to admirable effect: it strengthens the impression of blasphemy against love and fertility, makes deformity license depravity, and, most important, allegorizes the birth of a political monster in the present by recalling that of a physical monster in the past, 'Like to a chaos, or an unlick'd bear-whelp'. But it is not all specifically birth-imagery – about Richard having teeth and the dogs howling. The sense of violent struggle, of unnatural energies breaking free, is best caught in lines that are not explicitly about birth at all:

> And I — like one lost in a thorny wood
> That rents the thorns and is rent with the thorns,
> Seeking a way and straying from the way;
> Not knowing how to find the open air,
> But toiling desperately to find it out —
> Torment myself to catch the English crown;
> And from that torment I will free myself
> Or hew my way out with a bloody axe.

III.2.174–81

It is from the kennel of England's womb that this hell-hound is to bite itself free. At the end of the soliloquy Richard promises the audience a performance more entertaining than any heroic fantasy or medieval Trojan legend; he will outplay all politic dissemblers, 'add colours to the chameleon', 'Change shapes with Protheus' and 'set the murderous Machiavel to school'. The ground is prepared for *Richard III*, where for three Acts the comic idiom will dominate the tragic, with politics a kings' game best played by cunning actors.

But the continuity with the mood of *Richard III* is deliberately fractured and the tragic mode made to dominate the comic in the scene of Henry's death. The King opposes Richard's tongue and sword with a moral force that Shakespeare makes all but transcendent and the 'scene of death' that 'Roscius' — the actor and devil Richard — performs at last, comes near to a tragic consummation. Yet the qualifications 'all but' and 'comes near' are, after all, necessary. The brute facts of history will not allow a satisfying tragic outcome; Shakespeare cannot pretend that the martyrdom of an innocent king appeased the appetite of providence or exhausted the sophisticated savagery that Richard stands for.

Nor can Hall's dynastic myth be enlisted to reassure us that all will be well when the White Rose is wedded to the Red — that will only be possible at the end of *Richard III* when, in a kind of postscript to the complete tetralogy, Richmond will step into the Elizabethan present and address an audience sufficiently remote from Henry's reign. As it is, the plays of *Henry VI* are not, as it were, haunted by the ghost of Richard II, and the catastrophes of the civil wars are not laid to Bolingbroke's charge; the catastrophic virtue of Henry and the catastrophic evil of Richard are not an inescapable inheritance from the distant past but are generated by the happenings we are made to witness.

The questioning of the ways of God and the roles of good and evil in English history will be reopened in *Richard III*, but in the interim *Part Three* ends, as tragedies remotely derived from fertility rites of course should, with some elaborate imagery of autumn reaping. It is fitting that Richard should be standing by to blast the harvest and to boast himself a Judas.

NOTES

1. Richard Simpson, 'The Politics of Shakspere's Historical Plays', *Transactions of the New Shakspere Society* (1874). A similar approach is made by L. B. Campbell.

2. Quoted in E. K. Chambers, *Shakespeare* (1930), II, 188.

3. T. M. Raysor (ed.), *Coleridge's Shakespearean Criticism* (1930), I, 138.

4. See J. Pearce, 'An Earlier Talbot Epitaph', *Modern Language Notes* (1944), page 327.

5. pages 585–625 in the 1587 edition. These are the 'first phase' as they supply almost all the material of *Part One*. *Part Two* uses pages 622–43, and *Part Three* pages 643–93.

6. Raphael Holinshed, *Chronicles*, second edition, 1587, reprint of 1807–8, III, 161.

7. W. G. Boswell-Stone, *Shakespeare's Holinshed* (1896), pages 205–7.

8. Here it is Bedford who formally rebukes the quarrelsome lords; the play's homely figure of the mayor is borrowed from Fabyan.

9. For example, John Bale, *The Temptation of our Lord* (see *Works*, edited by J. S. Farmer, page 155), and *The Conflict of Conscience* (see Hazlitt-Dodsley, VI, 35).

10. The only mocking lines spoken of Joan by the French are Alençon's at I.2.119; the English messenger calls her 'holy prophetess' at I.4.102.

11. This play (edited by Richard Simpson in *The School of Shakspere*, 1878) treats the ups and downs of Elidure's reign with challenging irreverence. The extant edition is of 1606, but the original may antedate *Henry VI*.

12. Hall's titles pass from the 'troublesome season' of Henry VI to the 'prosperous reign' of Edward IV. Shakespeare's judgement of Edward is harsher than that of any of the chroniclers.

13. John Foxe, *Actes and Monuments* (1583), page 706.

14. *The Populace in Shakespeare* (1949), pages 101 ff.

15. See Stone, pages 271, 277–8, for the relevant chronicle passages.

16. *A Mirror for Magistrates*, edited by Lily B. Campbell (1938), page 171.

17. In *Henry VI, Part Three*, I.1.9, the elder Clifford is said by York, his stage killer, to have been slain by common soldiers. Since *Henry VI, Part Two*, V.2, and *Part Three*, I.3, are both indebted to a passage in Hall (see Stone, page 297) it is possible that Shakespeare revised the earlier scene to motivate Clifford's killing of Rutland.

18. *The Union of the Two Noble and Illustre Families of Lancaster and York* (1548), reprint of 1809, page 256.

19. The peroration of *Gorboduc* and the first stanza of *The Civil Wars*.

20. See notes to IV.8.38–50 in Hart's Arden and Wilson's New Cambridge editions.

FOUR

Angel with Horns:
The Unity of *Richard III**

A. P. Rossiter

'Let's write "good angel" on the devil's horn'
Measure for Measure, II.4.16

IN the Second Part of *Henry IV* (III.1) the King and Warwick are talking away the midnight, or the King's insomnia; and the King remembers how Richard spoke like a prophet of the future treachery of the Percies. Warwick replies that those who look for rotations in history can indeed appear to be prophets:

> There is a history in all men's lives,
> Figuring the natures of the times deceas'd;
> The which observ'd, a man may prophesy,
> With a near aim, of the main chance of things
> As yet not come to life, who in their seeds
> And weak beginning lie intreasured.
> Such things become the hatch and brood of time.
>
> III.1.80–86

Richard, he explains, had observed 'the necessary form' of the events he had seen happen; and from that he could 'create a perfect guess' of some that were to ensue as 'the hatch and brood of time'.

Men have always looked for such a predictability in history: it gives the illusion of a comfortably ordered world. They have also often read – and written – historical records to show that the course of events has been guided by a simple process of divine

---

*From *Angel with Horns* by A. P. Rossiter, edited by Graham Storey (1961), pages 1–22. Copyright © Longmans, Green & Co. Ltd, 1961. Reprinted by kind permission of the publishers, Theatre Arts Books, New York, and Longmans, Green & Co. Ltd, London.

justice, dispensing rewards and punishments here on earth and seeing to it that the wicked do *not* thrive like the green bay-tree (as the Psalmist thought), and that virtue is not 'triumphant only in theatrical performances' (as the humane Mikado put it: being a Gilbertian Japanese, not an Elizabethan Christian). The story-matter of the Henry VI plays and of *Richard III* accepted both of these comforting and comfortable principles.

When I say 'story-matter' I mean what the chronicles gave the author (or authors) of these four plays, and I wish to remain uncommitted as to whether their *plots* (and especially that of *Richard III*) work entirely within those reassuring limitations.

I am averse to source-study, as material for lectures. Yet sad experience of human nature (and perhaps of historians) leads me to remind you how the Richard III myth ('*story*') came to reach Shakespeare. In the play, you remember, the Bishop of Ely, Morton, plots with Buckingham and runs away to join Richmond (Henry Tudor). He duly became one of Henry's ministers; and Thomas More grew up in his household – and later wrote the life of Richard III. It would only be human if Morton recounted all the worst that was ever said of the master he had betrayed: it is not surprising that Edward Halle should accept More's account, in writing his vast book on the 'noble and illustre families of Lancastre and York'; and still more human that Raphael Holinshed (whom no one could call a historian) should copy extensively from Halle – and so leave room for all those since Horace Walpole who have had doubts about the historical character of this terrible monarch and the events of his times.

To think that we are seeing anything like sober history in this play is derisible naïvety. What we are offered is a formally patterned sequence presenting two things: on the one hand, a rigid Tudor *schema* of retributive justice (a sort of analogy to Newton's Third Law in the field of moral dynamics: 'Action and reaction are equal and apposite'); and, on the other, a huge triumphant stage-personality, an early old masterpiece of the art of rhetorical stage-writing, a monstrous being incredible in any sober, historical scheme of things – Richard himself.

I will talk about the first, first. The basic pattern of retributive justice (or God's vengeance) is well enough illustrated in Holinshed, in the passage telling how Prince Edward (Henry VI's son and Margaret's) was murdered at the Battle of Tewkesbury. The Prince was handed over to Edward IV on the proclamation of a promise that he would not be harmed; he was brought before the King, asked why he 'durst so presumptuously enter into his realm' and replied courageously 'To recover my father's kingdom and heritage' (and more to that purpose) – but let Holinshed say the rest:

At which words king Edward said nothing, but with his hand thrust him from him, or (as some saie) stroke him with his gantlet; whom incontinentlie, George duke of Clarence, Richard duke of Glocester, Thomas Greie marquesse Dorcet, and William lord Hastings, that stood by, suddenlie murthered; for the which cruell act, the more part of the dooers in their latter daies dranke of the like cup, by the righteous iustice and due punishment of God.

There you have the notional pattern, in little, of the whole framework of *Richard III*: Clarence – 'false, fleeting, perjured Clarence' (who took the sacrament to remain true to Henry VI of Lancaster and deserted him); Gray – one of the group of Queen Elizabeth Woodeville's relations, who fall to Richard and Buckingham next after Clarence; Hastings, who says he will see 'this crown of mine cut from my shoulders | Before I'll see the crown so foul misplaced' (on Richard's head) – and *does* (if a man can be said to see his own decapitation). Holinshed really understates the matter in writing 'the more part of the dooers ... dranke of the like cup'; for of those he names, everyone did. On the one hand, that is what *Richard III* is about: what it is composed of. A heavy-handed justice commends the ingredients of a poisoned [cup].

This notional pattern of historic events rigidly determined by a mechanical necessity is partly paralleled by, partly modified by, the formal patterns of the episodes (or scenes) and the language. By 'formal patterns' I mean the unmistakably iterated goings-on in scenes so exactly parallel that if the first *is* passable on a modern stage as quasi-realistic costume-play stuff, the second (repeating it always *more* unrealistically) cannot be. The two wooing-scenes (Richard with Anne and Elizabeth) are the simplest case;

but in the lamentation-scenes – where a collection of bereft females comes together and goes through a dismal catalogue of *Who was Who* and *Who has lost Whom* (like a gathering of historical Mrs Gummidges, each 'thinking of the old 'un' with shattering simultaneity) – there, even editors have found the proceedings absurd; and readers difficult. When Queen Margaret, for example, says:

> I had an Edward, till a Richard killed him;
> I had a husband, till a Richard killed him:
> Thou hadst an Edward, till a Richard killed him;
> Thou hadst a Richard, till a Richard killed him.
>
> IV.4.40–43

a reader may *just* keep up (and realize that the last two are the Princes in the Tower, so that Queen Elizabeth is being addressed); but when the Duchess of York takes up with

> I had a Richard too, and thou didst kill him;
> I had a Rutland too, thou holp'st to kill him
>
> IV.4.44–5

it is likely that you are lost, unless your recollection of a *Henry VI* and the ends of Richard, Duke of York, and his young son (Edmund) is unusually clear.

It is not only the iteration of scene that is stylized: the stiffly formal manipulation of echoing phrase and sequence of words within the scenes is even more unrealistic. A closely related parallelism exists in the repeated occurrence of a sort of 'single-line traffic' in sentences: the classicist's *stichomythia*. One speaker takes from the other exactly the same ration of syllables, and rejoins as if under contract to repeat the form of the given sentence as exactly as possible, using the maximum number of the same words or their logical opposites, or (failing that) words closely associated with them. I describe the game pedantically, because it *is* an exact and scientific game with language, and one of the graces and beauties of the play Shakespeare wrote. If we cannot accept the 'patterned speech' of *Richard III*, its quality must remain unknown to us. 'Early work' is an evasive, criticism-dodging term. Early it may be; but the play is a triumphant contrivance in a manner which cannot properly be compared with that of any other tragedy – nor of any history, except *Henry VI, Part Three* (where the manner takes shape, and particularly in III.2) and *King John* (which is not half so well built or integrated as this).

I have emphasized the stylization of verbal patterning (with its neatly over-exact adjustments of stroke to stroke, as in royal tennis), because the sequence of most of the important events offers very much the same pattern. I might remark, in passing, that these verbal devices were offering to the Elizabethans an accomplished English equivalent to the neat dexterities they admired in Seneca (a point made by T. S. Eliot years ago; though he did not examine how the dramatic ironies of the action run in parallel with these counter-stroke reversals of verbal meaning, and form a kind of harmony). But we miss something more than Shakespeare's rhetorical game of tennis if merely irritated by, e.g.:

> ANNE I would I knew thy heart.
> RICHARD 'Tis figured in my tongue.
> ANNE I fear me both are false.
> RICHARD Then never was man true.

> I.2.192–5

Those reversals of intention (*heart–tongue*; *false–true*) are on precisely the pattern of the repeated reversals of human expectation, the reversals of events, the anticipated reversals (foreseen only by the audience), which make 'dramatic irony'. The patterned speech of the dialogue – the wit that demonstrates that a sentence is but a cheveril glove, quickly turned the other way – is fundamentally one with the ironic patterns of the plot. 'Dramatic irony' here is verbal *peripeteia*.

You will see that simply exemplified if you read Buckingham's speech at the beginning of Act II, where he calls a curse on himself if ever he goes back on his reconciliation with the Queen (and is quite specific about it); then turn straight to his last lines in V.1, when he is on the way to execution: 'That high All-seer which I dallied with'. He has got exactly what he asked for. He did not mean the words he used, but they have been reversed into actuality, in exactly the same way as verbal terms are reversed in the tennis-court game of rhetoric.

The same irony plays all over *Richard III*. It lurks like a shadow behind the naïvely self-confident Hastings; it hovers a moment over Buckingham when Margaret warns him against 'yonder dog' (Richard), and, on Richard's asking what she said, he replies, 'Nothing that I respect, my gracious lord' (I.3.295) – and this at a time when Buckingham is under no threat whatsoever.

Its cumulative effect is to present the personages as existing in a state of total and terrible uncertainty. This is enhanced if we know the details of what comes into the play from *Henry VI, Part Three*, but is there even if we know only a few bare essentials of what has gone before. We need to know who Margaret is; how Lancaster has been utterly defeated, and King Henry and his son murdered; how Clarence betrayed his King and returned to the Yorkists; and how Richard, his younger brother, has already marked him as his immediate obstruction on his intended way to the crown. We need to know too that the Duchess of York is mother to that unrewarding trio, Edward IV, Clarence, Gloucester; that Edward IV has married an aspiring commoner, Elizabeth Grey (*née* Woodeville); and that she has jacked up her relations into nobility. Beyond those half-dozen facts we do not need back-reference to *Henry VI, Part Three* for any but the finer points – so far as the essential ironies of the plot go.

Far more important than these details is the simple over-riding principle derived from the Tudor historians: that England rests under a chronic curse – the curse of faction, civil dissension, and fundamental anarchy, resulting from the deposition and murder of the Lord's Anointed (Richard II) and the usurpation of the House of Lancaster. The savageries of the Wars of the Roses follow logically (almost theologically) from that; and Elizabeth's 'All-seeing heaven, what a world is this!' says but half. It is a world of absolute and hereditary moral ill, in which *everyone* (till the appearance of Richmond-Tudor in Act V) is tainted with the treacheries, the blood, and the barbarities of civil strife, and internally blasted with the curse of a moral anarchy which leaves but three human *genera*: the strong in evil, the feebly wicked, and the helplessly guilt-tainted (such as the Princes,

Anne – all those despairing, lamenting women, whose choric wailings are a penitential psalm of guilt and sorrow: England's guilt, the individual's sorrow). The 'poor painted queen's' 'what a world' needs supplementing with the words of the pessimistically clear-sighted Third Citizen:

> All may be well; but if God sort it so,
> 'Tis more than we deserve or I expect.
>
> II.3.36–7

I have in effect described the meaning of the framework of the play: presented it as 'moral history', to be interpreted in abstract terms. But the play itself is also a symphonic structure which I can only describe in terms of music: a rhetorical symphony of five movements, with first and second subjects and some Wagnerian leitmotives. The play-making framework is Senecan revenge, the characterization largely Marlovian; but the orchestration is not only original, but unique. It can be sketched like this.

The first movement employs five 'subjects': Richard himself, his own overture; the wooing-theme (to be repeated in the fourth movement); Richard among his enemies (repeating the duplicity with which he has fooled Clarence); Margaret's curse; and the long dying fall of Clarence. It occupies the whole of Act I.

The second movement includes Act II and scenes 1–4 of Act III. It begins with the King's feeble peace-making – in which Buckingham invites his curse – and its other subjects are: a lamentation after the King's death (repeated in the fourth movement); the fall of the curse on Rivers, Grey, and Vaughan (when the curse is remembered), and on Hastings (the curse briefly recalled again). The future subject of Richard's moves against the Princes is introduced between-whiles.

The third movement cuts across the Act-divisions and runs from III.5 to IV.3. Its main subject is the Gloucester–Buckingham plot for the crown, with the magnificently sardonic fooling of the London *bourgeoisie* with a crisis-scare, a brace of bishops, and the headline-story that here is a highly respectable unlibidinous monarch for decent England. On its success, Anne is called to be Queen, and thus to meet the curse she herself called on Richard's wife before he wooed her in that humour and won her (the first movement is here caught up). Buckingham now makes himself one of Richard's future victims by showing reluctance for the plot against the Princes, and Richard throws him off with a snub. The Princes are dealt with (the account of Forrest and Deighton echoing that of the murderers of Clarence, one of whom had a temporary conscience); and Richard concludes with a brisk summary and prospectus:

> The sons of Edward sleep in Abraham's bosom,
> And Anne my wife hath bid this world good night;
>
> IV.3.38–9

and so, since Richmond plans to marry 'young Elizabeth, my brother's daughter', 'To her go I, a jolly thriving wooer' (Richard's last jocularity). The movement ends with the first murmurs of Richmond. Previously there has been slipped in the trivial-sounding prophecy about 'Rouge-mount', besides Henry VI's prophecy (IV.2.94 ff.). The flight of the Bishop of Ely (Morton) really troubles Richard.

The fourth movement brings down the curse on Buckingham (V.1 is obviously misplaced, so the movement runs from IV.4 to V.1 inclusive). Mainly it repeats themes heard before: with a long lamentation-scene (the Blake-like weeping Queens); a repetition of Margaret's curse with the curse of Richard's mother added; the second wooing-scene; the subject of Nemesis repeated by Buckingham. In it the sound of Richmond's advance has become clearer; and Richard's self-command and certainty begin to waver.

The fifth movement is all at Bosworth: the fall of the curse on Richard himself. There is the dream-prologue of the procession of contrapuntal Ghosts (including all those so qualified from the four previous movements) and, like all ghosts, they are reminiscent and repetitive. The play ends with the epilogue to the Wars of the Roses – spoken by Queen Elizabeth's grandfather – calling a blessing on the English future, and inverting the opening lines of Richard's prologue:

> Now is the winter of our discontent
> Made glorious summer. . . .
>
> I.1.1–2

The deliberateness of this highly controlled workmanship needs but little comment. I shall take up a single musical phrase: one that intertwines its plangent undertones throughout the whole symphony, a true leitmotive.

At first sight, Clarence's dream (I.4.9 ff.) appears to contribute little to the play, nothing to the plot; and it may seem a rhetorical indulgence, even if we accept Mr Eliot's judgement that it shows 'a real approximation in English to the magnificence of Senecan Latin at its best. ... The best of Seneca has here been absorbed into English'.[1] But first recollect the setting. Clarence has been sent to the Tower, by the machinations of the Queen's party (so he thinks), and he is confident that his brother Richard will stand good friend to him. He believes Richard's worried 'We are not safe, Clarence, we are not safe'; cannot possibly see the ironical joke Richard is cracking with himself; has no idea that he has been first on Richard's list since that moment in *Henry VI, Part Three* (V.6.84) when his brother muttered, 'Clarence, beware; thou keep'st me from the light'.[2] (A line that follows a passage predetermining the gulling of both Clarence and Anne to follow:

> I have no brother, I am like no brother;
> And this word 'love', which greybeards call divine,
> Be resident in men like one another,
> And not in me! I am myself alone.)

Clarence had not been there to hear that: knows nothing of the typically sharp reversal of Richard's solemnly hypocritical fooling now with:

> Go, tread the path that thou shalt ne'er return.
> Simple plain Clarence, I do love thee so
> That I will shortly send thy soul to heaven,
> If heaven will take the present at our hands.

> I.1.117–20

Clarence has his nightmare in the Tower: a vision prophetic of doom, and thick with curdled guilt. He dreams that Richard blunderingly knocks him overboard from a vessel; he drowns; goes to hell; and his guilt-sick mind spews up its own evil:

KEEPER
    Awaked you not in this sore agony?
CLARENCE
    No, no, my dream was lengthened after life.
    O then began the tempest to my soul!
    I passed, methought, the melancholy flood,
    With that sour ferryman which poets write of,
    Unto the kingdom of perpetual night.
    The first that there did greet my stranger soul
    Was my great father-in-law, renownèd Warwick,
    Who spake aloud, 'What scourge for perjury
    Can this dark monarchy afford false Clarence?'
    And so he vanished. Then came wandering by
    A shadow like an angel, with bright hair
    Dabbled in blood, and he shrieked out aloud,
    'Clarence is come – false, fleeting, perjured Clarence,
    That stabbed me in the field by Tewkesbury.
    Seize on him, Furies, take him unto torment!'

                                   I.4.42–57

It is as fine a passage in that style as English can offer: calculated to leave its solemn music in even half-attentive ears. In the second movement of the play (II.2.43 ff.), Queen Elizabeth announces the King's death:

    If you will live, lament; if die, be brief,
    That our swift-wingèd souls may catch the King's,
    Or like obedient subjects follow him
    To his new kingdom of ne'er-changing night.

It is scarcely a proper-wifely expectation of the fate of her husband's spirit: but the echo of 'Unto the kingdom of perpetual night' is the effect intended, not Elizabeth's notions. The actors who put together the Quarto text of 1597 showed that they appreciated, if clumsily, the author's intention. They made it 'To his new kingdom of perpetuall rest': catching the echo rightly, while missing the point.

    The same 'dark monarchy' awaits all these people: they are the living damned. That is the translation of this echo-technique of leitmotives; and why I call the play's anatomy 'musical'. Nor is that all: the phrase returns again. But before I come to that, remark how Hastings philosophizes on his fall at the end of the second movement:

> O momentary grace of mortal men,
> Which we more hunt for than the grace of God!
> Who builds his hope in air of your good[3] looks
> Lives like a drunken sailor on a mast,
> Ready with every nod to tumble down
> Into the fatal bowels of the deep.

III.4.96–101

We have heard that surging rhythm before. And with it the feeling of being aloft, in air, unbalanced: the rhythm of Clarence dreaming:

> As we paced along
> Upon the giddy footing of the hatches,
> Methought that Gloucester stumbled, and in falling
> Struck me, that thought to stay him, overboard
> Into the tumbling billows of the main.

I.4.16–20

Pattern repeats pattern with remarkable exactitude. 'Into the fatal bowels of the deep' is where the giddy Hastings also goes. 'O Lord! Methought what pain it was to drown' might be extended to all these desperate swimmers in the tide of pomp and history. The elaboration of the dream is no mere exercise in fine phrase on Latin models: it offers a symbol of choking suspense above black depths (the ocean, and perpetual night) which epitomizes the 'momentary grace' of all these 'mortal men' and women. And the sea as figure of 'the destructive element' appears again in Elizabeth's lines in the second wooing-scene:

> But that still use of grief makes wild grief tame,
> My tongue should to thy ears not name my boys
> Till that my nails were anchored in thine eyes;
> And I, in such a desperate bay of death,
> Like a poor bark of sails and tackling reft,
> Rush all to pieces on thy rocky bosom.

IV.4.230–35

'Bay' of death suggests also an animal at bay; just plausibly relevant, since Richard (the boar) would be at bay when she *could* scratch his eyes out. But the repetition of the rather too emphatic anchors and the eyes from Clarence's dream is much more striking.

You will find a further echo of the 'night-motif' in the last movement. Richard suspects Stanley (confusingly also called Derby), and reasonably so: for he was husband to the Countess of Richmond, Henry Tudor's mother, the famous Lady Margaret Beaufort; and therefore keeps his son, George Stanley, as hostage. Before Bosworth, he sends a brisk message to warn the father of the black depths beneath the son; and again Shakespeare sounds his doom-music from the Clarence sequence:

> bid him bring his power
> Before sunrising, lest his son George fall
> Into the blind cave of eternal night.
>
> V.3.60–62

Need I remark that Clarence was 'George' too, and lightly called that by Richard when he was afraid that King Edward might die before he signed his brother's death-warrant?

> He cannot live, I hope, and must not die
> Till George be packed with post-horse up to heaven.
>
> I.1.145–6

I could further exemplify the play's tight-woven artistry by taking up that very remarkable prose-speech on 'conscience' by Clarence's Second Murderer (I.4.136 ff.), and following the word into Richard's troubled mind in Act V before Margaret's curse attains its last fulfilment. But to reduce attention to Richard himself in his own play, beyond what I am already committed to by my insistence on taking the play as a *whole* (as a dramatic pattern, not an exposition of 'character'), would be to do it – and Shakespeare – an injustice.

Richard Plantagenet is alone with Macbeth as the Shakespearian version of the thoroughly bad man in the role of monarch and hero; he is unique in combining with that role that of the diabolic humorist. It is this quality which makes it an inadequate account to say that the play is 'moral history', or that the protagonists are the personality of Richard and the curse of Margaret (or what it stood for in orthodox Tudor thinking about retributive justice in history) – for all that these opposed 'forces' *are* central throughout. The first movement establishes both, and emphatically. First, Richard, stumping down the stage on his unequal legs, forcing his hitched-up left shoulder and his withered arm on us, till we realize that *this* is what the 'winter of our discontent' in *Henry VI, Part Three* has produced, *this* the proper 'hatch and brood of time'; and then, Richard established, his cruel and sardonic effectiveness demonstrated on Clarence and Anne, there arises against his brazen Carl Orff-like music the one voice he quails before (if but slightly): the sub-dominant notes of Margaret and her prophecy of doom, to which the ghosts will walk in the visionary night before Bosworth. It is a conflict between a spirit and a ghost: between Richard, the spirit of ruthless will, of daemonic pride, energy and self-sufficiency, of devilish gusto and *Schadenfreude* (he *enjoys* wickedness even when it is of no practical advantage to his ambitions or to securing himself by murder: it may be only wickedness in *words*, but the spirit revealed is no less evilly exultant for that); and the ghost, as I call her – for what else is Margaret, Reignier's daughter picked up on a battlefield by Suffolk and married to that most etiolated of Shakespeare's husbands, Henry VI, but the living ghost of Lancaster, the walking dead, memorializing the long, cruel, treacherous, bloody conflict of the years of civil strife and pitiless butchery?

You can, of course, see more there if you will. Make her the last stage or age of woman-in-politics: she who has been beautiful, fiercely passionate, queenly, dominating, master of armies, *generalissima*; now old, defeated, empty of everything but fierce bitterness, the illimitable bitterness and rancour of political zeal. What did Yeats write of *his* equivalent symbol? It is in *A Prayer for my Daughter*. For her he prays:

> An intellectual hatred is the worst,
> So let her think opinions are accursed.
> Have I not seen the loveliest woman born
> Out of the mouth of Plenty's horn,
> Because of her opinionated mind
> Barter that horn and every good
> By quiet natures understood
> For an old bellows full of angry wind?

Margaret is that, if you like; but, not to go beyond Shakespeare, I cannot but think that when the old Duchess of York sits down upon the ground for the second lamentation-scene (to tell 'sad stories of the death of kings'), the *author's* mind ran more upon Margaret as he wrote:

> Dead life, blind sight, poor mortal-living ghost . . .
> Brief abstract and record of tedious days,
> Rest thy unrest on England's lawful earth,
> Unlawfully made drunk with innocents' blood!

IV.4.26, 28–30

Here Shakespeare devises a new variation on the Senecan visitant from another world howling for revenge, by making the spectre nominal flesh and blood; the tune of the Dance of Death to which all dance to damnation is played by Margaret; and one aspect of the play is our watching the rats go into the Weser, compelled by that fatal tune.

But Richard himself is not simply the last and most important (and worst) of the victims – if those justly destroyed can be called 'victims'. That is just where the label 'moral history' is inadequate. For Richard has grown a new dimension since his abrupt and remarkable development in *Henry VI, Part Three*: he has become a wit, a mocking comedian, a 'vice of kings' – but with a clear inheritance from the old Vice of the Moralities: part symbol of evil, part comic devil, and chiefly, on the stage, the generator of roars of laughter at wickednesses (whether of deed or word) which the audience would immediately condemn in real life. On the one hand, his literary relations with the Senecan 'Tyrant' (author of 'In regna mea Mors impetratur', etc.) are clear enough; as they are with the Elizabethan myth of 'the murderous Machiavel' ('feared am I more than loved | Let me be feared', etc.): enough has been written on them. But only the medieval heritage – from the comic devils with their *Schadenfreude*, and the Vice as comic inverter of order and decency – can fully explain the new Richard of this apparent sequel to the *Henry VI* series.

I have said that the Christian pattern imposed on history gives the simple plot of a cast accursed, where all are evil beings, all deserve punishment. Look, then, with a believing Tudor eye, and ought you not to *approve* Richard's doings? *Per se*, they are the judgement of God on the wicked; and he

> *Ein Teil von jener Kraft*
> *Die stets das Böse will, und stets das Gute schafft.*[4]

But that is not all. Richard's sense of humour, his function as clown, his comic irreverences and sarcastic or sardonic appropriations of things to (at any rate) *his* occasions: all those act as underminers of our assumed naïve and proper Tudor principles; and we are on his side much rather because he makes us (as the Second Murderer put it) 'Take the devil in [our] mind' than for any 'historical-philosophical-Christian-retributional' sort of motive. In this respect a good third of the play is a kind of grisly *comedy*; in which we meet the fools to be taken in on Richard's terms, see them with his mind, and rejoice with him in their stultification (in which execution is the ultimate and unanswerable practical joke, the absolutely final laugh this side of the Day of Judgement). Here, Richard is a middle-term between Barabas, the Jew of Malta (*c.* 1590), and Volpone (1606). He inhabits a world where everyone deserves everything he can do to them; and in his murderous practical joking he is *inclusively* the comic exposer of the mental shortcomings (the intellectual and moral deformities) of this world of beings depraved and besotted. If we forget to pity them awhile (and he does his best to help us), then his impish spirit urges us towards a positive reversal of 'Christian charity' until the play's fourth movement (which is when the Elizabethan spectator began to back out, I take it) – or even beyond that point.

An aspect of Richard's appeal, which has, I fancy, passed relatively unexamined,[5] is one that we can be confident that William Shakespeare felt and reflected on. I mean the appeal of the actor: the talented being who can assume every mood and passion at will, at all events to the extent of making others believe in it. Beyond question, all our great actors have regarded the part as a fine opportunity. The extent to which the histrionic art (as Shakespeare thought and felt about it) contributed to the making of this great stage-figure is to me more interesting.

The specific interest here is the *power* that would be in the hands of an actor consummate enough to make (quite literally) 'all the world a stage' and to work on humanity by the perfect simulation of every feeling: the appropriate delivery of every word and phrase that will serve his immediate purpose; together with the complete dissimulation of everything that might betray him (whether it be his intentions, or such obstructive feelings as compunction, pity, or uncertainty of mind). This appears at once when Gloucester first takes shape as the man self-made to be King, in the long soliloquy in *Henry VI, Part Three* (III.2.124 ff.). The closing lines are specifically on histrionic genius:

> Why, I can smile, and murder whiles I smile,
> And cry 'Content!' to that which grieves my heart,
> And wet my cheeks with artificial tears,
> And frame my face to all occasions.
>
> III.2.182–5

And then, after a little bragging prospectus on his intended deadliness, he ends:

> I can add colours to the chameleon,
> Change shapes with Protheus for advantages,
> And set the murderous Machiavel to school.
> Can I do this, and cannot get a crown?
> Tut, were it farther off, I'll pluck it down.
>
> III.2.191–5

M. R. Ridley notes here that 'Machiavelli . . . seems to have been to the Elizabethans a type of one who advocated murder as a method of cold-blooded policy'.[6] It is true that that marks off one point of difference between the 'Senecan' tyrant-villainy (which is primarily for revenge) and the 'Machiavellian' (which is for power, or self-aggrandizement: 'We that are great, our own self-good still moves us'): though I do not think that the distinction can be maintained, if you read Seneca. But surely Ridley's note misses the point, in its context? What the 'Machiavel' allusion represents is, I believe, Shakespeare's recognition that the programme set before the Prince in *Il Principe* is one that demands exactly those histrionic qualities I have just described: a lifelong, unremitting vigilance in relentless simulation and impenetrable deception. There, precisely, lies the super-humanity of the Super-

man. The will-to-power is shorn of its effective power without it.
He is an *artist* in evil.

Now Richard in his own play shows this power – these powers
– to perfection. Except to the audience, he is invisible; but the
audience he keeps reminded not only of his real intentions, but
equally of his actor's artistries. The bluff plain Englishman,
shocked at ambitious go-getters and grievingly misunderstood, is
perfectly 'done' before the Queen's relations:

> Because I cannot flatter and look fair,
> Smile in men's faces, smooth, deceive, and cog,
> Duck with French nods and apish courtesy,
> I must be held a rancorous enemy.
> Cannot a plain man live and think no harm,
> But thus his simple truth must be abused
> With silken, sly, insinuating Jacks?
>
> I.3.47–53

A little later, it is: 'I am too childish-foolish for this world'
(I.3.141); and even 'I thank my God for my humility' (II.1.74).

Then, left to himself and the audience, after egging on all their
quarrels:

> But then I sigh, and, with a piece of Scripture,
> Tell them that God bids us do good for evil;
> And thus I clothe my naked villainy
> With odd old ends stolen forth of Holy Writ,
> And seem a saint, when most I play the devil.
>
> I.3.333–7

The stage direction, '*Enter two Murderers*', caps this nicely. It is
not simply that Richard is a hypocrite and (like other stage-
villains) tells us so. The actor's technique of 'asides' is the essence
of his chuckling private jokes – made to 'myself alone'. (You
might say that Shakespeare is giving not merely 'the acting of
drama', but also 'the drama of consummate *acting*'.)

The same reminders, nudging the audience's attention, appear
in his swift-switched actual asides: e.g., his thoroughly unholy
reception of his mother's blessing, spoken as he gets up off his
dutiful knees:

> Amen! And make me die a good old man!
> That is the butt-end of a mother's blessing;
> I marvel that her grace did leave it out.

II.2.109–11

Or, again, we have Richard's insinuating equivocations in talking to the prattling little Princes; in one of which he acknowledges his theatrical-historical legacy from the Moralities:

> Thus, like the formal Vice, Iniquity,
> I moralize two meanings in one word.

III.1.82–3

Over and above this there is that striking passage (III.5.1–11) where he and Buckingham are working up a crisis (appearing ill-dressed in old rusty armour, as if they had armed in desperate haste), when Richard specifically inquires whether Buckingham can 'do the stage-tragedian':

RICHARD
> Come, cousin, canst thou quake and change thy colour,
> Murder thy breath in middle of a word,
> And then again begin, and stop again,
> As if thou wert distraught and mad with terror?

BUCKINGHAM
> Tut, I can counterfeit the deep tragedian,
> Speak and look back, and pry on every side,
> Tremble and start at wagging of a straw;
> Intending deep suspicion, ghastly looks
> Are at my service, like enforcèd smiles;
> And both are ready in their offices,
> At any time to grace my stratagems.

It is all sardonically jocular; but nothing shows more clearly the artist's delight in his craft: call it illusion or deception, it makes no odds. It is this dexterity that his other rapid reversals of tone keep us aware of; whether he is half-amazedly rejoicing in his conquest of Anne, or poking unfilial fun at his mother (a performance more shocking to Elizabethans than to our more child-foolish days).

Yet again, there is that admirable moment when the Londoners are being fooled into believing that he must be persuaded to be king; when Buckingham pretends to lose patience, with 'Zounds! I'll entreat no more!' And Richard, bracketed aloft with two Bishops, is distressed: 'O, do not swear, my lord of Buckingham' (III.7.219). (It is like the moment in *Eric or Little by Little* (Chapter 8) when Eric refers to the usher as a 'surly devil'; and the virtuous Russell exclaims: 'O Eric, that is the first time that I have heard you swear.') It is this unholy jocularity, the readiness of sarcastic, sardonic, profane, and sometimes blasphemous wit, the demonic gusto of it all, which not only wins the audience over to accepting the Devil as hero, but also points us towards the central paradox of the play. And, through that, to a full critical awareness of its unity: with a few remarks on which I shall conclude.

To begin with Richard. On the face of it, he is the demon-Prince, the cacodemon born of hell, the misshapen toad, etc. (all things ugly and ill). But through his prowess as actor and his embodiment of the comic Vice and impish-to-fiendish humour, he offers the false as more attractive than the true (the actor's function), and the ugly and evil as admirable and amusing (the clown's game of value-reversals). You can say, 'We don't take him seriously.' I reply, 'That is exactly what gets most of his acquaintances into Hell: just what the devil-clown relies on.' But he is not only this demon incarnate, he is in effect God's agent in a predetermined plan of divine retribution: the 'scourge of God'. Now by Tudor-Christian historical principles, this plan is *right*. Thus, in a real sense, Richard is a King who 'can do no wrong'; for in the pattern of the justice of divine retribution on the wicked, he functions as an avenging angel. Hence my paradoxical title, 'Angel with Horns'.

The paradox is sharpened by what I have mainly passed by: the repulsiveness, humanely speaking, of the 'justice'. God's will it may be, but it sickens us: it is as pitiless as the Devil's (who is called in to execute it). The contrast with Marlowe's painless, dehumanized slaughterings in *Tamburlaine* is patent.

This overall system of *paradox* is the play's unity. It is revealed as a constant displaying of inversions, or reversals of meaning: whether we consider the verbal patterns (the *peripeteias* or reversals of act and intention or expectation); the antithesis of false and true in the histrionic character; or the constant inversions of irony.

Those verbal capsizings I began by talking about, with their deliberate reversals to the opposite meaning in equivocal terms, are the exact correlatives of both the nature of man (or man in power: Richard) and of the nature of events (history); and of language too, in which all is conveyed.

But, start where you will, you come back to history; or to the pattern made out of the conflict of two 'historical myths'. The orthodox Tudor myth made history God-controlled, divinely prescribed and dispensed, to move things towards a God-ordained perfection: Tudor England. Such was the *frame* that Shakespeare took. But the total effect of Shakespeare's 'plot' has quite a different effect from Halle: a very different meaning. Dr Duthie may write, 'But there is no doubt that Shakespeare saw history in the same light as Halle saw it'.[7] I say there *is* doubt. Dover Wilson has nothing to offer but what he summarizes from Moulton, but his last sentence points my doubting way: 'it appears, to me at least, unlikely that Shakespeare's "main end" in *Richard III* was "to show the working out of God's will in English history" '.[8] (The quotation he is discussing is from Tillyard's *Shakespeare's History Plays* (1944), page 208.) He can go no further because his own limitations on *Henry IV* inhibit his ever observing that the comic Richard has no more place in Halle's scheme than Falstaff has.

The other myth is that of Richard the Devil-King: the Crookback *monstrum deforme, ingens* whom Shakespeare *found* as a ready-made Senecan tyrant and converted into a quite different inverter of moral order: a ruthless, demonic comedian with a most un-Senecan sense of humour and the seductive appeal of an irresistible gusto, besides his volcanic Renaissance energies. They are themselves demoralizing: *Tapfer sein ist gut*[9] is the antithesis of a Christian sentiment.

The outcome of this conflict of myths was Shakespeare's display of constant inversions of meaning; in all of which, two systems of meaning impinge and go over to their opposites, like the two 'ways' of the cheveril glove. This applies equally to words and word-patterns; to the actor-nature; to dramatic ironies; and to events, as the hatch and brood of time, contrasted with opposite expectations.

As a result of the paradoxical ironic structure built from these inversions of meaning – built above all by Richard's demonic appeal – the naïve, optimistic, 'Christian' principle of history, consoling and comfortable, modulates into its opposite. The 'Christian' system of retribution is undermined, counterbalanced, by historic irony. (Do I need to insist that the coupling of 'Christian' and 'retribution' itself is a paradox? That the God of vengeance is *not* a Christian God; that his opposite is a God of mercy who has no representation in this play. If I do, I had better add that the so-called 'Christian' frame is indistinguishable from a pagan one of Nemesis in which the 'high All-seer' is a Fate with a cruel sense of humour.)

But do not suppose I am saying that the play is a 'debunking of Tudor myth', or that Shakespeare is disproving it. He is not 'proving' anything: not even that 'Blind belief is sure to err | And scan his works in vain' (though I think that is *shown*, nevertheless). Contemporary 'order'-thought spoke as if naïve faith saw true: God was above God's Englishmen and ruled with justice – which meant summary vengeance. This historic myth offered absolutes, certainties. Shakespeare in the Histories always leaves us with relatives, ambiguities, irony, a process thoroughly dialectical. Had he entirely accepted the Tudor myth, the frame and pattern of order, his way would have led, I suppose, towards writing *moral history* (which is what Dr Tillyard and Dr Dover Wilson and Professor Duthie have made *out* of him). Instead, his way led him towards writing *comic history*. The former would never have taken him to tragedy: the latter (paradoxically) did. Look the right way through the cruel-comic side of Richard and you glimpse Iago. Look back at him through his energy presented as evil, and you see Macbeth. And if you look at the irony of men's struggles in the nets of historic circumstance, the ironies of their pride and self-assurance, you will see Coriolanus; and you are past the great tragic phase and back in history again.

NOTES

1. *Selected Essays* (1932), page 90; reprinted from the Introduction to *Seneca His Tenne Tragedies* (1927).
2. This contradicts R. G. Moulton, *Shakespeare as a Dramatic Artist* (1885), page 92, who says Richard is *not* 'ambitious' (as Macbeth is): 'never found dwelling upon the prize in view'. This presumes a complete disconnexion between *Henry VI, Part Three* and *Richard III*. No such assumption is acceptable nowadays – nor was it sensible even then.
3. 'fair' in the Quarto.
4. 'A part of that Power which always wills evil and yet always brings about good' (Goethe's *Faust*).
5. [J. Middleton Murry, *Shakespeare* (1936), pages 125–6, quotes the theatrical metaphors and remarks briefly on the conception of Richard as an actor.]
6. New Temple edition, page 140.
7. G. I. Duthie, *Shakespeare* (1951), page 118.
8. *Richard III* (New Cambridge edition, 1954), page xlv.
9. 'To be bold is good.'

FIVE

Richard's Divided Heritage in *King John**

William H. Matchett

IN 'Commodity and Honour in *King John*' (*University of Toronto Quarterly*, April 1960, 341–56) Mr James Calderwood demonstrates the essential role of those themes in Shakespeare's play. I should like to confirm, strengthen, and extend his perceptive analysis through a discussion of structure. In brief, my argument is as follows: The plot of *King John* is built around the question of who should be King of England and thus of what constitutes a 'right' to the throne. In the first Act, three characters are shown to have particular claims to the crown. With the death of Arthur, the failure and eventual collapse of John, and, through the course of the play, the growth of the Bastard in his perception of the distinction between commodity and true honour, it would appear that the Bastard is being groomed to take over as the rightful king. The final scenes, however, with their surprising introduction of a new claimant of unknown character and ability, defeat this expectation and shift the emphasis from the original question to a deeper consideration of the requirements of honour. The very qualities which constitute the Bastard's claim to the throne lead to his repudiation of personal ambition and his kneeling to Prince Henry. True honour, a matter not of prestige and power but of duty, is decided, in this play, upon the basis of what is best for England. The Bastard, in kneeling, renounces his recently established 'right' to the throne and thus ensures his already suffering country against civil war. True honour makes him the best of subjects in a unified England and this, in the

*From *Essays in Criticism* Volume XII, No. 3 (July 1962), edited by F. W. Bateson, Christopher Ricks, and Stephen Wall, pages 231–53. Copyright © William H. Matchett, 1962. Reprinted by kind permission of the editors of *Essays in Criticism*.

logic of the play, is more important than the character of the King.

A crux in this reading of the play, as it is in Calderwood's discussion of the central themes, is the weight of meaning it finds in the Bastard's kneeling to Prince Henry. Speeches at that place, as critics will point out, do not sustain the argument that the Bastard, in kneeling, is renouncing a personal claim to the crown. Similarly, both Calderwood and I interpret V.6 as a scene in which Hubert is inviting the Bastard to seize the throne, while critics may claim that the text of that scene does not justify such a reading. I would agree that the speeches in these two key scenes do not deal explicitly with the issue as I see it, but I hope to demonstrate that Shakespeare is working by means of dramatic implication. The speeches are understatements (not, it is worth pointing out, contradictions) of the issue, while the main weight of meaning in the actions and speeches is carried by their relationship to the inevitable expectations aroused by the structure of the play.

I

King John enters his play as a usurper. Unlike his mother, he offers no objection to Chatillon's reference to his 'borrow'd majesty' (I.1.4),[1] and even Eleanor's objection is a political gesture, not an assertion of principle, as is clear as soon as Chatillon has left the stage. When Chatillon urges Arthur's right to the throne (based, of course, upon primogeniture), John's response is not an argument but the cold question 'What follows if we disallow of this?' (16). The dramatic image is unmistakable. Chatillon three times uses the word 'right' for Arthur's claim; John's only rebuttal is force, 'war for war and blood for blood' (19). Eleanor also, though she disapproves of 'ambitious Constance' (32), speaks of 'the right and party of her son' (34). Finally, when John couples 'Our strong possession and our right' (39), Eleanor immediately distinguishes them, leaving John's position dependent upon 'Your strong possession much more than your right' (40). John is king *de facto* but not *de jure*.

It is necessary to insist upon this initial image in the play because critics, pointing to Holinshed and Richard I's will, have shown that John had in fact a legitimate claim to the throne.

Historically perhaps, but not here. John's claim to the throne is his presence on it and the issue raised is one of possession v. right.

The remainder of the Act, devoted to introducing the Bastard, repeats the national situation on a domestic scale. The Bastard is also in possession of an estate to which another, his half-brother Robert, is the rightful heir. Our sympathies, like John's, are of course with the 'good blunt fellow' (71); under the influence of these sympathies, however, both 'right' and 'honour' begin to twist in our hands. Robert's assumed moral right to his inheritance is denied by John in the name of another right, the legal fiction of the Bastard's legitimacy. Everyone concerned knows that Robert, for lack of sufficient proof, like Arthur, for lack of sufficient power, is being 'legally' cheated. Though he happens to have truth on his side and to be fighting for his right, Robert is, dramatically, a deserving victim both because of his unprepossessing appearance, especially in comparison with the Bastard, and his willingness to sacrifice his mother's good name, however undeserved, for his own gain.

But the Bastard, unlike John, is not permitted to enjoy his dishonourably held possessions. To save him for his later role in the play, he is presented with a choice between 'honour' and possessions. He chooses 'honour' (here merely 'reputation') and his ambitious choice immediately pays off, for John knights him – 'Arise Sir Richard, and Plantagenet' (162). There is in his response an impetuous decisiveness, uncalculating, heedless of consequences, a little naïve. He is not one to ask 'What follows if we disallow of this?' but says at once, 'I'll take my chance' (151). In appearance already judged 'perfect Richard' (90), the image of his father, he further convinces his grandmother of his parentage by his blunt, bawdy, and attractive enthusiasm:

BASTARD [*to Robert*]
    Brother by th' mother's side, give me your hand:
    My father gave me honour, yours gave land.
    Now blessed be the hour [punning with *whore*], by night or day,
    When I was got, Sir Robert was away!

ELEANOR
    The very spirit of Plantagenet!

163–7

Though we have not yet seen Arthur, it is clear that the first Act has set up three characters as each being in a special relation to kingship through his share in Richard's heritage: the nephew, Arthur, the throneless rightful king; the brother, John, who has usurped the throne; and the bastard son, who, with neither right to nor possession of the throne, has nevertheless inherited the self-reliant decisiveness of a true king. For the memory of Coeur-de-lion haunts this play as the mythically heightened image of a good and heroic king. A little cuckolding on the side merely proved his manliness, and it is the manliness of 'this same lusty gentleman' (108), his son, that is played off against the debility of Sir Robert's son by the same mother. Coeur-de-lion triumphantly combined what has now been divided, his right going to the child, Arthur, his throne to the man, John, and his personal qualities to the youth, Sir Richard, the son who now has his name. The division is an imbalance demanding resolution: which – right, possession, or character – is the essential ingredient for a king? Arthur has been denied his right and John's possession is threatened; only the Bastard cannot be alienated from his inheritance, for it is intrinsic and he can boast 'I am I, howe'er I was begot' (175).

There would seem to be a contradiction, then, between the Bastard's self-sufficient character and his pursuit of an honour which is merely reputation. So there is. His discovery and handling of this contradiction is a primary development in the play. But the reputation he has chosen is one to which he has in fact a right: gambling on future 'chance', he trades his spurious respectability for an honest reputation as a royal bastard. He has made the right choice for the wrong reason; he has yet to add insight to the character which is already his. It is safe to say that the first Act leaves the audience more interested in what will happen to the Bastard than in the immediate challenge to John, which, in the absence of Arthur, has as yet been somewhat abstract.

2

The second Act, however, is concerned almost completely with the dynastic struggle, and the Bastard, though he attempts once, unsuccessfully, to control the action, serves primarily as an observant commentator. His simple presence as an observer needs to be stressed since, in the shade of his lively comments, one might overlook its importance: his political education is beginning and he has much to learn. By the end of the Act the once naïve young man has found the proper name for the political motivation he observes.

The point at issue between John and Arthur, so clearly stated in the first Act, becomes more ambiguous when looked at more closely in the second; we meet Arthur in circumstances which overshadow his right. While his immaturity and weakness may attract some personal sympathy, sympathy for his cause is dissipated as we observe the company he keeps. King Richard's rightful heir is first seen agreeing to 'Embrace', 'love', 'welcome' and 'forgive' (11–12) Austria, the man who killed King Richard. Instead of avenging England's honour, which he is of course too weak to do, Arthur – or Constance through Arthur – is seeking to further his cause and to force his way into Angiers by embracing England's enemies. The patriotic determination to 'follow arms' till England, 'That water-walled bulwark, still secure | And confident from foreign purposes ... Salute thee for her king' (27–31) rings falsely from the tongue of one who is not merely a foreigner but the very foreigner who wears the lion-skin of England's last rightful king. After his first brief, formal (and no doubt prompted) speech, Arthur speaks only twice more in the Act, both times in brief and vain attempt to pacify his mother, who does his fighting and decision-making for him. He is too retiring, but Constance – especially since she is not above the suspicion that she fights primarily for personal power – is overbearing. Arthur is a pawn surrounded by an unscrupulous, self-seeking league. Were he to gain his right and become king, the results would presumably be disastrous for England.

For, though the word 'right' is used sixteen times in the Act,[2] it is eclipsed by the recurring threat of the bloodshed to which the issue is leading: 'blood' and its cognates ('bleed', 'bleeding', 'bloody'), used only four times in the first Act's foreshadowing of this result, appear in the second Act no less than twenty-six times.[3] While the issue of dynastic 'right' is being shown to be far from simple, its very existence unresolved is being shown to invite, or indeed ordain, carnage.

But the attack on Angiers is interrupted by the arrival of John and the English forces. The first battle is verbal, with the opponents paired: John *v*. France, Eleanor *v*. Constance, and the Bastard *v*. Austria. Opposed to France – ' 'Tis France, for England' – John appears in a new light – 'England, for itself' (202). We realize again – especially now that we have seen poor Arthur – that, usurper or not, John *is* the King. The meeting of the two rulers, each backed by an army and mouthing 'Peace', is, however, a bit of political farce, no less so for being true to the life of power politics: each subverts the peace he claims to desire, since each will have it only on his own terms. John's self-righteous claim is no criterion; 'God' is a mere political gambit, one which can be used equally by France in citing Arthur's right: 'in the name of God | How comes it then that thou art call'd a king' (106–7). (And Hubert, demurring from both positions, will claim, 'A greater power than we denies all this' (368).)

The women's exchange is close to hair-pulling, especially Eleanor's unjustified slur on Arthur as 'thy bastard' (122) and her witty play on Constance's desire to be 'queen' (123) – *royal queen*, and *chess queen* ('check the world') – which oversteps any pretence of royal dignity in its third significance, *quean*. Constance, with Arthur's right on her side, is nevertheless forced on to the defensive and, frustrated, becomes increasingly violent. First Austria – 'Peace!' (134) – then Arthur – 'Good my mother, peace!' (163) – then John – 'Bedlam, have done' (183) – and finally France – 'Peace, lady!' (195) – seek to quiet her, her three allies using the same maligned word in the attempt to reconcile her to the etiquette of political duplicity.

The Bastard's immediate antipathy to Austria, motivated of course by the lion-skin, contrasts his sense of honour directly with Arthur's and, by extension, with John's. Whatever the moral masquerades of the others, the Bastard, as Richard's son, has a legitimate personal grudge against Austria.

France brings the general verbal violence back to the practical here-and-now of Angiers and suggests discovering 'Whose title they admit, Arthur's or John's' (200). The decision of the men of Angiers then, though not necessarily a final resolution of the main issue, has its dramatic importance as a test case. Hubert – for, though as yet unnamed, it is he who is the citizen-spokesman for Angiers (as Wilson first made clear and Honigmann has adopted) – gives an answer that has all the appearance of eminent sense: 'we are the king of England's subjects . . . he that proves the king, | To him will we prove loyal' (267–71). John, after an exasperated appeal to his simple logic – 'Doth not the crown of England prove the king?' (273) – adduces the thirty thousand Englishmen who accompany him. It is, of course, a double argument: that so many Englishmen follow him attests his moral right to the English throne; that so many men follow him attests his threat to Angiers. France cannot match the moral half of this claim though he can match the threat with 'As many and as well-born bloods' (278). But Hubert remains adamant:

> Till you compound whose right is worthiest,
> We for the worthiest hold the right from both.

> 281–2

After the frustrated kings indulge in a brief and bloody, but fruit-less skirmish, Hubert for a third time maintains his seemingly sensible neutrality:

> One must prove greatest: while they weigh so even
> We hold our town for neither, yet for both.

> 332–3

But, however sound the arguments which might convince a modern man of the virtues of neutrality, Hubert's position is unacceptable in *King John*. This is not the moral superiority of 'A plague a'both your houses!' with which Mercutio, 'the Prince's near ally', rejects the parochial quarrel that has caused his death (*Romeo and Juliet*, III.1.106–9); this is the willingness of common citizens to accept either of two contradictory national loyalties. It has the sound sense of self-preservation – and perhaps today that seems enough – but it is meant to have little else; as comes increas-ingly clear in Hubert's progressive responses, it is not a moral position at all, but a refusal to face the issue. (That the issue is not resolvable in the terms in which it has been set does not, appar-ently, excuse a man from involvement.) At no time is Hubert concerned with Arthur's rights. He faces the straight power politics of England and France. His first response sounds fine till probed: 'he that proves the king, | To him will we prove loyal.' What kind of loyalty is this? Like 'honour' in the first Act, it is not the real article, but a calculated substitute; what ought to be the warm and total response of a committed man is here the small change of a self-indulgent apathy. What 'proves the king' is precisely the issue that Hubert avoids, and his restatements, 'the worthiest' or 'greatest', are equally hollow, assuming only that might makes right. Hubert abdicates the citizen's duty to act according to his best moral lights and, selfishly holding himself aloof, leaves the decision to naked force.

It is in contrast with Hubert that one is to understand the Bastard's behaviour. Loyally (he declared his loyalty to John with his entering line in the first Act), unselfishly and also, one must add, unthinkingly, he urges on the battle which seems to him the sole way of settling the issue:

> Cry 'havoc!' kings; back to the stained field ...
> Then let confusion of one part confirm
> The other's peace; till then, blows, blood, and death!
>
> 357, 359–60

But, though superior to Hubert here in his loyalty and his freedom from selfish calculation, the Bastard is not himself facing any moral issues. His response is warm and total, but it is not yet what one would call perceptive. He, no less than Hubert, leaves the decision to naked force; the difference is his willingness to involve himself on the side to which he is loyal. After Hubert's fourth refusal, the Bastard, unable to stomach men who can stand coldly before 'industrious scenes and acts of death' (376), makes his 'wild' (395) suggestion that the kings join forces against Angiers before turning back to their own quarrel. It is his first venture into political strategy, and his 'Smacks it not something of the policy?' (396) shows his naïve pride in what he is pleased to consider his approach to political wisdom.

But what is the rash response of naïve loyalty in the Bastard as an individual becomes insane ruthlessness when it is accepted and given royal authority by John:

> France, shall we knit our powers
> And lay this Angiers even with the ground;
> Then after fight who shall be king of it?
>
> 398–400

To such inhuman nonsense has the political stalemate led.

Hubert, fortunately for Angiers, has another suggestion: the marriage of John's niece, Blanche, to the Dauphin, Lewis. The Bastard reacts with disgust to Hubert's rhetoric, which has usurped the place of his own strategy, but both kings see in the plan a way of saving face while abandoning their sterile enmity. With the few gestures owed to respectability, the political match is arranged. Lewis plays the game with a will and his ability to switch so rapidly from enemy to lover, patently insincere, gilding his political opportunism with the language of a sonneteer, is in sharp contrast not only with the Bastard's disgusted and less-flexible sincerity, but with the honesty of his bride-to-be. Blanche plays only a brief role in the play, but it is a crucial one for, though she is almost as much as Arthur a political pawn, she has something to teach the Bastard. Without loss of dignity or feminine propriety, she is hardly less plain-spoken – when called upon to speak – than he is:

> My uncle's will in this respect is mine: ...
> Further I will not flatter you, my lord,
> That all I see in you is worthy love,
> Than this: that nothing do I see in you ...
> That I can find should merit any hate.
>
> 510, 516–18, 520

To marry Lewis is her duty, and therefore she will marry Lewis. When John asks for formal assent, she pronounces herself 'bound in honour still to do | What you in wisdom still vouchsafe to say' (522–3). This is the only appearance of the word 'honour' in the second Act, and its first appearance in the play as a high-minded sense of personal obligation, a trait of character rather than a mere claim for public approval. Blanche is controlled by her honour, whatever the personal consequences. The Bastard is silent but his education has now truly begun, as comes clear when he is left alone at the end of the scene.

In his well-known soliloquy – 'Mad world! mad kings! mad

composition!' (561) – with new insight, he gives the name, missing so far in the play, to the primary motivating force behind what we have seen: 'Commodity, the bias of the world' (574), commodity, the unprincipled self-interest which perverts 'all indifferency, … direction, purpose, course, intent' (579–80), and brings the noblest-sounding resolutions to the most ignominious results. This speech is clearly crucial in the play, as others before Calderwood have recognized, but there has been much disagreement as to what it is meant to imply. Though the Bastard is disgusted by commodity, he has been thought to advocate it, and, indeed, his final words are: 'Gain, be my lord, for I will worship thee!' (598).

Many of the problems commentators have with this speech seem to me to arise from attempts to make of it a summation of the Bastard's character, a final position rather than a stage in his development. He is not static, and it is enough in the second Act that he has begun to consider where he is. What was blind loyalty now sees madness on both sides. For the first time he is critical of John. Though he is wrong in his estimate of King Philip's original motive, accepting the public declaration for the fact, the important point is that he is beginning to judge for himself, and no longer just following chance. The word 'honourable' in the Bastard's mouth now, though we may demur from 'honourable war', is not what it was in the first Act, but what he has learned from Blanche.

After this insight into the kings, there is surely a hesitation (between lines 586 and 587) while, in his honesty, the Bastard recognizes its application to himself:

> And why rail I on this commodity?
> But for because he hath not woo'd me yet.

> 587–8

Must we demand conversion at the very incipience of self-knowledge? The Bastard, realizing that he has been living in the very spirit he has condemned in the kings, concludes most humanly by reversing his complaint and turning their conduct into a rationalization for his own. But he has found a name for such conduct; he has seen 'commodity' and its opposite. Never again can he remain unconscious in following chance. It is enough for now. It is a place to end a scene but not a play.

The brief scene which follows and concludes the Act (traditionally III.1.1–74) brings Constance the news of her loss of support. 'I have a king's oath', she insists (10), but we have seen what such an oath is worth. Arthur has only a single line: 'I do beseech you, madam, be content' (42). His cause would appear to be lost; the Act thus ends with John's possession of the throne apparently secure and the primary suspense once again is that of what is likely to happen next to the Bastard.

3

The third Act, however, quickly introduces a new challenge to John. Pandulph's entry is abrupt, but John's response is even more so. To the legate's greeting – 'Hail, you anointed deputies of heaven!' (62 [136]), clearly meant as an immediate assertion of the Pope's claim to superior authority – John returns his thoroughly and anachronistically Protestant answer. Having just won his victory over Arthur, John is carried away into attempting to brazen out another which, could he win it, would leave him even stronger. The stakes are high. John must carry France with him in this reckless rebellion or suffer not only excommunication but, what makes it a political threat, loss of the very support which he has just purchased to seal the possession of his kingdom against the threat of Arthur's right. The ensuing struggle is not spiritual, but political jockeying, with Pandulph merely another power politician, his weapons excommunication and incitement to political purge of the excommunicant.

When Pandulph can argue that 'indirection ... grows direct, | And falsehood falsehood cures' (202–3 [276–7]), he is a master politician at the furthest remove from the Bastard. But the Bastard has been presented with no special problem by all this. Remaining loyal to John, he has been more concerned with his animosity for Austria, whom he continues to bait, than with Pandulph. Blanche, however, is trapped between her loyalty to her uncle and her new loyalty to her husband. She is hardly more in this scene than a formalized image of the dilemma of loyalties; her having acted honourably has not protected her from subsequent suffering.

Two brief images of importance must emerge from the chaos of the staged battle: the Bastard enters with Austria's head, having achieved his revenge; and Hubert is entrusted by John with the custody of their prisoner, Arthur. There are no speeches to explain Hubert's presence as John's follower; we can only look for the implications. France having broken the league, Hubert has apparently remained loyal to the injured party. A possible further implication of the entry with Arthur is that Hubert himself has been responsible for Arthur's capture. The battle over, these same characters return to the stage. John commissions the Bastard to precede him to England and 'shake the bags | Of hoarding abbots' (III.2.17–18 [III.3.7–8]). More attention has gone to debating the degree of Protestantism of this commission – which is hardly a remarkable one, given John's defiance of the Pope – than in recognizing its obvious structural function. For the sake of his dramatic development, the Bastard cannot be permitted to witness John's charge to Hubert. Sending him to England gets him off the stage; sending him to rob the monasteries adds another touch to John's defiance and to the Bastard's own character. Clearly the issue between Church and Crown has not touched him. He is still John's loyal follower with a responsible commission – one from which he presumably stands to gain a percentage for himself. Thus his earlier choice has begun to pay off in cash as well as title.

The Bastard gone and Eleanor claiming Arthur's attention, John turns and fawns on Hubert. The warmth of his approach – 'O my gentle Hubert, | We owe thee much!' (III.2.29–30 [III.3.19–20]) – has, I believe, a double motivation. John is not merely flattering Hubert in order to bring him to murder Arthur, but indeed owes Hubert much, just as he says – owes him the very capture of Arthur, as the former appearance implied. John is promising a reward already due and hinting for just one further service. Hubert's response, moving from his noncommittal 'I am much bounden to your majesty' (39 [29]) to his more fervent declaration of love, is not unclouded. Whatever the circumstances that determined him, he is no longer in a position to maintain his neutrality; he has made, or been forced to make, his choice, and the loyalty then so coldly promised to the stronger must now be delivered. After a number of false starts, John finally manages the

most pointed of commissions, as though his will were less tainted
through showing naked so briefly:

KING JOHN
  Death.
HUBERT My lord?
KING JOHN   A grave.
HUBERT   He shall not live.
KING JOHN   Enough.

76 [65–6]

John leaves the promised reward unspecified, but the more
significant ambiguity lies in the sinister irony of his final statement
to Arthur that Hubert will attend on him 'With all true duty'
(83 [73]). True to whom? to what? and in what sense? The nature
of 'true duty' – whether Hubert's, John's, the Bastard's, Blanche's,
King Philip's, Pandulph's, Lady Faulconbridge's, or that of others
yet to appear – is precisely what is at issue in this play, whether
we call it that, or loyalty, or honour.

In the final scene of the third Act, Pandulph, the master strategist,
shows the defeated French how they yet stand to win. John, he
points out, cannot rest while Arthur lives. Arthur is John's
prisoner and John must kill him, thus freeing Lewis to claim the
English throne through Blanche and simultaneously driving the
English to revolt. John, as we know, has already headed directly
into the trap Pandulph has described, but, should John eliminate
himself along with Arthur, we are left with a claimant whom
Pandulph has not imagined: the English Bastard will be on hand
to contest the issue, and he, we feel, should take precedence over
the foreigner. As though to heighten the developing contrast, the
final comment of the willing Lewis – 'Strong reasons makes strange
actions' (182) – is a direct affirmation of commodity.

4

The fourth Act closes the trap, with complications no one could
have foreseen. However unexpected, and even illogical, the shift
in intent from murder to blinding – or, more likely, to murder as
an 'accident' during blinding – the resultant stage business is an
image of the moral situation, an image which is echoed and re-
echoed in the lines. The dilemma of conflicting loyalties is here

most acute, with Hubert, the very man who thought he could hold himself aloof from commitment, now caught between the claims of political allegiance and those of simple compassion. It is his 'duty' that is iron:

ARTHUR
  Must you with hot irons burn out both mine eyes?
HUBERT
  Young boy, I must.
ARTHUR   And will you?
HUBERT   And I will.

39–40

Human sympathy is the living eye that Hubert must put out. Hubert, with his irons and backed by two burly accomplices, concealed but at hand, is brute power; the child Arthur is powerless innocence, wronged right.

Arthur's insistence upon his own innocence and upon his loving attendance when Hubert's head once ached drives the scene dangerously close to the sentimental. To maintain his helplessness, there can be no one else to defend him, and, in the economy of the play, there has been no time for a scene demonstrating the attendance he is forced to cite, a bit priggishly, in his own behalf. In the difficulty of putting goodness on the stage, Shakespeare makes of Arthur, as he did of Blanche, a formal image of victimized virtue, Arthur the image of suffering innocence as Blanche was of suffering integrity. Perhaps the ultimate horror in the viciousness of 'this iron age' (60) is the recognition by innocence that its own appearance must be suspect: 'Nay, you may think my love was crafty love, | And call it cunning' (53–4). But Hubert is unable to proceed and, surprising no one more than himself – 'Yet am I sworn' (123) – he spares Arthur. His choice of a higher duty over a lower creates no moral millennium; it involves him immediately in duplicity – he must lie to John – and in 'Much danger' (133).

In the second scene, the English lords, who have formed John's silent retinue throughout the play, now first have a hand in the action, detaching themselves from John as Pandulph foretold. They are ostensibly objecting to the 'wasteful and ridiculous excess' (16) of a second coronation which John has just staged. (The unspoken implication is that John has been reasserting his authority after the excommunication, enforcing a new oath of allegiance to counteract Pandulph's having freed his followers from their former oaths.) Behind their cold acceptance, however, lies an obvious discontent. Their very worry about John's 'safety' (50), in requesting freedom for Arthur, has about it more of threat than of concern. Hubert's entrance before John's reply (as the Folio has it, rather than following that reply, where most editors have seen fit to place it) plainly implies, as Honigmann points out, that John grants their request as a matter of hypocritical policy, assured by Hubert's appearance that Arthur is dead. The nobles' well-justified suspicion leads them to depart with all the dignity of outraged principle. But, as Calderwood demonstrates, it becomes clear in the next scene that this apparent dependence upon principle has been the commodity of traitors.

Before we see them again, however, we have a new view of the Bastard. His increasing maturity is evident. He is no less open, no less loyal, but he makes his decisions more slowly, suspending judgement without hiding his grounds for suspicion. He is more critical. He speaks to John with more than a hint of annoyance –

> if you be afeard to hear the worst,
> Then let the worst unheard fall on your head –
>
> 135–6

an annoyance which must arise from his close inspection of John and his disappointment with what he sees. He has met the lords

> going to seek the grave
> Of Arthur, whom they say is kill'd tonight
> On your suggestion.
>
> 164–6

This report clearly invites denial from John, and the Bastard's suspicions cannot but increase when the invitation is not accepted. John instead claims ambiguously, 'I have a way to win their loves again' (168), and sends the Bastard to bring them back. His first response is merely a sober acceptance of the charge – 'I will seek them out' (169) – quite unlike his earlier enthusiasm, but John's reminder of the need to reconcile 'subject enemies' (171) in the face of a French invasion restores his usual zeal. His loyalty to England takes precedence over any doubts he is feeling about John.

John's 'way to win their loves again' is presumably explained in his immediate attempt to put the blame for Arthur's supposed death upon Hubert. Even while struggling to clear himself of the responsibility, John, with no sympathy for the boy, shows merely his own dismay at the outcome. Learning that Arthur lives, he expresses no joy, but thinks only of his own advantage: 'Doth Arthur live? O, haste thee to the peers' (260). It is obvious, however, that Hubert has best served his king, both morally and politically, by disobeying him.

What John wanted was Arthur's death without the responsibility for it. The consequences of the alleged death have no sooner forced him to welcome the news that Arthur is yet alive than Fate gives him exactly what he first wanted: the third scene begins with Arthur's accidental death while leaping from the wall to escape. But it is too late and the thing John wanted becomes its own opposite. Though, as it turned out, he lacked the power, he is left with the responsibility – or at least the alleged responsibility, which is equally harmful.[4]

Arthur's body lies unfound on the stage, however, while the skein is tangled still further. The lords, who appeared to be leaving the King on the basis of outraged principle, turn out to have been already in correspondence with Pandulph. They know the French plans and are deserting John to save their skins; Arthur's supposed death was a pretext for treason, not a cause of revulsion. The justice of their pretext cannot excuse such hypocrisy. They have just renewed their oaths to the king they are deserting. In contrast, though he shares the same suspicions, the Bastard puts his duty to England first: 'Whate'er you think, good words, I think, were best' (28). Given England's danger and the absence of evidence that Arthur is dead, 'there is little reason in your grief' (30).

Discovery of Arthur's body will confirm all suspicions, and the audience waits in suspense for the Bastard's reaction while the lords indulge in self-justifying superlatives of horror. 'Sir Richard, what think you?' Salisbury asks (41), but he and Pembroke both favour him with their own I-told-you-so's before – following surely a lengthy pause – he answers, simply and directly:

> It is a damned and a bloody work;
> The graceless action of a heavy hand,
> If that it be the work of any hand.

57–9

His conditional conclusion, which in John would be but a final attempt to protect his own false position, is in the Bastard a sign of his increasing wisdom. It is under-girded for the audience by their knowledge that he is right to withhold final judgement, for the death was in fact accidental. But this rational contingency can only strike the eager lords as pussy-footing, and Salisbury returns the Bastard's 'If' with indignant scorn. The lords, carried away by their own performance, join in a 'holy vow' (67) for revenge. In spite of the evidence, they are mistaken; whatever John's unsuitability, they are taking a vow that can only be seen as traitorous.

Hubert's untimely message that Arthur lives can hardly be expected to convince them of their error. The Bastard is forced to defend Hubert from their wrath, though his 'If' is still unresolved. Shown Arthur's body, Hubert weeps, which the hypocrites naturally take for hypocrisy, but, held off by the Bastard, they cannot attack him, and they leave to join the Dauphin at Saint Edmundsbury.

Though willing to defend Hubert from attack while the facts are unclear, the Bastard has not abandoned his own strong suspicions. Hubert, in spite of his choice of a higher duty, is entangled in circumstantial evidence. The Bastard demands a direct answer – 'Knew you of this fair work?' (116) – indicates both his stand if the answer is *yes* –

> There is not yet so ugly a fiend of hell
> As thou shalt be, if thou didst kill this child –

123–4

and his honest opinion – 'I do suspect thee very grievously' (134). This is the new, more thoughtful, less hot-headed but no less forthright man that the Bastard has grown to be, a far cry from the unthinking enthusiast he was in the first Act. Having accepted Hubert's protestation of innocence, however, he is left with his suspicions of John. The issues surrounding Arthur's death are more complex, more confused and human, than most critics have been willing to allow, and the Bastard's reaction is the appropriate one for any conscientious man:

> I am amaz'd, methinks, and lose my way
> Among the thorns and dangers of this world.
>
> 140–41

The moral life is never, for a perceptive man, a simple choice between black and white, but life in a maze. The ambiguity of the Bastard's ensuing soliloquy reflects the ambiguity of the issues themselves, and his conclusion the necessity to act in spite of it. He recognizes both Arthur's right to the throne and the fact that the very question of right is now irrelevant; that 'England' is dead, but that England remains to suffer,

> and vast confusion waits,
> As doth a raven on a sick-fall'n beast,
> The imminent decay of wrested pomp.
>
> 152–4

This is what commodity has cost England. But, though he realizes now that John's pomp was wrested, the Bastard sees no choice but continuing loyalty: 'I'll to the king' (157).

5

The fifth Act begins with the King reduced to a most unkingly posture, however, yielding his crown to Pandulph. True, he receives it back at once, but only as the Pope's vassal, and we cannot fail to realize how far he has fallen from his earlier proud defiance. There is no religious issue here, but once again a simple political bargain, a yielding to force: John's immediate response to the brief ceremony is 'Now keep your holy word: go meet the French' (5). He sees himself as re-establishing his own rule in his kingdom, where his people have been 'Swearing allegiance ... To stranger blood' (10–11), but, remembering his

assurance that 'no Italian priest | Shall tithe or toll in our domin-
ions' (III.1.79–80), we realize that we have witnessed him doing
precisely what he blames in his subjects.

The Bastard, upon his arrival with bad news, is again closely
observing John and controlling his disgust only with difficulty.
After mentioning military reversals and the nobles' treachery, he
concludes

> And wild amazement hurries up and down
> The little number of your doubtful friends.
>
> 35–6

He is reporting not merely a general but a pointedly personal
condition ('I am amaz'd'), and though others may be 'doubtful
friends' because they are both fearful and untrusting, he is a
trustworthy and fearless friend tormented by doubt. John's assumption that Arthur yet lives sounds to the Bastard like the sheerest
hypocrisy and almost leads to a break. Given the Bastard's suspicions, 'some damn'd hand' (41) is dangerously blunt, backing
down no whit before John's face from the firm position already
taken (IV.3.57–9). There is a crescendo of excitement, with John,
in horror and guilt, attempting again to put the blame on Hubert,
and the Bastard, having accepted Hubert's innocence, responding
with a direct insinuation of John's responsibility for murder:

> KING JOHN
> That villain Hubert told me he did live.
> BASTARD
> So, on my soul, he did, for aught he knew.
>
> 42–3

The final pronoun, clearing Hubert, accuses John. This exchange,
in which tempers have risen on both sides, must be followed by a
long, electric silence, while John cringes and the Bastard cools to
consider what he is doing. England must again be uppermost in
his thoughts, for he stops, as it were, in midstream in his attack
and turns to rallying John's spirits for the battle with the invaders.
This self-control, this ability to quell his passionate outrage in
order to undertake what is required by a higher loyalty, demonstrates the maturity the Bastard has reached. His moral superiority

to John is clear; it is one of his glorious moments and prepares us to accept what follows.

Though he has, technically, misjudged the detail of Arthur's death, he has not in fact misjudged John. He pleads now only that the man act with the outer semblance of the king in order to inspire his followers. But John has abandoned his authority to Pandulph and, pleased merely to have retained his throne, considers it a 'happy peace' (63). Such peace with an invading army horrifies the Bastard – 'O inglorious league!' (65) – and leads to so overwhelming a remonstrance that John, having just yielded to Pandulph, yields again, this time to the Bastard. John, a king incapable of kingship, is finally replaced in action by the man most capable of it.

The little ceremony by which John and Pandulph exchanged oaths is succeeded in the second scene by another little ceremony in which the Dauphin and the traitorous nobles do the same. These are the formalizations of allegiance, the hollow rites which political practice substitutes for the living loyalty exemplified by such a man as the Bastard.

The Bastard's new role is mirrored in the stage direction: always before he has been on his own, but now, as Regent, he enters '*attended*'. Though he speaks of 'the scope | And warrant limited unto my tongue' (122–3), it is but a way of postponing action until he learns how things stand; once he knows the situation, he assumes full authority. The King of and for whom he speaks – who 'is prepar'd' (130), who 'doth smile' (134) at the invasion, 'the gallant monarch' (148), 'warlike John' (176) – is of course not the man John but a verbal image of the king England needs at the moment. The image is not a mere fiction, however, for it is personified in the Bastard himself; though not the King, he wields the King's authority and speaks for England.

As though to ensure this distinction, the brief third scene shows us, in direct contrast to 'warlike John', the utter impotence of the man beneath the public image. Ill with a fever, he is ordered off the field by the Bastard lest his very appearance dishearten the soldiers. The kingly role has been entirely transferred. The Bastard 'alone upholds the day' (V.4.5).

The fourth scene twists the ironic complications of meaningless oaths and meaningful loyalty about as far as they can go. The dying Melun, breaking an oath (his to the Dauphin) which broke an oath (the Dauphin's and his to the English nobles) which broke an oath (theirs to John), reveals to the nobles that the Dauphin intends to execute them as soon as the battle is over. Abandoning their 'holy vow', they hasten to return to John. Who is to disentangle true honour from such a skein as this? But Melun, saving their lives, says that he does so for the love of 'one Hubert' (40), and because he himself had an English grandfather. This personal loyalty stands out above the meaningless oaths as a return to sanity and honour. The men saved by his love for Hubert are, however, the very men who misjudged and misused Hubert for their own selfish ends. They are saved by love for the man they scorned; the cutting of the skein carries overtones of Christian forgiveness.

Hubert it is who brings to the Bastard the news that John is dying. No time is wasted in the play on the mechanics of John's death; poisoning by a monk is supplied by history as Shakespeare knew it; his attention, however, is not on John but on the effect of John's approaching death on the Bastard. As they meet in the night, Hubert's 'Who art thou?' (V.6.9) is precisely the question which remains to be settled, and the Bastard's 'Who thou wilt' (9), coupled with the reminder of his Plantagenet blood, stresses the possibility toward which the play has apparently been aiming. We have seen Hubert grow from his attempt at a coldly rational avoidance of the problem of choice between loyalties to a realization that a man is forced to commit himself and can only hope to do so honourably. We have seen the Bastard grow from a naïve enthusiast following chance to a man of mature insight and ability. What Hubert brings the Bastard now is, in effect, an invitation to take the throne, to assume the role he has in fact been filling and for which the character he inherited from his father has proven so eminently fitted. It is all understated, but the implications are clear:

> I left him almost speechless; and broke out
> To acquaint you with this evil, that you might
> The better arm you to the sudden time.

24–6

Hubert foresees a struggle, and he wants the Bastard to have the throne. A struggle with whom? 'The lords are all come back' (33). Clearly they must not gain control. But then a new complication is introduced: 'And brought Prince Henry in their company' (34). This is the first mention in the play that John has a son and heir; the Bastard is (and many in the audience are) presumably reminded; dramatically it is startling news, further snarling the problem of moral choice.[5]

Prince Henry is apparently, like Arthur earlier, a young successor surrounded by a self-seeking league.[6] The Bastard is in the identical situation which faced John upon the death of Richard and the question is, will he, like John, usurp the throne? However self-seeking such a move might appear, it could clearly be considered also, given the Bastard's truly kingly character, to be for England's own good. The Bastard's immediate response is a prayer, as much for England as for himself:

> Withhold thine indignation, mighty heaven,
> And tempt us not to bear above our power!

37–8

It is not a decision, but it is surely an aspiration not to be misled by the temptations of commodity. He is, in fact, not even willing at the moment to entertain the possibility. His immediate revelation that he has lost 'half my power this night' (39), half of his army having been wiped out by a perverse tide, has been taken as showing that he is forced to his dynastic decision only by his inability to muster sufficient strength to seize the throne from the combined forces of the returning noblemen. It is rather the explanation to Hubert of his prayer that heaven withhold its indignation. His worry is, as always, for England, facing the invader now with decimated forces. The invasion, not the succession, is his business at the moment. And the question is doubly untimely, for John is still 'the king' (43).

But the audience knows, as the Bastard does not, that Lewis also has suffered grievous losses quite apart from the battle. Structurally, it remains only for John to die and the Bastard to reach his decision. Shakespeare first shows us Prince Henry, however, though the lines give us almost no clue as to how the author directed his company to have that part played. Prince

Henry's few speeches leave him sounding a sensitive enough young man facing the death of his father, but it would be equally possible to play him as a weakling reminiscent of Arthur or as a young man of promising strength of character. And the effect he creates will naturally cast its light on the Bastard's decision. I think director and actor are called upon to attempt a compromise: Henry must be kept young enough to underline the similarity between the Bastard's choice and that which originally faced John; at the same time he must show some vitality and promise, for a suggestion of his complete dominance by the former traitors would be out of key with the generally hopeful conclusion of the play. This ambiguity of effect in the Prince's role is in part indicative of the fact that our attention is no longer on the question of what a king ought to be but has shifted over to that of how, given this situation, the Bastard ought to act.

John, who commenced the play as a successful usurper, dies miserably as he listens to the Bastard's news of England's losses. Even as John lies dying, his faithful follower pays him the compliment of not tempering the truth. And, though 'God He knows how we shall answer' Lewis (60), John is no sooner dead than the Bastard turns to rallying the defence. But defence is not necessary, for the others know that Lewis has already sued for peace. There remains then but the single question, and it is quickly settled: the Bastard turns and kneels to Prince Henry. Whether the Prince combines the true kingly character with the possession and right here acknowledged, we are given little chance of knowing. That, however, is not the point. The very strength of character which made the Bastard the most worthy of Richard's heirs leads him to relinquish any divisive personal ambitions and to acknowledge a true duty to support the new king. This is the heir who alone remains of those who were established in the first Act as having a share in Richard's heritage; this is the young man who once said 'Gain, be my lord, for I will worship thee!'; this is the efficient commander who, as John failed, has actually been wielding the royal power. In spite of all these indications of a contrary denouement, he kneels to Prince Henry. In a world of self-seekers, his conception of honour has grown until he is capable of this self-denying loyalty to England. It is, of course, one of the tragic ironies of politics that a man may be cut off from authority by the very act which best demonstrates his worthiness to wield it.

Though it takes a paragraph – and could take more – to sketch the implications of the Bastard's kneeling, he is not to be seen as one who has thought it all through. He is impulsive at the close as he was at the beginning, but his impulses now are those of one whose original promise has come to maturity. His closing speech, with its ringing final couplet – 'Nought shall make us rue | If England to itself do rest but true!' – has sometimes been dismissed as a platitudinous set-piece. It is so only if we cannot see that the play has demonstrated the moral complexity of the problem of loyalty while the Bastard (and to a lesser extent Hubert) has shown us the self-denying acceptance of a higher duty which true loyalty demands from the man of honour.

NOTES

1. All citations are from the Arden edition, edited by E. A. J. Honigmann (London, 1954), because I am convinced by his arrangement of the Act- and scene-divisions. Where these differ from the traditional arrangement, I give a second reference to that, as found in J. D. Wilson's Cambridge edition (1936).

2. Nine times as Arthur's; once – 'God and our right!' (299) – the French king, in Arthur's name, claiming for himself in English what English kings are supposed to claim in French; once (548) Arthur's right given to Constance; once (335) John claiming right for himself; and twice (139 and 236) with a different meaning altogether.

3. Four times, it is true, in reference to lineage; five times, with greater richness of connotation, in reference to vital existence; but the remaining seventeen times in reference to the butchery of war.

4. The moral responsibility may, of course, be disputed, with the emphasis either on the accident or on the justified fear of John which forced Arthur to take the chance.

5. The structure of the play is not affected by whether or not the audience 'knows all the time' that John must, historically, be followed on the throne by his son Henry. Whether or not the audience is surprised by the conclusion, the fact remains that the

play, in its original division of claimants to the throne and its eventual elimination of two of them, seems to be moving toward the coronation of the third and only frustrates that expectation at the last minute by introducing the hitherto unmentioned heir.

6. Where, when, and how the lords made contact with the Prince is unmentioned. It would not be out of line with their duplicity and the complications of V.4 to think of them as having been holding him in reserve as a future resource against Lewis.

SIX

King Richard the Second's Tragedy*

Peter Ure

WHEN at first examined, the design of *Richard II* may appear unexpected. The play is in four unequal phases:

(i) I.1–II.1.223. Richard as king; the political crises with which he is faced (shown as derived in part from earlier events), and his lack of wisdom in dealing with them.

(ii) II.1.224 to the end of III.1. Bolingbroke's invasion, and the transference of real power.

(iii) III.2 to the end of V.1. Richard's deposition, or what can perhaps be called his 'passion'.

(iv) V.2 to the end. Bolingbroke as king; his mastery in a political crisis.

These phases are not as mechanical or clear-cut as their tabulation may suggest; in the first part of IV.1, which echoes the trial-by-combat scenes of the first Act, Bolingbroke is manifestly ruling, while the most absorbing scene of the last phase develops Richard's suffering to its conclusion in death. Such counterpointing preserves unity and sequence without disorganizing the four-part design; the first two phases seem especially deliberate.

This view of the design serves to show, at least, what Shakespeare was *not* concerned to do, and why our expectations may be baffled. The play, although it touches upon this subject, is not about a struggle for power between two royal houses, nor even between two royal men, despite contrasts in temperament and politics. Shakespeare could have written a play of political intrigue, and made the military action which accompanies it a good

---

*From the Introduction to the new Arden Shakespeare edition of *King Richard II* (1961), pages lxii–lxxxiii. Copyright © Methuen & Co. Ltd, 1961. Reprinted by kind permission of the author and the publishers, Methuen & Co. Ltd, London.

deal more uncertain and exciting – the material was there in Holinshed. Instead, he placed the emphasis on Richard's nature and behaviour, and gave his play the order and unity of biography. He did this even at the risk of exaggerating what might be thought to be, by a dramatist chiefly concerned with dynastic and military conflict, a disadvantage of the original story: the fact that Richard was so largely a passive victim of events, and Bolingbroke so easy a victor. Shakespeare gives them even less to do in the fields of conquest and intrigue than his history permitted. He chose to do this, and makes his choice clear to the audience.

The first phase works towards, as its climax, a striking demonstration of Richard's unfitness for his kingly office. He has, first, the legacy of past mistakes to contend with. These mistakes are brought to dramatic life in the dead-and-gone business of Gloucester's murder which has come alive again in the person of the avenging nephew, and his challenge to the murderer's wretched tool, Mowbray; meantime, the Duchess of Gloucester, a lamenting chorus, serves to revivify for the audience the shock and horror, as well as the plangent dynastic issues, attendant upon the tyrant's buried act.

On the whole, Richard deals with this situation creditably enough. Since Coleridge gave the lead, many commentators have read Richard's 'insincerity, partiality, arbitrariness and favouritism',[1] as well as Mowbray's bluster and Bolingbroke's tenacity, between the lines of the challenge scenes. John Palmer perhaps has it both ways:

The more vigilant spectator may detect a subtle difference in Richard's addresses to the two men. Surely there is a touch of irony in his words to Bolingbroke:

> Cousin of Hereford, as thy cause is right,
> So be thy fortune in this royal fight!
>
> I.3.55–6

and a touch of affectionate approval in his valediction to Mowbray:

> Farewell, my lord. Securely I espy
> Virtue with valour couchèd in thine eye.
>
> I.3.97–8

But these are hints to the wary. The simple onlooker is absorbed by the knightly courtesy of it all and is as eager for the fight as the champions themselves.[2]

It is possible that the scenes yield these hints to the wary in a measure as great as some commentators have claimed, but they are taken only at the cost of neglecting the broad theatrical effect. Shakespeare gives little sign, as he tries to breathe life into the chivalric forms that he found in Holinshed, that Richard steps out of the part prescribed for a monarch faced with a trial by combat between two of his nobility. The challenge scenes are not, to any of the actors engaged in them, much more, of course, than a political performance staged to the common view, serious enough perhaps, but with the kind of gravity that attends upon the operation of a fairly stereotyped social institution. All this is indicated by the formal arrangement and character of the speeches and gestures, a stiffness which suggests very cleverly that the lines of procedure have been laid down in advance, probably by a committee. Richard plays his appointed part. His attempts to make peace – prescribed as necessary for the validity of what was a strictly legal process – which are rejected by the angry knights, as they had full right within the process to do, are Gaunt's attempts, too; the old man, unlike the young, is not accused of weakness or 'levity of tone'.[3]

What we are to understand by the stopping of the trial is even more of an open question. Hayward thought that the incident was a contrived anti-climax, thoughtlessly devised by Richard so that he might indulge in irresponsible splendours, and many critics, such as Craig, have agreed with him: 'he loves the pomp of his office, else he would hardly have suffered Bolingbroke and Mowbray to meet'.[4] Yet Shakespeare does not seem at this stage to be exploiting a fact of history, from which he could hardly escape, to the detriment of Richard, nor is there any hint in the sources available to Shakespeare that the trial was a thoughtless display, terminated by an act of royal petulance. Indeed, *if* Shakespeare had read Froissart, he would know that order and public safety made this last act advisable, and, *if* Shakespeare knew anything of the ordinances of the trial by combat, he would know that its termination at any stage was one of the royal umpire's allowed acts of authority. Whatever his sources said or, in the case of Holinshed, left unsaid on the point, Shakespeare was free to make thoughtlessness and petulance a part of Richard's character here. Whether he did, depends not on our estimate of the wisdom or folly of the historical Richard, measured with the foresight of one who knows the rest of the story, nor even on hints to the vigilant spectator, but on unprejudiced theatrical effect, even if this means ranging ourselves with that humble creature, Palmer's simple onlooker. From his point of view, Richard's sudden regaining of the initiative, and the submissions which follow it, can be seen as a ruler's stroke: it deflates the quarrelling magnates, and is explicitly justified by that highest of all Elizabethan arguments, the avoidance of civil tumult. It permits, so clear is the ascendancy Richard has now established, the remission of four years from Bolingbroke's exile: this is an act of mercy whose kingly and politically unforced nature is emphasized by Shakespeare's rendering of it as a free response to Gaunt's pleas rather than (as it is in Froissart) a shrewd calculation by the Council.

It is not difficult for the actor who plays Richard, and who knows what comes next, to 'twinkle' with a consciousness of mischievous intentions and to make every one of the few sentences which he speaks in these scenes bristle with hints of the 'skipping king [who] ambled up and down'.[5] But it is, I think, more correct to believe that Shakespeare intended, with a larger theatrical effect in mind, to show Richard playing the part of majesty with a fair efficiency in these first scenes, the more dramatically to reveal his profounder unfitness for the role in the later ones. In Richard's sudden lapse of tone in the last scene of the first Act, it is unlikely that we see disclosed the 'true' motive for the act of state which exiled the two rivals: for there is no indication that Shakespeare's monarch, like Froissart's, knew of Bolingbroke's wooing of the commonalty until it is manifested in his conduct when he departs for exile. But we do see a glittering autocrat when he is no longer concerned to keep up public appearances. The scene has a broken opening, a cheap irony, a naturalistic speech, full of sneers, and some quite sinister frankness and brutality; all this would have been impossible in the public context of the preceding scene, which asks for rehearsed gestures and harmless formulae. A general relaxation occurs when Richard is no longer kinging it. Is there even to be observed, perhaps, an offending gap between the public and the private character? This is one reason why the scenes are juxtaposed.[6]

This shock and disharmony are followed by the scene in which we are directly told for the first time about Richard's mismanagement of himself and his kingdom. Gaunt, our informer, has been shown so far as an orthodoxly loyal subject, a counsellor of patience to the Duchess and to his son. Loyal, time-honoured, and dying, he is to be believed without reservations when he paints *his* picture of a king who 'Mingled his royalty with capering fools'. Richard does not hear the great speech on the ruin of England, perhaps because Shakespeare avoided having to show a lack of response on Richard's part that would have prejudiced the beholder too finally against him. But it is the background to the more strictly technical reproaches of both Gaunt and York that follow, and, reinforced by the dynastic appeal to the great past of Richard's line, help to prepare for the climax towards which this first phase of the play has been moving. For Richard totally fails to raise himself to Gaunt's level, or even to respond to the good sense of York's argument[7] at II.1.195–9:

> Take Hereford's rights away, and take from Time
> His charters and his customary rights.
> Let not tomorrow then ensue today.
> Be not thyself; for how art thou a king
> But by fair sequence and succession?

This makes plain that his act of state in this scene, the seizure of Gaunt's property, is to be seen as a paramount folly that matches nothing he has done so far. Our sense of this is induced by the spectacle of the prince, in wilful choler, rejecting the advice of the good counsellors, who speak with a special authority. The good courtier, wrote Castiglione, must

understand how to behave himselfe readily in all occurrents to drive into his Princes heade what honour and profit shall ensue to him and to his by justice, liberallitie, valiantnesse of courage, meekenesse, and by the other vertues that belong to a good prince, and contrariwise what slander, and damage commeth of the vices contrarie to them.

Richard rejects the good courtiers' persuasions to justice; thereby the scene makes its impact and reveals the defectiveness of this prince.[8] Other inferences from it – such as 'Richard should not have gone to Ireland, leaving an unsettled land behind him', or 'Richard should not have appointed York Lord Governor because York's allegiance has been shaken' – are of minor force beside the king's rejection of the good counsellors. For Shakespeare did not expect his audience to exercise the kind of logic that comes more readily to the historian; by watching where Shakespeare places the dramatic emphasis – using invented material to achieve it – we may at least avoid confusing the dramatic character with the historical personage. What the audience is left with is the reflection that a prince who so cavalierly rejects the advice of grave persons must be deficient in the qualities that nourish kingship.

This is allowed to hang in the air of the second phase of the play, which deals with the transference of power. Here, Shakespeare has greatly compressed his scale of time and has omitted all the business of the intrigue culminating in the Archbishop of Canterbury's mission to Bolingbroke in France which might have compromised the swift pace of the action. The struggle for power is of the most perfunctory kind. When we encounter Bolingbroke in II.3, he is already deep in the country receiving the access of powerful followers, while York's incompetence and the Queen's forebodings in the previous scene have already made plain how little of a fight he is likely to have. All this is designedly contrasted with the defection of Richard's own companies. Power slides from the absent and silent Richard with the speed of an avalanche: this is not a play about how power is gained by *expertise*, nor even about how cunning overcomes stupidity – Richard is simply not there, either to provide the one, or counter the other. The phase ends with an act of quasi-regal authority by Bolingbroke – the execution of the favourites – which indicates how completely he has taken over from Richard. Shakespeare so arranges matters that, when Richard re-enters in III.2 to begin the third phase, the phase of his suffering, he is a man whom the audience knows, after this series of bloodless victories and defeats, to be a king without power ready to receive the bad news that he is so. It is by now clear where the centre of interest is to lie: not in an intrigue, nor in the confrontation of tyrant and usurper, but, as Coleridge said, in 'a history of the human mind'.[9]

This design must control our understanding of how Shakespeare wished us to read Richard's character. The second scene of the third Act is crucial in any interpretation of this. Richard lands in Wales, his mind tense and large with the knowledge that his kingdom has been invaded; he hears, hard upon each other, of the disasters to his cause: that the Welsh have deserted him, the favourites been taken, and the Lord Governor gone over to the enemy; Aumerle tries to keep his spirits up, only to have the comfort dashed away by the next piece of ill news. At the end of the scene there is nothing Richard can do except shut himself up in the neighbouring castle. The audience already knows, before the scene begins, the worst that he is yet to learn; their interest is not in the news itself, but in his reception of it. They also know that Richard cannot now act against Bolingbroke: any expectation of that kind has been stripped from them as efficiently as Bolingbroke has stripped from Richard the apparatus of physical power. The audience is prepared for action only in the field of mind, for, as it turns out, the dizzying alternation of hope and despair.

The situation in which Richard now finds himself is that of a king, deprived of physical power, who retains a circumscribed personal liberty and the sacred name and attributes pertaining to his kingship. Amongst these we must include a Queen. The rest of this phase of the play is to be concerned with how he gives even these things one by one into the hands of the usurper; it is not until the last phase that life itself is required of him. It is sometimes said that Shakespeare shows up Richard's weakness and unfitness for the throne by indicating his preference for words over action, his temperamental inability to implement Carlisle's saying:

> My lord, wise men ne'er sit and wail their woes,
> But presently prevent the ways to wail.

> III.2.178–9

This judgement – which overlooks the fact that even the Bishop falls silent when the final disaster of York's desertion is reported – does not seem to accord with Shakespeare's intention so far as that is apparent in his design. It is in the first phase of the play that

Richard's unfitness has been shown, his political misjudgement, the burdensome legacy of past mistakes and brutal disregard of present advice: all defects in the princely character and failures to rise to the level of his function. It is these that are the sufficient causes of the loss of power that has followed upon them in the swift retribution of the second phase. But in this third phase, which this scene initiates, Shakespeare is not now dealing with the causes, already adequately set out in political terms, but with the effects on Richard of the new situation. That part of his fall which was political and entailed the loss of power has been accomplished; there remains that aspect of it which trenches upon a sacred tragedy, the divesting of royalty of its mysterious panoply. It is the wish to set this last in a clear and free light, as a thing that happened to a man who was also a king, which, we may conjecture, shaped the design of the play as a whole. Shakespeare bundled the narrative of causes away into the first two and a half Acts so that he might more fully set forth the drama of the sufferer constrained to reduce himself from king to man by shedding the 'great glory' of the Name.

Hence it is that we meet for the first time in this scene the new, the expressive Richard. It is hardly just to read back his loquacity here into one of the causes of a loss of power already adequately accounted for by his political misjudgement and defects as a prince. Richard is a new character here in the sense that the play's design has now developed to the point where it is laid down for him that he must give voice to what is in him; more narrowly, that he must say what he feels all the time about his situation, or many successive situations: his appearance on the walls of Flint Castle, his abdication, his parting with Isabel, his death in the prison; and these are contrived about him by Bolingbroke, nor can he alter them save as Bolingbroke directs. That is to say, to survive at all as the protagonist of a poetic drama designed, as this one is, with a helpless king at its centre, Richard has to use words or, more accurately, poetry.

But the poetry in Richard is there because he is a character in a poetic drama, not because Shakespeare thought that Richard II lost his kingdom through a preference for blank verse over battles, or, as Mark Van Doren puts it, because he loved poetry 'more than power and more than any other person'.[10]

This is not to deny that there is a large element of conscious expressiveness and calculated gesture in the Richard who is drawn for us in the last two and a half Acts of the play. These show that Shakespeare wished us to see him as akin in some respects to the poet and the actor. Richard's ability to see his story as story is an aspect of this conscious expressiveness, comparable to that of Thomas Mann's Joseph or of Brutus and Cassius when they reflect, the one on the glory, the other on the pitiableness of their deed:

> How many ages hence
> Shall this our lofty scene be acted over,
> In states unborn, and accents yet unknown!
>
> *Julius Caesar*, III.1.111–13

So Richard can see his fall as a mirror for princes (III.2.155 ff.), or compare it to that of 'glistering Phaeton', or of Christ, or urge Isabel: 'Tell thou the lamentable tale of me'. It is a part of the drawing of his character, too, that this expressiveness is sometimes shown to fall short of the effect he intends, or to induce self-disgust. In III.3 Aumerle is reduced to tears by the genuine pathos of the first half of Richard's speech (III.3.143–59):

> Aumerle, thou weepest, my tender-hearted cousin.

But Richard goes too far in the rococo image which follows; tears turn to embarrassment:

> Well, well, I see
> I talk but idly, and you laugh at me.
>
> III.3.170–71

Another of Richard's miscalculations occurs at the end of the mirror episode, where he needs time to recover from Bolingbroke's curt demolition of the mirror-smashing gesture (IV.1.292–3) before he can turn Bolingbroke's own quibble upside down. The soliloquy in prison ends with a movement of self-disgust at a too abundant fancy: 'I stand fooling here' (V.5.60).

Akin to this kind of miscalculation is a strong element of corrupt fantasy in Richard. This is not, I conceive, the same as saying with Van Doren that he is the 'great poet of the play', albeit a 'minor poet'. He is a man, as Yeats remarked,[11] full of capricious fancy; in his sorrow he behaves like a 'fantastic', a changeful, restless figure imperfectly governed by the reason to which he should be subject: 'how many chimeras, antics, golden mountains and castles in the air do they build unto themselves!'[12] 'Meethinkes', says Phantaste in Jonson's *Cynthia's Revels*:

I should wish my selfe all manner of creatures. Now, I would bee an empresse; and by and by a dutchesse; then a great ladie of state; then one of your *miscelany* madams; then a waiting-woman; then your cittizens wife; then a course countrey gentlewoman; then a deyrie maide; then a shepheards lasse; then an empresse againe, or the queene of *fayries*. . . . [13]

So Richard, too, longs for other roles than that which fate constrains him to play:

> Thus play I in one person many people,
> And none contented.

> V.5.31–2

But it is quite another thing to claim that because Richard 'thinks in images',[14] Shakespeare therefore wished us to think of him as a poet, or even as a bad poet because his images sometimes misfire,[15] with the corollary that 'Richard's fall is due . . . to his preference for words over deeds'.[16] The design of the play, as already exposed, shows that Richard's fall *is* due to a specific deed, a rash act which he was warned to avoid and which springs not from a corrupt fancy but from a failure in duty and the understanding of his function. The poetry which he speaks thereafter is Shakespeare's medium, which he uses to show – and by means of images to show as lustrously as possible – what is going on in Richard's mind and heart. This is why it is legitimate to use the images which Shakespeare puts into his mouth as clues to the way he reacts to his situation and from them to draw conclusions about his nature as a whole. The sun-images, used by him and by others of him, express his and their feeling for the splendour of the royal office[17]; the image of mother and child (III.2.8 ff.) shows that his intense love of country is touched with a feminine feeling[18]; the images of earth and the grave show how ready he is to decline into the ultimate of sorrow, and that of the clock how discrowning seems to him to have robbed him of life itself. Richard D. Altick has brilliantly collated these and others to bring out their interrelation and the force they acquire through studied repetition.[19]

In expressiveness Bolingbroke contrasts with Richard. Shakespeare has made use of the fact that his design – 'The Tragedy of King Richard the Second' – is shaped to set out as fully as possible the passion of the deposed monarch, rather than the struggle between two rivals, and therefore throws Bolingbroke into a subordinate position. This subordination does not mean that he is simply flatter and obscurer than Richard; his flatness and obscurity become attributes of his character. This is most keenly felt in the deposition scene, where Bolingbroke's silence seems to have a positive quality.

To identify precisely this quality is difficult. Elsewhere in the play, Bolingbroke has at his command the florid and formal language of the politician and patriot; as Tamburlaine 'plays the Orator' against Theridamas, so Bolingbroke can use enticing argument to draw York into his camp.[20] His fair discourse has been 'as sugar' to Northumberland, and, as Dr Tillyard notes,[21] there is a 'plain and understandable passion' in his language when he recounts his wrongs in III.1. Yet, compared with the full and free expression of what is in Richard's mind, Bolingbroke's mind and motives are in shadow.[22] This is why the view, held by some commentators,[23] that the whole play is built on the contrast in character between Richard and Bolingbroke needs to be defined. It is true that the two men are manifestly contrasted in respect of their success as princes. Richard's chief act as prince is, as we have seen, one which makes plain his unfitness to hold the sceptre which inheritance has bestowed upon him; Bolingbroke's mastery in the kingly office is emphasized in the challenge scene of IV.1 and throughout the fifth Act, where his tempering of mercy with justice shows that he understands the duties classically prescribed for the wise ruler.[24] Thus, when the two men are compared as rulers and magistrates, it is plain that Bolingbroke knows how and what to do:

> And with that odds he weighs King Richard down.
>
> III.4.89

But the metaphor of the balance, as a means of discerning the structure of the play, will not work over the whole of it. We do not know about Bolingbroke's sensations as he takes the heavy weight of the crown on his head as we do about Richard's when he puts it off.[25] On all that aspect of the event which touches not simply the transference of executive power, but the divinity which hedges and sanctions it, Bolingbroke is silent. It is a theme of which Richard makes much; if we are to trust the design of the tragedy, which orders the free unfolding of this subject in terms of Richard's suffering, as well as the whole scheme of the history plays, it is one with which Shakespeare and his audience were deeply concerned; yet Bolingbroke evades it. Are his silence and evasion, then, to be interpreted as Shakespeare's method of indicating that Bolingbroke is indifferent to the accredited sanctions of power, so long as he can grasp the reality of it; that he is depicted as the new man whose embryonic 'Counter-Renaissance' world is destined to overthrow the medievalism of Richard's?[26] This is a persuasive view, and is supported by much in the play, so that some sense that an old order is giving place to a new is present to most of its readers: Richard says

> my time
> Runs posting on in Bolingbroke's proud joy
>
> V.5.58–9

and in the 'new spring of time' of the fifth Act, York appears as a pathetic survival of an old winter of discontent. Yet we cannot be perfectly confident that Shakespeare could have felt the contrast between old pageantry and new principles in so contemporary a fashion as Dr Tillyard suggests. It may have been that Shakespeare created a Bolingbroke partially inarticulate because the usurper's springs of action puzzled him, as they did Daniel:

> Doubtfull at first, he warie doth proceed
> Seemes not t'affect, that which he did effect,
> Or els perhaps seemes as he ment indeed,
> Sought but his owne, and did no more expect:
> Then fortune thou art guilty of his deed,
> That didst his state aboue his hopes erect,
> And thou must beare some blame of his great sin
> That left'st him worse then when he did begin.[27]

Hazlitt, by contrast, held that Shakespeare portrayed him as 'seeing his advantage afar off, but only seizing it when he has it within reach, humble, crafty, bold, and aspiring, encroaching by regular but slow degrees'.[28] Bolingbroke, certainly, though he may have inherited Gaunt's lands, does not inherit his moral role. Shakespeare seems almost ostentatiously to avoid pressing it upon him by omitting the scene of his first landing in England: here we might have expected some declaration of policy and some affirmation of his country's good to countervail Richard's landing at Harlech and his own patriotic slogan when we last saw him. It is difficult to be as confident as Hazlitt that we can read a policy so circumscribed with shadow as this. Right up to the deposition scene he is not represented as seeking more than his hereditary rights as Gaunt's son and the punishment of those who have wronged him. Yet the pursuit of those rights involves him in defiance of the anointed king's authority; though York himself weakens, there is no answer, except denial of the premises on which it is based, to York's rebuke at II.3.105–13:

> BOLINGBROKE My gracious uncle, let me know my fault.
> On what condition stands it, and wherein?
> YORK Even in condition of the worst degree,
> In gross rebellion and detested treason.
> Thou art a banished man, and here art come
> Before the expiration of thy time
> In braving arms against thy sovereign!

Bolingbroke's reply:

> As I was banished, I was banished Hereford;
> But as I come, I come for Lancaster

(which Shakespeare did not find in Holinshed) sounds suspiciously like a piece of chicanery hastily run up for the occasion. Bolingbroke's appeal to his father's shade (II.3.116 ff.) may remind us that Gaunt himself, if his advice to the Duchess of Gloucester (I.2.37–41) is any guide, would have rejected it, and Bolingbroke is certainly ready to lift an angry arm against God's minister (III.3.42 ff.) although the threat becomes characteristically ambiguous a moment later (III.3.58–60) and when Northumberland rephrases it (III.3.101 ff.). It may be fair to conclude from all this that indifference to what Richard feels so deeply about is the positive quality of Bolingbroke's silence during the deposition scene, but

Shakespeare does not seem to have provided enough evidence about Bolingbroke's state of mind for us to conclude with Hazlitt that we are to see him as plotting for supreme power from the first. The contrast between Bolingbroke as an efficient ruler and Richard as an unwise one contributes to the play's structure and helps to balance the last phase against the first. But a similar balance is not found in that region where deeper motives and sanctions greater than that of physical power are exposed; it is Richard who brings these to life and awareness; against his exposition of them we cannot set the outward man who is Bolingbroke – his impulses are hidden from us; his conduct is ambiguous, partly because such ambiguity is for him an instrument of policy and partly, perhaps, because of his creator's irresolution. 'To find out right with wrong – it may not be', says York: Bolingbroke's apparent total unawareness of the dilemma may be due to a settled determination to get what he wants at the cost of ignoring it or merely to Shakespeare's unwillingness to sound his motives too deeply. Whatever the reason, the effect – and this perhaps is the calculation that lies behind the whole unbalance – is to throw all the light upon Richard: his 'right' is the burden of his thoughts, and he is the uninterrupted expositor of it.

He introduces the theme in the central scenes of the third Act. His inability to resist Bolingbroke or his demands sets him free, as it were, both to fall back upon the divinity of his kingship as a last resource and to bring it to our awareness, not as a mere theory of sovereignty, but as an active component in the situation as a whole and in his own suffering. In its former relation, York had begun to propound the theme in the preceding Act: Bolingbroke and his company are rebels, *nemine contradicente*; neither their power, nor York's inability to resist it, cancels out the fact of their treason:

> I cannot mend it, I must needs confess,
> Because my power is weak and all ill-left.
> But if I could, by Him that gave me life,
> I would attach you all and make you stoop
> Unto the sovereign mercy of the King.

II.3.152–6

York speaks as a subject, as Carlisle is later to do. When this theme of powerless, but divinely ordained, right overcome by powerful

183

wrong is transferred from the subject, who infers from it the future punishment of the sinners, to the king himself, who incarnates the right, and is transmuted by his personality, it becomes at once a spring of faith and a cause of suffering. By its nature, since it supposes that the rightful king is a deputy appointed by God and not by the election of power, it is a faith which supports Richard when power is diminished or gone:

> show us the hand of God
> That hath dismissed us from our stewardship;
> For well we know no hand of blood and bone
> Can grip the sacred handle of our sceptre
> Unless he do profane, steal, or usurp.
> And though you think that all, as you have done,
> Have torn their souls by turning them from us,
> And we are barren and bereft of friends,
> Yet know, my master, God omnipotent,
> Is mustering in his clouds on our behalf
> Armies of pestilence; and they shall strike
> Your children yet unborn and unbegot,
> That lift your vassal hands against my head
> And threat the glory of my precious crown.

> III.3.77–90

But it is a faith which is, as faiths generally are, at times held with this kind of sublime and richly figured confidence, but at other times has to struggle in Richard's mind with the facts that seem to contradict it: in this case, the paradox of the rightful king who is without power to substantiate his right. Thus arises Richard's suffering. There is a kind of denial of his faith which springs from the difficulty of holding it when the startling fact of the *king's* helplessness seems to mock at its truth or efficacy:

> Cover your heads, and mock not flesh and blood
> With solemn reverence. Throw away respect,
> Tradition, form, and ceremonious duty;
> For you have but mistook me all this while.
> I live with bread, like you; feel want,
> Taste grief, need friends. Subjected thus,
> How can you say to me I am a king?

> III.2.171–7

Richard suffers, too, in performing the acts which his dilemma enforces upon him because they make him conscious of their contradiction of his claims:

> O God, O God, that e'er this tongue of mine,
> That laid the sentence of dread banishment
> On yon proud man, should take it off again
> With words of sooth!
>
> III.3.133–6

and this leads to the striving to escape from the dilemma, the wish to be no longer the 'god on earth' who is so manifestly at the mercy of his subjects:

> O that I were as great
> As is my grief, or lesser than my name,
> Or that I could forget what I have been,
> Or not remember what I must be now!
>
> III.3.136–9

Yet Richard can recover from this mood enough to affirm the confidences of the next scene, to collapse again, and in the end, even after his resignation, to feel that his own act has betrayed his faith and to suffer because he seems to have committed a kind of voluntary apostasy:

> Mine eyes are full of tears. I cannot see.
> And yet salt water blinds them not so much
> But they can see a sort of traitors here.
> Nay, if I turn mine eyes upon myself
> I find myself a traitor with the rest.
> For I have given here my soul's consent
> T'undeck the pompous body of a king;
> Made glory base, and sovereignty a slave;
> Proud majesty, a subject; state, a peasant.
>
> IV.1.243–51

These alternating states, this personal accent and hypertension of grief surely result from Shakespeare's attempt to give us a man who is really suffering. The kind of attention, or the degree of respect, we pay to this suffering will partly depend on our estimate of how far Shakespeare established Bolingbroke's ascendancy in physical power and Richard's weakness as a ruler early in the play. I have suggested that the design is in fact of this kind, leaving the last half of the play largely occupied with the fate of a king deprived of power through his own defects (which are measured against their absence in Bolingbroke) yet hedged about with divinity. If this issue seemed important enough to Shakespeare for it to shape his design and be built into the fabric of his protagonist, Richard's agonies over it are evidently amongst the things which the dramatist wanted us to contemplate at length and in detail. The very fact that we have been encouraged early and firmly to decide that Richard is deficient in the qualities that nourish kingship suggests that we are now to see him as a king who is tragic because this deficiency, and its consequence in loss of power, has not freed him, for himself at least, from the burden of majesty.

It is to make us pay attention to this that Shakespeare at first takes sides between Bolingbroke and Richard, making the latter quickly and deservedly lose power and even underlining the success of the former as ruler. He does this not for the sake of making a political point but in order to create the conditions of outer and inner turbulence proper to a protagonist of stature. Through them the protagonist's sufferings become not merely those of a prince who falls pathetically from high place into darkness, like the heroes of the old *casus* stories, but also those of one in whom belief strives with weakness within while enemies without affront it by their power to force him, as they eventually do, to seem to deny it by his own acts. Similarly, the purpose of Richard's speeches on the inviolability of his right, delivered against the background of Bolingbroke's advancing army and of total loss of power, is not to proclaim the Tudor doctrine of majesty in the teeth of the odds, nor even, as Irving Ribner suggests,[29] to make it sound silly, but to tell us what Richard is feeling and move us with the spectacle. This also is the purpose of Richard's collapses into despair and repudiations under stress. The alternating moods go to make up a man rather than to expose the relativity of a doctrine. It is the design that makes all this life in the character possible by bringing about at an early stage the condition: unarmed and deficient majesty versus armed and able usurpation. It is doubtful if we can even ask about this play Ribner's question 'What is the precise political position taken by Shakespeare in the conflict between Richard II and Bolingbroke?',[30] because this is a question about the condition artificially detached from the character which is its reason for being.

But just as Richard's miscalculations and capricious fancy give us an insight into his weakness, so the kind of attention we pay to his sufferings will be to some extent determined by what commentators have diagnosed as the theatricality with which he expresses them. 'He throws himself into the part of the deposed monarch', says Pater, '[and] falls gracefully as on the world's stage'.[31] Here again we are in danger of confusing Shakespeare's medium, which is a play designed to cast light above all others on to Richard, with the dramatic character. The gracefulness, the enthusiasm, the loquacity, the taking of the centre of the stage, and the consciousness of onlookers are Shakespeare's own powers and the means which he uses to give us Richard as fully and centrally as he can; they are not attributes of the character, for Richard is no more an actor than he is a poet.[32] We are not to suppose that because a character in a play speaks a great deal, he is necessarily fond of the sound of his own voice, or because he continually takes the centre of the stage, that he necessarily enjoys playing a part. The Richard who luxuriates in his own destruction is a product of some such suppositions; it also springs from an unwillingness to recognize the appeal of the tradition of the 'complaint' and the *Mirror for Magistrates*, from which Richard's lamentations and reproaches in part descend.[33] It is not Richard who stages the impressive and symbolical scenes in which he appears, as G. A. Bonnard claims,[34] but Shakespeare, who desired to set before us the honoured spectacle of the fallen king.

There is another way in which play-acting or theatricality may be said to be an element in the character. The scenes, including the deposition scene, in which Richard appears in the last half of the play are stage-managed by Bolingbroke in the sense that his power and decisions prescribe the scope of Richard's actions. Richard must play the part set down for him, and he shows from time to time a weary and baffled consciousness of this: 'What must the King do now?' (III.3.143 ff.). The bitter irony is manifest if we remember Queen Elizabeth's remark on her death-bed about 'must' not being a word which may be used to princes.

> What says King Bolingbroke? Will his majesty
> Give Richard leave to live till Richard die?
> You make a leg, and Bolingbroke says 'Ay'.

III.3.173-5

Here Richard caricatures the set nature of the characters' behaviour. That actions previously planned are now being performed is emphasized, especially in the deposition scene, by the way in which they are represented as done for the benefit of an audience within the play:

> Fetch hither Richard, that in common view
> He may surrender.

IV.1.155-6

Richard is to confess his crimes in order that men may 'deem' that he is 'worthily deposed' (IV.1.226) or 'The commons will not then be satisfied' (IV.1.271). Bolingbroke is the silent *régisseur*, who intervenes only occasionally to modify the course of the piece. And we learn from York how marked is this element of staging in Richard's humiliation (V.2.23 ff.). The device emphasizes the helpless yet central position of Richard, the man with the pistol at his ribs.

Bolingbroke, as Leonard F. Dean expresses it,[35] has in this way turned the state itself into a theatre; he has assigned his part to Northumberland, and, in the deposition scene, he has set down a part for Richard, too, to play. From Bolingbroke's point of view, if it is true that the seizure of power is all that matters to him, Richard has become, indeed, a mere actor in his play, since, in resigning his crown before the assembled parliament and placing it in the usurper's hands, he passively does what is expected of him. If it is true that Bolingbroke cares nothing about the divine sanctions of power, the way in which Richard performs the act – emphasizing his own grief (IV.1.190 ff.) and shame (IV.1.246 ff.) and betrayal (IV.1.233 ff.) – hardly amounts to more than a nuisance, an in-indulgence in sorrow springing from the weakness of temper that made Richard a bad king; it is sentimentalizing, and confirms Bolingbroke in what we may suppose to be his view that the Name without the reality is a shadow without substance: let Richard be king of sorrows if he will, Bolingbroke will be king in England. But Bolingbroke's 'play' is not Shakespeare's, and it is a mistake, made by some commentators, to suppose that the two coincide. The Bishop's prophecy preceding the act of dis-crowning (IV.1.136 ff.), the conspiracy that follows it, Richard's warning to Northumberland (V.1.55 ff.), and, of course, Henry IV's own disturbed conscience later on, show something of the woe that has been engendered and make it plain that, if Boling-broke takes the Name to be only a shadow, disarmed before the untitled holder of power and of no force in politics, Shakespeare does not, and never expected his audiences to do so either.

It is not only this which shows that our point of view is not to be identified with the attempt to reduce Richard's status to that of mere play-actor. For, except on the level of his confirmation in real power through a public act of abdication, the level of his immediate concern, Bolingbroke is actually in very imperfect control of his leading actor. It is the contrast between what Richard has to do with the way he does it that brings out the shocking paradox of the *helpless king*, the king who 'must'. Marlowe's *Edward II* has this too:

> They give me bread and water being a king;
>
> V.5.61

and it has been Richard's area of suffering ever since he was intro-duced in his more expressive form in III.2. But here it is climactic; for in this scene, by performing what Pater called an 'inverted rite',[36] the king must shed the glory of his name and so, as it were, try to shatter the paradox that has caused him to suffer and yet, because one part of it affirmed his right, has allowed him to hope. We can imagine, perhaps, that Bolingbroke would have liked to run the deposition as he managed the execution of the favourites, or to contrive some effect akin to that of the challenge scenes of the first Act, where, as I have suggested, the stiffness of the language and gestures argues that the characters are following obediently a pro-cedure laid down in advance. But Richard, so far as the audience is concerned, knocks awry Bolingbroke's carefully staged profes-sional spectacle. With all the weaknesses of his feminine sensibility and capricious fancy upon him, he moves us to pity[37] in verse the contrast of which with the formal vigour of the verse in the challenge scenes is the measure of Shakespeare's attempt to give him the voice of a man who is really in pain. And this remains true even though Shakespeare learnt later on, in *Lear*, to write verse which is much more expressive of the agonies of fallen majesty.

The episode of the looking-glass towards the end of the deposition scene is the most remarkable of Richard's departures from the role set down for him by Bolingbroke. It wrenches attention inwards to Richard, the more designedly in that it seems to complete a movement apparent throughout the whole scene. This begins in a very public and external way with the yells and threats of the appellants, modulates to Carlisle's appeal to God and men's consciences, and thence to Richard's profoundly personal rendering of the formal act of abdication, in which the crown becomes an image of his grief (IV.1.180–88) and the bystanders not witnesses but participators in a crime (IV.1.167–75). Northumberland tries to drag Richard back towards the public and the formal, towards Bolingbroke's 'theatre'; but the movement, with Richard in command of it, has gathered too much momentum, and his efforts are in vain. Richard sends for the looking-glass, the double-edged symbol of vanity and truth-telling.[38]

The episode points forward to the solitary and self-communing Richard of the prison soliloquy. There is something deliberately unexplained, something therefore impulsive and compulsive, about his wish to have the mirror at this moment, and something intense and private in his act of looking at it, for this, too, is a kind of soliloquy, his first. It is also thematically linked with the prison soliloquy in that it touches the question whether Richard, in divesting himself of the name of king, has anything at all left by which to live: for the 'great glory' was the source of his hopes, even though, conjoined with his helplessness (the *King must*), it was the ground of his suffering. The sending for the mirror is a movement towards asking the question 'What am I like now I have given everything away?' (see IV.1.265–6), but has behind it, perhaps, the question 'Am I anything at all?' The first question is a move towards self-knowledge, and even repentance:

> I'll read enough
> When I do see the very book indeed
> Where all my sins are writ; and that's myself.
>
> IV.1.272–4

This is but faintly hinted at (and again at V.5.47–9).[39] But the thought of the mirror is a close neighbour to the thought of annihilation:

> O that I were a mockery king of snow,
> Standing before the sun of Bolingbroke,
> To melt myself away in water-drops!
>
> IV.1.259–61

When the mirror lies to him about his inward condition, he smashes it.[40] He does this, perhaps, simply because of the analogy between its behaviour and that of his flattering followers, and thereby repudiates them and his own folly when he encouraged them in the past. But the smashing is also an act of self-destructive violence, for he has destroyed the image of the face with which he must henceforth live in as manly a fashion as he can:

> A brittle glory shineth in this face.
> As brittle as the glory is the face,
> For there it is, cracked in an hundred shivers.
> Mark, silent King, the moral of this sport:
> How soon my sorrow hath destroyed my face.
>
> IV.1.286–90

Repudiation of the past self may also be a mere destruction of the self, unless the penitent has the power to contrive a new being. There is no sign that Richard possesses this power. In the prison soliloquy he can picture himself only as something less than a man, an automaton, the Jack of the clock that moves as Bolingbroke bids (V.5.50–60), or at best his beast of burden (V.5.92–3). If Richard did ask himself the question 'Am I, unkinged, anything?' the answer came back 'Nothing at all':

> Then am I kinged again; and by and by
> Think that I am unkinged by Bolingbroke,
> And straight am nothing.
>
> V.5.36–8

This is only the confirmation of a truth recognized by sixteenth-century statists: the balm cannot be washed off; the anointed cannot become a man who lives 'with bread like you'; for the mark of his divinity is in the bone, and he must either rule or die. Richard's actual death is courageous, or perhaps perfunctory, but it does not alter this.

The play, then, is not simply about a weak but legitimate monarch out-generalled by an able usurper. By showing us this subject in terms of Richard's suffering, Shakespeare adds a further dimension; and extends this beyond the mere pathos of a spectacular fall from glory to dishonour. Shakespeare seems to have used all the skill then at his command to give voice to the inwardness of his protagonist and to show him alive and exciting within the area of his peculiarly exact and individual tragic dilemma: the king who must. As Hazlitt said, 'the part of Richard himself gives the chief interest to the play', and with it all the more important problems of its interpretation connect.

NOTES

1. *Coleridge's Shakespearean Criticism*, edited by T. M. Raysor (London, 1930), II, 153.

2. *Political Characters of Shakespeare* (London, 1945), page 130.

3. *The Tragedy of King Richard II*, edited by C. H. Herford (London, 1893), page 116.

4. H. Craig, *An Interpretation of Shakespeare* (New York, 1948), page 128. In further discussion of the trial, Craig writes: 'If Mowbray had won, Bolingbroke would have been silenced. If Bolingbroke had won, the King would have been rid of a follower who, he feared, would betray him, and he would have been at least no worse off as regards Bolingbroke. Then, too, in the decision of the council, which Richard had dictated, he follows the one course of conduct that was sure to do injustice to both appellants; and, most cruelly and unnaturally, he inflicts the heavier penalty on Mowbray, who had no ulterior motive and had been honest and faithful.' All this is perhaps true, but it is a historian's judgement about the Richard II of history; it does not necessarily apply to the character in Holinshed or in Shakespeare.

5. As Palmer (page 131) suggests that he should.

6. For discussion of the juxtaposition of scenes, see W. B. C. Watkins, *Shakespeare and Spenser* (Princeton, 1950), page 78.

7. On this, as a factor leading directly to the rebellion, see G. C.

Reese, 'The Question of the Succession in Elizabethan Drama', *Studies in English* (Texas, 1942), page 79.

8. Our understanding of the rejection is also guided, of course, by Gaunt's previous insistence on Richard's susceptibility to the influence of the bad counsellors, the flatterers.

9. *Coleridge's Shakespearean Criticism* (1930), II, 281.

10. *Shakespeare* (New York, 1939), page 89. Van Doren's section on the play carries the conception of 'Richard as poet' about as far as it will go. A similar conception seems to underlie, though less clearly, the censures of Swinburne (*Three Plays of Shakespeare* (London, 1909), pages 59 ff.) and the sympathies of Yeats in 'At Stratford-on-Avon' in *Ideas of Good and Evil* (in *Collected Works*, Volume VI (1908), or *Essays* (1924), pages 117 ff.). Yeats rightly pointed out the pleasure which commentators take in scolding Richard: Hardin Craig's pages in *An Interpretation of Shakespeare* maintain the tradition.

11. *Collected Works* (Stratford-on-Avon, 1908), VI, 123.

12. Burton, *Anatomy of Melancholy*, I. 2. 3. 2 (London, 1881 edition), page 166.

13. *Ben Jonson*, edited by Herford and Simpson, IV, 104–5.

14. W. Clemen, *The Development of Shakespeare's Imagery* (London, 1951), page 60.

15. 'A dilettante in poetry as well as in kingship' (Herford, op. cit., page 28).

16. R. D. Altick, 'Symphonic Imagery in *Richard II*', *Publications of the Modern Language Association of America* LXII (1947), 351.

17. These have been much studied. Oscar Wilde seems to have been the first to note the connexion between Richard's sun-badge (see III.3.178) and the sun-imagery, in 'The Truth of Masks' (*Works* (London, n.d.), page 1241. I owe this reference to J. C. Maxwell). See also P. Reyher, 'Le Symbole du Soleil . . .', *Revue de l'Enseignement des Langues Vivantes* (June 1923); C. Spurgeon, *Shakespeare's Imagery* (Cambridge, 1935), pages 233–8; *Richard II*, edited by J. Dover Wilson (Cambridge, 1951), pages xii, xiii; S. Kliger in *Studies in Philology* XLIV (1948), 196–202; Clemen, op. cit., page 59.

18. *Coleridge's Shakespearean Criticism* (1930), I, 155.

19. Altick, op. cit.

20. cf. Palmer, op. cit., page 149. On York's character in general Coleridge's observations (op. cit., I, 153, 154) are not likely to be bettered; Swinburne (op. cit., pages 72–3) allows the pleasure of vituperation to carry him too far.

21. *Shakespeare's History Plays* (London, 1944), page 259.
22. B. Stirling's 'Bolingbroke's "Decision" ', *Shakespeare Quarterly* II (1951), is a persuasive attempt at reading them.
23. E. Dowden: 'The interest of the play centres ... in the personal contrast between the falling and rising kings' (*Shakespeare* (1912 edition), page 88); Herford: 'the action is merely a prolonged duel between Richard and Bolingbroke' (*Shakespeare* (1912), page 28); F. S. Boas: 'In the detailed contrast of character between [Richard and Bolingbroke] lies the cardinal interest of the play' (*Shakespeare and his Predecessors* (1918 edition), page 250).
24. See E. T. Sehrt, *Vergebung und Gnade bei Shakespeare* (Stuttgart, 1952), pages 111–16.
25. In later plays both Henry IV and Henry V are shown as fully conscious of the burden of the diadem: see especially *Henry IV, Part Two*, IV.5.23 ff. and 159 ff.
26. See Tillyard, op. cit., pages 257 ff. For Shakespeare's literary use of such countervailing themes, see some suggestive remarks by H. Haydn, *The Counter-Renaissance* (New York, 1950), pages 652–3.
27. Samuel Daniel, *The First Fowre Bookes of the civil warres* (London, 1595), I, stanza 94; Daniel continues his speculations for a further six stanzas.
28. *The Characters of Shakespear's Plays* (*Complete Works*, edited by P. P. Howe, IV, 275).
29. 'The Political Problem in Shakespeare's Lancastrian Tetralogy', *Studies in Philology* XLIX (1952) , 179–81.
30. ibid., page 171.
31. 'Shakespeare's English Kings' in *Appreciations* (1944 edition), page 206; Chambers thinks that Richard is 'himself a born actor', and Craig (op. cit., page 128) that he 'spent his life not living, but playing parts'.
32. No more – and no less – than Brutus or Cassius. All are conscious of 'bearing a part', their role in life. There is an element of theatricality in Richard just as there is an element of corrupt fancy: but to describe Richard as an actor is to allow a useful metaphor to get out of control. The same thing happens when we describe him as a poet. It is not helpful to say that he is playing the part of a fallen king when he *is* a fallen king, even though we may consider that his behaviour in that condition is unmanly or consciously overdone; he does not bleed in sport; cf. Clemen, op. cit., page 55; and for a similar point about Macbeth, K. Muir's Arden edition of *Macbeth* (1951), page lx.

33. See W. Farnham, *The Medieval Heritage of Elizabethan Tragedy* (Berkeley, 1936), pages 416 ff.

34. 'The actor in Richard II', *Shakespeare-Jahrbuch* lxxxvii–lxxxviii (1952), 99.

35. '*Richard II*: the State and the Image of the Theatre', *Publications of the Modern Language Association of America* LXVII (1952).

36. 'It is as if Shakespeare had had in mind some inverted rite, like those old ecclesiastical or military ones, by which human hardness, or human justice, adds the last touch of unkindness to the execution of its sentences' (op. cit., page 205).

37. As Dryden thought: see *Essays*, edited by W. P. Ker, I, 226–7.

38. As iconographers have shown, the mirror is the attribute of *Vanitas*: on this, see G. F. Hartlaub, *Zauber des Spiegels* (Munich, 1951), and H. Schwarz, 'The Mirror in Art', *Art Quarterly* (Detroit) XV (1952), 97–118. The epithet which Richard uses for it, *flattering* (and therefore lying), is very commonly attached to looking-glasses of any kind: e.g. in Lyly, Daniel, Heywood, Webster, and Burton (for references see my article in *Philological Quarterly* XXXIV (1955), 220); Elizabeth I on her death-bed rejected a 'flattering' glass and called for a 'true' one (see J. Nichols, *Progresses of Queen Elizabeth* (London, 1823), III. 614). The mirror also has the property of reflecting the true state of things: hence its use as a book-title for works (*specula*) of moral instruction (*Mirror for Magistrates* etc.), which is also very common; on this see E. Curtius, *European Literature and the Latin Middle Ages* (London, 1953), page 336, L. B. Campbell, *Shakespeare's 'Histories'* (San Marino, California, 1947), pages 107–8, M. Doran, *Endeavors of Art* (Madison, 1954), page 72, R. Bradley, 'Speculum Backgrounds in Medieval Literature', *Speculum* XXIX (1954), 100–115, and cf. *Julius Caesar*, I.2.55–8. Shakespeare may have been conscious of both these connotations of the mirror here.

39. cf. V.1.24–5. Dr Johnson thought that Richard's self-reformation was radical: 'In his prosperity we saw him imperious and oppressive, but in his distress he is wise, patient and pious'; cf. Stopford Brooke, *On Ten Plays of Shakespeare* (London, 1905), pages 97–8.

40. For a discussion of the light thrown by the references to music in V.5 on Richard's inward condition, see L. Spitzer, 'Classical and Christian Ideas of World Harmony', *Traditio* III (1945), 335.

SEVEN

King Richard the Second:
An Actor's Approach*

Sir John Gielgud

'RICHARD II' is a ceremonial play. In spite of its long list of characters only a few are of the first importance, and most of these are very broadly treated, especially in the early scenes. The young King himself, though his personal beauty and the subservient manner in which he is treated, as he sits idly on his throne, must draw all eyes to him immediately, is only lightly sketched at first in a few rather enigmatic strokes. It is not until after his return from Ireland, almost halfway through the play, that his inner character begins to be developed in a series of exquisite cadenzas and variations. In these later scenes, the subtleties of his speeches are capable of endless shades and nuances, but (as is nearly always the case in Shakespeare) the actor's vocal efforts must be contrived within the framework of the verse, and not outside it. Too many pauses and striking variations of tempo will tend to hold up the action disastrously and so ruin the pattern and symmetry of the text.

The actor of Richard cannot hope at any time during the action to be wholly sympathetic to the audience. Indeed he must use the early scenes to create an impression of slyness, petty vanity, and callous indifference. But he must also show himself to be innately well-bred, sensitive to beauty (as *he* understands it, though he cannot himself see the beauty of the dying Gaunt), lonely in his remote position of kingship, young, headstrong, frivolous, and entirely out of sympathy with the older men who try so vainly to advise him and control his whims.

In the later scenes, however, the lovely lines he has to speak can

---

*Chapter 3 ('King Richard the Second') of *Stage Directions* (1963). Copyright © John Gielgud, 1963. Reprinted by kind permission of the publishers, Heinemann Educational Books Ltd, London.

hardly fail to win a certain sympathy for him, and he gradually becomes more understandable and so more pitiable. But owing to his utter lack of humour and his constant egotism and self-posturing, there is always a risk that he may become tedious and irritating to the audience unless the finer shades of his character are very subtly portrayed.

It is essential for an actor playing Richard to find the exact line of his disintegration. First, by grading the successive scenes as they follow one another, with their shifting changes of mood expressed in a continually minor key, and then by developing the detail and constructive pattern of the speeches as they become more elaborate and involved.

Richard is one of the rare parts in which the actor may indulge himself, luxuriating in the language he has to speak, and attitudinizing in consciously graceful poses. Yet the man must seem, too, to be ever physically on his guard, shielding himself, both in words and movement, from the dreaded impact of the unknown circumstances which, he feels, are always lying in wait to strike him down. He is torn between the intrinsic weakness of his nature and the pride and fastidiousness of his quality and breeding. He strives continually to retain his kingly dignity, to gain time by holding it up to the light before his enemies (as he will actually hold up the mirror later on in the deposition scene), while he prepares inwardly to face the shock of the next humiliation. Finally, cast out into the empty darkness of his prison, he is forced to realize at last that neither his personal beauty nor the divine right of kingship can save him from inevitable horror, as he is forced to contemplate his private doom.

Thus the actor has a dual responsibility. He must present the external action as the King suffers his defeats – the news of his favourites' deaths, the surrender to Bolingbroke at Flint, the defiant shame of the deposition scene, and the agonies of farewell to his Queen. Yet he must somehow contrive at the same time to execute the poetic intricacies of the text with a full appreciation of its musical intention, using a completely lucid (and possibly stylized) method of vocal and plastic interpretation. The speaking of blank verse can only be projected, so as to hold an audience, by artificial and technical means – tone, emphasis, and modulation.

The task may seem an impossibly difficult one – to play, as it were, in two different styles at once, just as a singer has to do in opera. But this is actually a question of technique. A good actor experiences emotion at rehearsal – or imagines the experience of it vividly, which is not quite the same thing – and then selects, through trial and error, what he wishes to convey at each given moment of his performance. So he has always a double task – that of living in his role and at the same time judging his own effects in relation to his fellow players and the audience, so as to present an apparently spontaneous, living being, in a pattern carefully devised beforehand, but capable of infinite shades of colour and tempo, and bound to vary slightly at every performance. The actor is, after all, a kind of conjuror, and in a part like Richard he will find infinite opportunities to put his skill into practice, playing, as Richard himself plays, on the feelings of an audience until they are at one with the complicated nature of the character; then, even when they cannot condone his actions or sympathize with his misfortunes, they come at length to understand his intricate nature and can share in his unique experience.

Whether the scenes of the Aumerle conspiracy in the fourth Act should be retained or omitted in the theatre is a difficult question to decide. Many people think that they are not by Shakespeare, and that they may have been cobbled together by another hand to pad out the necessary playing time, when the deposition scene, owing to its dangerous political implications, was omitted in Elizabeth's day. Certainly the rhyming couplets in these scenes have a strong flavour of fustian melodrama, and many of the lines can seem ridiculous unless they are delivered with consummate power and tact. Also they make the play considerably longer. On the other hand they are of value to vary the somewhat monotonous tone and style of the main part of the text, and they serve to make a break in style, dividing the two great scenes of Richard's grief (the deposition scene and the farewell to the Queen) from his final soliloquy and fight to death in the prison. These episodes gain considerably in their effect if the King has been absent from the stage for two scenes beforehand. Also, of course, the Aumerle scenes contain the celebrated passage between York and his Duchess, describing Richard's entry into London in the power of

Bolingbroke, and the first references to the wildness of Prince Hal.

The opening scene of the play, though dramatically effective in reading, always presents considerable difficulties for a modern audience. The implications of the King's complicity in the murder of Gloucester (which has taken place before the action begins) are not easy to understand. Most of us are less familiar with history than the Elizabethans, who seem to have had a curiously detailed knowledge of the intricate topical events of the times chronicled by Holinshed and so faithfully followed in the Histories of Shakespeare. The opening quarrel between Mowbray and Bolingbroke is repeated with greater elaboration and formality in the tournament scene at Coventry, with only the short duologue between the Duchess of Gloucester and Gaunt to separate them. This intermediate scene also refers back almost exclusively to the murder of Gloucester, and it is difficult to make it interesting, since the Duchess appears without any introduction and is to have no further part in the action, though the account of her death some scenes later makes an effective moment for old York. In all this early part of the play the action is formalized and lacking in progression. The King's motives seem to be deliberately understated, while the characters of his Queen and various lords and favourites are very baldly indicated. Ceremony and fine speaking must combine to hold the interest of the audience. The vocal effects must be carefully orchestrated: Mowbray's fine tenor speeches, Bolingbroke's strong blustering tones, and the deep bass warning voice of Gaunt.

Unfortunately, throughout the tragedy, the verse seems to be too evenly distributed, and often with more music than sense of character. Everyone speaks in images, parentheses, and elaborate similes, whether gardeners, exquisites, or tough realistic nobles, and though this richness of metaphor gives, in reading, a beautiful, tapestried, somewhat Gothic effect (like an illuminated missal or a Book of Hours), the continually artificial style tends to become somewhat indigestible on the stage, and stands between the audience and their desire to get on more intimate terms with the characters and situations. It is therefore especially important to have actors for the chief parts who are strongly contrasted individual types as well as skilled speakers of verse.

The more simply the characters are played on broad, conventional (but not too melodramatic) lines, the scenes appearing to flow smoothly and swiftly with the correct stress and phrasing, but without too much elaboration, either of action, grouping, or pauses, the better will the beauty of the general pattern emerge and the interest of the audience be sustained. The actor of Richard may then be allowed, like the solo violin in a concerto, to take certain liberties with his cadenzas, developing their intricacies legitimately in an almost unlimited variety of pace and detail, in contrast to the more plodding ground bass of Bolingbroke, Northumberland, and the other nobles.

Many of the shorter scenes in the play can produce an exquisite effect; especially the famous episode of the Queen with the gardeners at Langley, for example, and the little duologue between the Welsh captain and Salisbury (which has something of the same sensitive yet sinister effect as the little scene in *Macbeth* in which the murderers wait for Banquo on the lonely heath). These passages should have a romantic, simple expressiveness in contrast to the formality of the great scenes which precede and follow them.

There are several difficult links in the action. The scene between Ross, Willoughby, and Northumberland after Gaunt's death, and the passage when the three favourites part for the last time on hearing of Bolingbroke's return, seem almost like choral exercises for three voices, and should, perhaps, be directed mainly from this point of view. The quarrel of the peers, before the entrance of Richard in the deposition scene, is difficult to stage without a dangerous risk of seeming ridiculous (the throwing down and picking up of gloves and so on), and it is advisable to make some discreet cuts to avoid bathos both here and in the Aumerle conspiracy scenes, if they are included. The character of York, used by Shakespeare as a kind of wavering chorus throughout the play, touching yet sometimes absurd, can be of great value, provided that the actor and director can contrive between them a tactful compromise between comedy and dramatic effect. To make him a purely farcical character (as has sometimes been attempted) weakens the play, and is quite opposed, it seems to me, to the intention of the dramatist. The women in the cast are very lightly drawn, and they are difficult parts for actresses to clothe with flesh and blood, though vocally and pictorially they can make a considerable effect – the two Duchesses old and proud, the little Queen so young and helpless – in the somewhat conventional episodes allotted to them.

Most of the characters, except Gaunt, York, Carlisle, and the two Duchesses, seem to be young and full of life, and there should be something of the same impetuous brilliance that is so wonderfully vivid in *Romeo and Juliet* in the way they glitter and struggle and hurl themselves towards their fates. *Richard II* is a play, above all, which must in performance be finely orchestrated, melodious, youthful, headlong, violent, and vivid. It must not be heavy or dragging, and the actors must know where they are going in their long speeches. Every effort must be made to contrast scene against scene. At first we must be made aware of the lightness of Richard's character, his fatal, obstinate frivolity, unchecked by the baleful warnings and implacable nobility of Gaunt. Then, as we reach the heart of the play, and the King's own heart and soul are gradually revealed to us by Shakespeare, we must see him forced, by the realization of his favourites' deaths and the desertion of his countrymen, reluctantly beginning to abandon his contemplative poetic fantasies, to face the brutal reality of Northumberland's hostility and the grim determination of the ruthless Bolingbroke.

The great problem, as in all Shakespearian plays, is to achieve a straightforward musical rendering of the verse, and yet to combine this with a sense of exciting actuality in the action. The events of the play must really seem to happen, and yet, as in an opera, the music of the lines must be neither slurred, dragged nor unduly hurried. In short, the technical brilliance of the poetic writing must be correctly balanced and simply executed, with the added colour of character and personality, while at the same time the shock of the actual events presented must appear to be spontaneous and realistically convincing. The poetry must be welded imperceptibly into the dramatic action to a point where the audience will accept the two together – and, if successfully managed, the two styles should support one another to create a complete harmony of effect.

EIGHT

The Structural Problem in
Shakespeare's *Henry the Fourth**

Harold Jenkins

... T H E first problem that confronts one in approaching *Henry IV*,
and the one about which I propose to be particular, has inevitably
introduced itself already. Is it one play or two? Some of you will
dismiss this as an academic question, the sort of thing that only
people like professors bother their heads about. Some of you will
look askance at it as a metaphysical question, which in a sense it is.
But it is also, surely, a practical question: how satisfactorily can
either the first part or the second be shown in the theatre without
the other? What is gained, or indeed lost, by presenting the two
parts, as the Old Vic are doing at the moment, on successive
evenings? And thus of course the question becomes a problem of
literary criticism. Until it has been answered, how can the dramatic
quality of *Henry IV* be fully appreciated, or even defined? Yet the
numerous literary critics who have attempted an answer to the
question have reached surprisingly opposite conclusions.[1]

Answers began more than two hundred years ago in the *Critical
Observations on Shakespeare* by John Upton, a man who deserves
our regard for trying to scotch the notion so strangely current in
the eighteenth century that 'Shakespeare had no learning'. Far from
accepting that Shakespeare's plays were the happy, or the not so
happy, products of untutored nature, Upton maintained that they
were constructed according to some principles of art; and his
examination of *Henry IV* suggested to him that each of its two
parts had, what Aristotle of course demanded, its own beginning,
middle, and end. Upton held it to be an injury to Shakespeare even

*From *The Structural Problem in Shakespeare's 'Henry the Fourth'* (1956),
pages 2–27. Copyright © Harold Jenkins, 1956. Reprinted by kind permission
of the publishers, Methuen & Co. Ltd, London.

to speak of a first and second *part* and thus conceal the fact that there were here two quite independent plays.[2] To this Dr Johnson retorted that these two plays, so far from being independent, are 'two only because they are too long to be one'. They could appear as separate plays, he thought, only to those who looked at them with the 'ambition of critical discoveries'. In these tart words Johnson shrewdly defined what, if not one of the deadly sins, is still a vice and one to which universities are prone. The 'ambition of critical discoveries', a natural human vanity unnaturally nourished in our day by the requirements of the Ph.D. thesis and the demand for 'publications', has been responsible for many interpretations of Shakespeare whose merit is in their being new rather than their being true. Yet one must not always accept the accepted. Dr Johnson's contemporaries did not all find it as plain as he did that *Henry IV* was just one continuous composition. It seemed probable to Malone that *Part Two* was not even 'conceived'[3] until *Part One* had been a roaring success. Capell, on the other hand, thought that both parts were 'planned at the same time, and with great judgment'.[4]

Among present-day scholars Professor Dover Wilson is on Johnson's side. He insists that the two parts of *Henry IV* are 'a single structure' with the 'normal dramatic curve' stretched over ten Acts instead of five. Professor R. A. Law, however, declares that *Henry IV* is 'not a single ten-act play', but two organic units 'written with different purposes in view'. On the contrary, says Dr Tillyard, 'The two parts of the play are a single organism.' *Part One* by itself is 'patently incomplete'. 'Each part is a drama complete in itself', says Kittredge flatly.[5] In short, some two centuries after Upton and Johnson, scholars are still about equally divided as to whether *Henry IV* was 'planned' as 'one long drama' or whether the second part was, as they put it, an 'unpremeditated sequel'. A new professor, his ambition already dwindling at Johnson's warning, might well lapse into melancholy, or even modesty. Modest or not, he can hardly escape the conclusion, reached by another eighteenth-century dignitary in a somewhat different situation, that 'much might be said on both sides'. Like Sir Roger de Coverley, he 'would not give his judgment rashly', yet like the late R. W. Chambers, whose pupil I am proud to have been, he may think that the modesty which forbears to make a judgement is disastrous.[6]

Words like 'planned' and 'unpremeditated' figure largely in this controversy; and of course they imply intention or the lack of it, and will therefore be suspect in those circles which denounce what is called 'the intentional fallacy'.[7] I am far from belonging to that school of criticism which holds that an author's own intention is irrelevant to our reading of his work; yet, as Lascelles Abercrombie says, aesthetic criticism must ultimately judge by results: a man's work is evidence of what he did, but you can never be sure what he intended.[8] This position, with the coming of the Freudian psychology, is finally inescapable, but in its extreme form it seems to me unnecessarily defeatist. When I find *Much Ado About Nothing* beginning with talk of a battle in which those killed are 'few of any sort, and none of name', I may infer that Shakespeare intended to write a comedy and not a realistic one at that. But if I wish to play for safety, I may use a phrase of Lascelles Abercrombie's own and speak – not of what Shakespeare intended, but of what he 'warned his audience to expect'.[9] If we leave aside for the present all question of Shakespeare's intention, what does *Henry IV* itself, as it begins and proceeds along its course, warn us to expect?

The short first scene, filled with reports of wars – wars this time in which multitudes are 'butchered' – makes an apt beginning for a history play. But its dialogue announces no main action. Yet certain topics, brought in with apparent casualness, naturally engage our interest. There is talk of two young men who do not yet appear, both called 'young Harry', yet apparently unlike. The first of them, Hotspur, is introduced as 'gallant', an epithet which is very soon repeated when he is said to have won 'A gallant prize'. The prisoners he has taken are, we are told, 'a conquest for a prince to boast of'. Already, before Prince Hal is even named, a contrast is being begun between a man who behaves like a prince though he is not one and another who is in fact a prince but does not act the part. The King makes this explicit. Hotspur, who has gained 'an honourable spoil', is 'A son who is the theme of honour's tongue', while the King's own son is stained with 'riot and dishonour'. In the second and third scenes the two Harries in turn appear. First, the Prince, already associated with dishonour, instead of, like Hotspur, taking prisoners in battle, plans to engage in highway robbery. Then, when he has arranged to sup next night in a tavern, he is followed on the stage by Hotspur telling how, when he took his prisoners, he was 'dry with rage and extreme toil'. This practice of juxtaposing characters who exhibit opposite codes of conduct is a common one in Shakespeare's drama. After the 'unsavoury similes' that Hal swaps with Falstaff, in which a squalling cat and a stinking ditch are prominent, there is Hotspur's hyperbole about plucking 'bright honour from the pale-faced moon'. It may not be a classical construction, but there is enough suggestion here of arrangement to justify Upton's claim for Shakespeare's art. We expect that central to the play will be the antithesis between these two young men and the lives they lead. And we shall find that this antithesis precipitates a moral contest which is an important aspect of the historical action of the drama.

The historical action presents Hotspur's rebellion. It is an action which develops with a fine structural proportion throughout *Part One*. The Act divisions, although they are not Shakespeare's of course, being first found in the Folio, may serve nevertheless as a convenient register of the way the action is disposed. In the first Act the rebel plot is hatched, in the second Hotspur prepares to leave home, in the third he joins forces with the other rebel leaders, in the fourth the rebel army is encamped ready to give battle, in the fifth it is defeated and Hotspur is killed. Meantime, along with the military contest between Hotspur and the King, the moral contest between the Prince and Hotspur proceeds with an equally perfect balance. The opposition of honour and riot established in the first Act is intensified in the second, where a scene of Hotspur at home preparing for war is set against one of Hal revelling in the tavern. The revelry even includes a little skit by Hal on Hotspur's conversation with his wife, which serves not only to adjust our view of Hotspur's honour by subjecting it to ridicule, but also to emphasize that the Prince is – with gleeful understatement – 'not yet of Percy's mind'. That he is not of Percy's mind leads the King in the third Act to resume his opening plaint: it is not the Prince but Percy, with his 'never-dying honour', who is fit to be a king's son. At this point the Prince vows to outshine his rival. He will meet

'This gallant Hotspur' – the words echo the opening scene – this 'child of honour', and overcome him. And so, when the rebels see the Prince in Act IV he is 'gallantly armed' – Hotspur's word is now applied to him – and he vaults upon his horse 'As if an angel dropped down from the clouds' – with a glory, that is, already beyond Hotspur. All that then remains is that the Prince shall demonstrate his new chivalry in action, which of course he does in the fifth Act, first saving his father's life and finally slaying Hotspur in single combat. Opposed to one another throughout the play, constantly spoken of together, these two are nevertheless kept apart till the fifth Act, when their first and last encounter completes in the expected manner the pattern of their rivalry that began in the opening words. The two have exchanged places. Supremacy in honour has passed from Hotspur to the Prince, and the wayward hero of the opening ends by exhibiting his true princely nature.

What then is one to make of the view of Professor Dover Wilson that the Battle of Shrewsbury, in which the Prince kills Hotspur, is not an adequate conclusion but merely the 'nodal point we expect in a third act'? If we do expect a 'nodal point' in a third Act, then *Henry IV, Part One* will not disappoint us. For there *is* a nodal point, and – I am tempted to say this categorically – it is in the third Act of *Part One* that it occurs. In this third Act, when the King rebukes his son, the Prince replies 'I will redeem all this . . .'; in the fifth Act he fulfils this vow at Shrewsbury, as is signalized by the King's admission that the Prince has 'redeemed' his 'lost opinion'. Again, in the third Act, the Prince swears that he will take from Hotspur 'every honour sitting on his helm'; in the fifth Act Hotspur is brought to confess that the Prince has won 'proud titles' from him.[10] More significantly still, the third Act ends with the Prince saying

> Percy stands on high,
> And either we or they must lower lie
>
> III.3.200–201

and then the fifth Act shows us the spectacle of the hero looking down upon his rival's prostrate form. The curve of the plot could hardly be more firmly or more symmetrically drawn. It does not seem easy to agree with Dr Johnson and Professor Dover Wilson that *Henry IV, Part One* is only the first half of a play.

If this were all there were to *Henry IV, Part One*, the matter would be simple. But the Prince's conquest of honour is only one aspect of his progress; the other is his break with the companions of his riots. Interwoven with the story of the Prince and Hotspur are the Prince's relations with Falstaff, and these, from Falstaff's first appearance in the second scene of the play, are presented in a way which leads us to expect a similar reversal. The essential thing about Hal is that, scapegrace that he is, he is the future king – the 'true prince', the 'sweet young prince', the 'king's son', the 'heir apparent', as Falstaff variously calls him, with whatever degree of mockery, in their first dialogue together. More than that, this dialogue is constantly pointing forward to the moment when he will come to the throne. 'When thou art King' – Falstaff uses these words four times in the first seventy lines and yet again before the scene is over. 'Shall there be gallows standing in England when thou art King?' 'Do not thou when thou art King hang a thief.' And so on. With these words ringing in our ears, then, we are continually being reminded of what is to come. The words seem, however, to refer to some vague time in the distant future. The Prince's reign will inescapably become reality, but it is at present apprehended as a dream. Falstaff's irrepressible fancy blows up a vast gaily-coloured bubble, and, as Bradley recognized,[11] it is because this bubble encloses the dreams of all of us that we feel for Falstaff so much affection. In our dreams we all do exactly as we like, and the date of their realization is to be when Hal is King. Then, everything will be changed – except of course ourselves. *We* shall go on as before, our friend Falstaff will continue his nocturnal depredations, but highwaymen will not be regarded as thieves and punishments will be abolished. Unfortunately, in the real world outside the bubble, it is not the law but we ourselves that should change, as Falstaff recognizes when he says, 'I must give over this life, and I will give it over ... I'll be damned for never a king's son in Christendom.' The joke of this is that we know that Falstaff will never give over, nor means to; but the joke does not quite conceal the seriousness of the alternatives – give over or be damned; and the idea of damnation continues to dance before

us, now and later, in further jests about Falstaff's selling his soul
to the devil, wishing to repent, and having to 'give the devil his
due'. What Falstaff's eventual doom is to be could be discerned
more than dimly by a mind that came to this play unfurnished by
literature or folk-lore. And none of us is quite as innocent as that.
We cannot help being aware of an archetypal situation in which a
man dallies with a diabolical tempter whom he either renounces or
is destroyed by; and to the first audience of *Henry IV* this situation
was already familiar in a long line of Christian plays, in some of
which man's succumbing to temptation was symbolized in his
selling his soul to the devil and being carried off to Hell. It is
because it is so familiar that it is readily accepted as matter for jest-
ing, while the jests give a hint of Falstaff's role in the play. I
merely pick out one or two threads in the very complex fabric of
the dialogue: you will be good enough, I trust, to believe that, in
spite of some dubious precedents in the recent criticism of other
plays, I am not seeking to interpret *Henry IV* as an allegory of sin
and damnation. Falstaff is not a type-figure, though within his vast
person several types are contained. And one of them is a sinner
and provokes many piquant allusions to the typical fate of sinners,
whether on the earthly gallows or in the infernal fire. There is also
an ambiguity, to use the modern jargon, which permits Falstaff
to be not only the sinner but the tempter as well. The jokes of a
later scene will call him indeed a devil who haunts the Prince, a
'reverend Vice', an 'old white-bearded Satan'. What I think the
play makes clear from the beginning is that neither as sinner nor
as tempter will Falstaff come to triumph. Even as we share his
dream of what will happen when Hal is King, we confidently await
the bursting of his bubble.

To strengthen our expectation even further is what we know of
history, or at least of that traditional world where the territories of
history and legend have no clear boundaries. The peculiarity of the
history play is that while pursuing its dramatic ends, it must also
obey history and steer a course reasonably close to an already known
pattern of events. The story of Prince Hal was perfectly familiar to
the Elizabethan audience before the play began, and it was the story
of a prince who had a madcap youth, including at least one escapade
of highway robbery, and then, on succeeding to the throne, banished

his riotous companions from court and became the most valorous king England had ever had. Not only was this story vouched for in the chronicles, but it had already found its way on to the stage, as an extant play, *The Famous Victories of Henry the Fifth*, bears witness, in however garbled a text. It is hardly open to *our* play, then, to depart from the accepted pattern, in which the banishment of the tavern friends is an essential feature. Moreover, that they are to be banished the Prince himself assures us at the end of his first scene with Poins and Falstaff in that soliloquy which generations of critics have made notorious.

> I know you all, and will awhile uphold
> The unyoked humour of your idleness.

I.2.193–4

The word 'awhile' plants its threat of a different time to come when a 'humour' now 'unyoked' will be brought under restraint. The soliloquy tells us as plain as any prologue what the end of the play is to be.

Yet although *Henry IV, Part One* thus from its first Act directs our interest to the time when Hal will be King, it is not of course until the last Act of *Part Two* that Pistol comes to announce 'Sir John, thy tender lambkin now is King'. It is not until the last Act of *Part Two* that the Prince is able to institute the new régime which makes mock of Falstaff's dream-world. And it is not of course till the final scene of all that the newly crowned King makes his ceremonial entrance and pronounces the words that have threatened since he and Falstaff first were shown together. 'I banish thee.' To all that has been said about the rejection of Falstaff I propose to add very little. The chief of those who objected to it, Bradley himself, recognized the necessity of it while complaining of how it was done. Granted that the new king had to drop his former friend, might he not have spared him the sermon and parted from him in private?[12] Yet Professor Dover Wilson is surely right to maintain that the public utterance is the essential thing.[13] From the first, as I have shown, interest is concentrated on the prince as the future sovereign and Falstaff builds hopes on the nature of his rule. Their separation, when it comes, is not then a reluctant parting between friends, but a royal decree promulgated with due solemnity. This is also the perfect moment for it, when the crown that has hovered over the hero from the beginning is seen, a striking symbol in the theatre, fixed firmly on his head. The first words of the rejection speech elevate him still further – 'I know thee not' – for the scriptural overtones here[14] make the speaker more than a king. The situation presents many aspects, but one of them shows the tempter vanquished and another the sinner cast into outer darkness. In either case the devil, we may say, gets his due.

The last Act of *Part Two* thus works out a design which is begun in the first Act of *Part One*. How then can we agree with Kittredge that each part is a complete play? Such a pronouncement fits the text no better than the opposite view of Johnson and Dover Wilson that *Part One*, though it ends in Hotspur's death and the Prince's glory, is yet only the first half of a play. If it were a question of what Shakespeare intended in the matter, the evidence provided by what he wrote would not suggest either that the two parts were planned as a single drama or that *Part Two* was an 'unpremeditated sequel'.

An escape from this dilemma has sometimes been sought in a theory, expounded especially by Professor Dover Wilson and Dr Tillyard, that what *Henry IV* shows is one action with two phases. While the whole drama shows the transformation of the madcap youth into the virtuous ruler, the first part, we are told, deals with the chivalric virtues, the second with the civil. In the first part the hero acquires honour, in the second he establishes justice. But I see no solution of the structural problem here. For though it is left to *Part Two* to embody the idea of justice in the upright judge, the interest in justice and law is present from the start. On Falstaff's first appearance in *Part One* he jibes at the law as 'old Father Antic'. And he goes further. Included within his bubble is a vision of his future self not simply as a man freed from 'the rusty curb' of the law but as a man who actually administers the law himself. 'By the Lord, I'll be a brave judge', he says, making a mistake about his destined office which provokes Hal's retort, 'Thou judgest false already.' It is in the last Act of *Part Two* that we have the completion of this motif. Its climax comes when on Hal's accession Falstaff brags 'the laws of England are at my commandment', and its resolution when the true judge sends the false judge off to prison. But it begins, we see, in the first Act of *Part One*. The Prince's achievement in justice cannot, then, be regarded simply as the second phase of his progress. Certainly he has two contests: in one he outstrips Hotspur, in the other he puts down Falstaff. But these contests are not distributed at the rate of one per part. The plain fact is that in *Henry IV* two actions, each with the Prince as hero, begin together in the first Act of *Part One*, though one of them ends with the death of Hotspur at the end of *Part One*, the other with the banishment of Falstaff at the end of *Part Two*.

Now, since the Falstaff plot is to take twice as long to complete its course, it might well be expected to develop from the beginning more slowly than the other. Certainly, if it is to keep symmetry, it must come later to its turning-point. But is this in fact what we find? Frankly it is not. On the contrary, through the first half of *Part One* the Hotspur plot and the Falstaff plot show every sign of moving towards their crisis together.

Both plots, for example, are presented, though I think both are not usually observed, in the Prince's soliloquy in the first Act which I have already quoted as foretelling the banishment of his tavern companions. It is unfortunate that this speech has usually been studied for its bearing on Falstaff's rejection; its emphasis is really elsewhere. It is only the first two lines, with the reference to the 'unyoked humour' of the Prince's companions, that allude specifically to them, and what is primarily in question is not what is to happen to the companions but what is to happen to the Prince. In the splendid image which follows of the sun breaking through the clouds we recognize a royal emblem and behold the promise of a radiant king who is to come forth from the 'ugly mists' which at present obscure the Prince's real self. Since Falstaff has just been rejoicing at the thought that they 'go by the moon . . . and not by Phoebus', it is apparent that his fortunes will decline when the Prince emerges like Phoebus himself. It is equally apparent, or should be, that the brilliant Hotspur will be outshone.[15] There is certainly no clue at this stage that the catastrophes of Hotspur and Falstaff will not be simultaneous.

Our expectation that they will be is indeed encouraged as the two actions now move forward. While Hotspur in pursuit of honour is preparing war, Falstaff displays his cowardice (I use the word advisedly) at Gad's Hill. While Hotspur rides forth from home on the journey that will take him to his downfall, the exposure of Falstaff's make-believe in the matter of the men in buckram is the foreshadowing of his. The news of Hotspur's rebellion brings the Falstaffian revels to a climax at the same time as it summons the Prince to that interview with his father which will prove, as we have seen, the crisis of his career and the 'nodal point' of the drama. That this interview is to be dramatically momentous is clear enough in advance: before we come to it, it is twice prefigured by the Prince and Falstaff in burlesque. But not only do the two mock-interviews excite our interest in the real one to come; the mock-interviews are in the story of the Prince and Falstaff what the real interview is in the story of the Prince and Hotspur. First, Falstaff, whose dream it is that he may one day govern England, basks in the make-believe that he is king; and then Hal, who, as we have so often been reminded, is presently to be king, performs in masquerade his future part. The question they discuss is central to the play: 'Shall the son of England prove a thief, and take purses?' Shall he in fact continue to associate with Falstaff? One should notice that although the two actors exchange roles, they do not really change sides in this debate. Whether he acts the part of king or prince, Falstaff takes the opportunity of pleading for himself. When he is king he instructs the prince to 'keep with' Falstaff; as prince he begs, 'banish not him thy Harry's company, banish not him thy Harry's company. Banish plump Jack, and banish all the world.' Falstaff's relations to the future king, a theme of speculation since the opening of the play, now come to a focus in this repeated word 'banish'. And when the Prince replies, 'I do, I will', he anticipates in jest the sentence he is later to pronounce in earnest. If it were never to be pronounced in earnest, that would rob the masquerade of the dramatic irony from which comes its bouquet: those who accept *Part One* as a play complete in itself wrongly surrender their legitimate expectations. In this mock-interview the Prince declares his intentions towards Falstaff just as surely as in his real interview with his father he declares his intentions towards Hotspur. One declaration is a solemn vow, the other a glorious piece of fun, but they are equally prophetic and structurally their function is the same. We now approach the turning-point not of one, but of both dramatic actions. Indeed we miss the core of the play if we do not perceive that the two actions are really the same. The moment at the end of the third Act when the Prince goes off to challenge Hotspur is also the moment when he leaves Falstaff's favourite tavern for what we well might think would be evermore. It is at the exit from the tavern that the road to Shrewsbury begins; and all the signposts I see indicate one-way traffic only. There should be no return.

The various dooms of Hotspur and Falstaff are now in sight; and we reasonably expect both dooms to be arrived at in Act V. What we are not at all prepared for is that one of the two will be deferred till five Acts later than the other. The symmetry so beautifully preserved in the story of Hotspur is in Falstaff's case abandoned. Statistics are known to be misleading, and nowhere more so than in literary criticism; but it is not without significance that in *Henry IV, Part One* Falstaff's speeches in the first two Acts number ninety-six and in the last two Acts only twenty-five. As for Falstaff's satellites, with the exception of a single perfunctory appearance on the part of Bardolph, the whole galaxy vanishes altogether in the last two Acts, only to reappear with some change in personnel in *Part Two*. Falstaff, admittedly, goes on without a break, if broken in wind; and his diminished role does show some trace of the expected pattern of development. His going to war on foot while Hal is on horseback marks a separation of these erstwhile companions and a decline in Falstaff's status which was anticipated in jest when his horse was taken from him at Gad's Hill. When he nevertheless appears at one council of war his sole attempt at a characteristic joke is cut short by the Prince with 'Peace, chewet, peace!' A fine touch, this, which contributes to the picture of the Prince's transformation: the boon companion whose jests he has delighted in is now silenced in a word. There is even the shadow of a rejection of Falstaff; over his supposed corpse the Prince speaks words that, for all their affectionate regret, remind us that he has turned his back on 'vanity'. But these things, however significant, are details, no more than shorthand notes for the degradation of Falstaff that we have so confidently looked for. What it comes to is that after the middle of *Part One*, *Henry IV* changes its shape. And that, it seems to me, is the root and cause of the structural problem.

Now that this change of shape has been, I hope I may say, demonstrated from within the play itself, it may at this stage be permissible to venture an opinion about the author's plan. I do not of course mean to imply that *Henry IV*, or indeed any other of Shakespeare's plays, ever had a plan precisely laid down for it in advance. But it has to be supposed that when Shakespeare began a play he had some idea of the general direction it would take, however ready he may have been to modify his idea as art or expediency might suggest. Though this is where I shall be told I pass the bounds of literary criticism into the province of biography or worse, I hold it reasonable to infer from the analysis I have given that in the course of writing *Henry IV* Shakespeare changed his mind. I am compelled to believe that the author himself foresaw, I will even say intended, that pattern which evolves through the early Acts of *Part One* and which demands for its completion that the hero's rise to an eminence of valour shall be accompanied, or at least swiftly followed, by the banishment of the riotous friends who hope to profit from his reign. In other words, hard upon the Battle of Shrewsbury there was to come the coronation of the hero as king. This inference from the play is not without support from other evidence. The Prince's penitence in the interview with his father in the middle of *Part One* corresponds to an episode which, both in Holinshed and in the play of *The Famous Victories of Henry the Fifth*, is placed only shortly before the old king's death. And still more remarkable is the sequence of events in a poem which has been shown to be one of Shakespeare's sources.[16] At the historical Battle of Shrewsbury the Prince was only sixteen years old, whereas Hotspur was thirty-nine. But in Samuel Daniel's poem, *The Civil Wars*, Hotspur is made 'young' and 'rash' and encounters a prince of equal age who emerges like a 'new-appearing glorious star'.[17] It is Daniel, that is to say, who sets in opposition these two splendid youths and so provides the germ from which grows the rivalry of the Prince and Hotspur which is structural to Shakespeare's play. And in view of this resemblance between Daniel and Shakespeare, it is significant that Daniel ignores the ten years that in history elapsed between the death of Hotspur and the Prince's accession. Whereas in Holinshed the events of those ten years fill nearly twenty pages, Daniel goes straight from Shrewsbury to the old king's deathbed. This telescoping of events, which confronts the Prince with his kingly responsibilities directly after the slaying of Hotspur, adumbrates the pattern that Shakespeare, as I see it, must have had it in mind to follow out. The progress of a prince was to be presented not in two phases but in a single play of normal length which would show the hero wayward in its first half, pledging reform in the middle, and then in the second half climbing at Shrewsbury the ladder of honour by which, appropriately, he would ascend to the throne.

The exact point at which a new pattern supervenes I should not care to define. But I think the new pattern can be seen emerging during the fourth Act. At a corresponding stage the history play of *Richard II* shows the deposition of its king, *Henry V* the victory at Agincourt, even *Henry IV, Part Two* the quelling of its rebellion in Gaultree Forest. By contrast *Henry IV, Part One*, postponing any such decisive action, is content with preparation. While the rebels gather, the Prince is arming and Falstaff recruiting to meet them. Until well into the fifth Act ambassadors are going back and forth between the rival camps, and we may even hear a message twice over, once when it is dispatched and once when it is delivered. True, this is not undramatic: these scenes achieve a fine animation and suspense as well as the lowlier feat of verisimilitude. But the technique is obviously not one of compression. Any thought of crowding into the two-hour traffic of one play the death of the old king and the coronation of the new has by now been relinquished, and instead the Battle of Shrewsbury is being built up into a grand finale in its own right. In our eagerness to come to this battle and our gratification at the exciting climax it provides, we easily lose sight of our previous expectations. Most of us, I suspect, go from the theatre well satisfied with the improvised conclusion. It is not, of course, that we cease to care about the fate of individuals. On the contrary, the battle succeeds so well because amid the crowded tumult of the fighting it keeps the key figures in due prominence. Clearly showing who is killed, who is rescued, and who shams dead, who slays a valiant foe and who only pretends to, it brings each man to a destiny that we perceive to be appropriate. We merely fail to notice that the destiny is not in every case exactly what was promised. There is no room now in *Part One* to banish Falstaff. A superb comic tact permits him instead the fate of reformation, in fact the alternative of giving over instead of being damned. It is a melancholy fate enough, for it means giving over being Falstaff: we leave him saying that if he is rewarded, he will 'leave sack, and live cleanly as a nobleman should do'. But since this resolution is conditional and need in any case be believed no more than Falstaff has already taught us to believe him, it has the advantage that it leaves the issue open, which, to judge from the outcry there has always been over the ending of *Part Two*, is how most people would prefer to have it left. Shakespeare's brilliant improvisation thus provides a denouement to *Part One* which has proved perfectly acceptable, while it still leaves opportunity for what I hope I may call the original ending, if the dramatist should choose to add a second part. I refrain, however, from assuming that a second part was necessarily planned before *Part One* was acted.

Part Two itself does not require extended treatment. For, whenever it was 'planned', it is a consequence of *Part One*. Its freedom is limited by the need to present what *Part One* so plainly prepared for and then left out. Falstaff cannot be allowed to escape a second time. His opposition to the law, being now the dominant interest, accordingly shapes the plot; and the law, now bodied forth in the half-legendary figure of the Lord Chief Justice, becomes a formidable person in the drama. The opening encounter between these two, in which Falstaff makes believe not to see or hear his reprover, is symbolic of Falstaff's whole attitude to law – he ignores its existence as long as he can. But the voice which he at first refuses to hear is the voice which will pronounce his final sentence. The theme of the individual versus the law proves so fertile that it readily gives rise to subplots. Justice Shallow, of course, claims his place in the play by virtue of the life that is in him, exuberant in the capers of senility itself. He functions all the same as the Lord Chief Justice's antithesis: he is the foolish justice with whom Falstaff has his way and from whom he wrings the thousand pounds that the wise justice has denied him. Even

Shallow's servant Davy has his relation to the law; and his view of law is that though a man may be a knave, if he is my friend and I am the justice's servant, it is hard if the knave cannot win. In this humane sentiment Davy takes on full vitality as a person; but he simultaneously brings us back to confront at a different angle the main moral issue of the play. Is he to control the law or the law him? In fact shall Falstaff flourish or shall a thief be hanged?

It has sometimes been objected that Falstaff runs away with *Part Two*. In truth he has to shoulder the burden of it because a dead man and a converted one can give him small assistance. *Part Two* has less opportunity for the integrated double action of *Part One*. To be sure, it attempts a double action, and has often been observed to be in some respects a close replica of *Part One* – 'almost a carbon copy', Professor Shaaber says. At exactly the same point in each part, for example, is a little domestic scene where a rebel leader contemplates leaving home, and in each part this is directly followed by the big tavern scene in which revelry rises to a climax. And so on. An article in a recent number of *The Review of English Studies* has even called *Henry IV* a diptych, finding the 'parallel presentation of incidents' in the two parts the primary formal feature. I do not wish to deny the aesthetic satisfaction to be got from a recognition of this rhythmic repetition; yet it is only the more superficial pattern that can be thus repeated. With history and Holinshed obliging, rebellion can break out as before; yet the rebellion of *Part Two*, though it occupies our attention, has no significance, nor can have, for the principal characters of the play. The story of the Prince and Hotspur is over, and the King has only to die.

The one thing about history is that it does not repeat itself. Hotspur, unlike Sherlock Holmes, cannot come back to life. But there are degrees in all things; conversion has not quite the same finality as death. And besides, there is a type of hero whose adventures always can recur. Robin Hood has no sooner plundered one rich man than another comes along. It is the nature of Brer Fox, and indeed of Dr Watson, to be incapable of learning from experience. In folk-lore, that is to say, though not in history, you can be at the same point twice. And it seems as if Prince Hal may be sufficient of a folk-lore hero to be permitted to go again through the cycle of riot and reform. In *Part Two* as in *Part One* the King laments his son's unprincely life. Yet this folk-lore hero is also a historical, and what is more to the point, a dramatic personage, and it is not tolerable that the victor of Shrewsbury should do as critics sometimes say he does, relapse into his former wildness and then reform again. The Prince cannot come into *Part Two* unreclaimed without destroying the dramatic effect of *Part One*. Yet if *Part Two* is not to forgo its own dramatic effect, and especially its splendid last-Act peripeteia, it requires a prince who is unreclaimed. This is *Part Two*'s dilemma, and the way that it takes out of it is a bold one. When the King on his deathbed exclaims against the Prince's 'headstrong riot', he has not forgotten that at Shrewsbury he congratulated the Prince on his redemption. He has not forgotten it for the simple reason that it has never taken place. The only man at court who believes in the Prince's reformation, the Earl of Warwick, believes that it will happen, not that it has happened already. Even as we watch the hero repeating his folk-lore cycle, we are positively instructed that he has not been here before:

> The tide of blood in me
> Hath proudly flowed in vanity till now.
>
> V.2.129–30

In the two parts of *Henry IV* there are not two princely reformations but two versions of a single reformation. And they are mutually exclusive.[18] Though *Part Two* frequently recalls and sometimes depends on what has happened in *Part One*, it also denies that *Part One* exists. Accordingly the ideal spectator of either part must not cry with Shakespeare's Lucio, 'I know what I know.' He must sometimes remember what he knows and sometimes be content to forget it. This, however, is a requirement made in some degree by any work of fiction, or, as they used to call it, feigning. And the feat is not a difficult one for those accustomed to grant the poet's demand for 'that willing suspension of disbelief ... which constitutes poetic faith'.

Henry IV, then, is both one play and two. *Part One* begins an action which it finds it has not scope for but which *Part Two* rounds off. But with one half of the action already concluded in

Part One, there is danger of a gap in *Part Two*. To stop the gap *Part Two* expands the unfinished story of Falstaff and reduplicates what is already finished in the story of the Prince. The two parts are complementary, they are also independent and even incompatible. What they are, with their various formal anomalies, I suppose them to have become through what Johnson termed 'the necessity of exhibition'. Though it would be dangerous to dispute Coleridge's view that a work of art must 'contain in itself the reason why it is so', that its form must proceed from within,[19] yet even works of art, like other of man's productions, must submit to the bondage of the finite. . . .

NOTES

Of the numerous critical writings on *Henry IV*, I have read most and learnt from many. So although my main thesis about its structure has not, as far as I am aware, been previously put forward, it necessarily incorporates some arguments which have. To my predecessors I gladly acknowledge my indebtedness. It is not least to some of those with whom I disagree – Professor Dover Wilson and Dr Tillyard; from their work on *Henry IV* I have derived much insight and stimulus. The most important discussions of the particular problem are, I think, the following:

Johnson, *Shakespeare* (1765), IV, 235, 355; C. H. Herford, *Shakespeare* (Eversley edition, 1899), VI, 253–4; C. F. Tucker Brooke, *The Tudor Drama* (1912), pages 333–5; R. A. Law, 'Structural Unity in the Two Parts of *Henry the Fourth*', *Studies in Philology* XXIV (1927), 223 ff.; J. Dover Wilson, *The Fortunes of Falstaff* (1943), page 4 and *passim*; E. M. W. Tillyard, *Shakespeare's History Plays* (1944), pages 264 ff.; Dover Wilson, *Henry IV, Part One* (New Cambridge Shakespeare, 1946), pages vii–xiii; M. A. Shaaber, 'The Unity of *Henry IV*', *Joseph Quincy Adams Memorial Studies* (1948), pages 217 ff.; H. E. Cain, 'Further Light on the Relation of *1* and *2 Henry IV*', *Shakespeare Quarterly* III (1952), 21 ff.; Law, 'Links between Shakespeare's History Plays', *Studies in Philology* L (1953), 175–82; Tillyard, 'Shakespeare's Historical Cycle: Organism or Compilation?', and Law, 'Shakespeare's Historical Cycle: Rejoinder', *Studies in Philology* LI (1954), 37–41; G. K.

Hunter, '*Henry IV* and the Elizabethan Two-Part Play', *Review of English Studies*, n.s. V (1954), 236 ff.

For further references, see *Henry IV, Part Two*, New Variorum edition, edited by M. A. Shaaber, pages 558–63.

1. For particulars of the most important, see the paragraph above, which will usually obviate the necessity of further reference in the notes to the works listed in it.
2. op. cit. (1746). See especially pages 11, 41–2, 70–71.
3. *Shakespeare*, Johnson-Steevens Variorum, second edition (1778), I, 300.
4. *Notes and Various Readings to Shakespeare* [1775], page 164.
5. *Henry IV, Part One*, edited by Kittredge (1940), page viii.
6. See *Beowulf, an Introduction to the Study of the Poem*, second edition (1932), page 390.
7. This is actually the title of an article by W. K. Wimsatt and M. C. Beardsley in the *Sewanee Review* LIV (1946), 468 ff., reprinted in Wimsatt's *The Verbal Icon* (1954).
8. *A Plea for the Liberty of Interpreting*, British Academy Shakespeare Lecture, 1930, page 6.
9. op. cit., page 22.
10. The connexion here is reinforced by the Prince's use of his earlier image: 'all the budding honours on thy crest | I'll crop'.
11. 'The Rejection of Falstaff', *Oxford Lectures on Poetry* (1909), pages 262–3.
12. op. cit., page 253.
13. *The Fortunes of Falstaff*, pages 120–21.
14. cf. Luke 13.25–7.
15. i.e. this first-Act soliloquy looks forward not only to the rejection of Falstaff but also to Vernon's vision of the Prince and his company before Shrewsbury, 'gorgeous as the sun at midsummer'.
16. See F. W. Moorman, 'Shakespeare's History Plays and Daniel's "Civile Wars"', *Shakespeare-Jahrbuch* XL (1904), 77–83.
17. Book III, stanzas 97, 109–10.
18. All this is very well exhibited by H. E. Cain (see the bibliography above). But his conclusion that the two parts therefore have no continuity is invalidated because, like many others, he is content to isolate particular elements in the problem and does not examine it whole. Except when the views of others are being quoted or discussed, the word 'Falstaff' does not occur in his article.
19. This is a synthesis of several passages in Coleridge. The words in

quotation marks are said of whatever can give permanent pleasure; but the context shows Coleridge to be thinking of literary composition. See *Biographia Literaria*, edited by J. Shawcross, II, 9. Also relevant are 'On Poesy or Art', ibid., II, 262; and *Coleridge's Shakespearean Criticism*, edited by T. M. Raysor (1930), I, 223–4.

NINE

Falstaff*

A. R. Humphreys

FALSTAFF'S transcendent prestige is reflected in a vast literature, and in such abundant reference as to occasion, in the *Shakspere Allusion-Book* index, the telling entry 'For the purpose of this Index Falstaff is treated as a work'. This eminence is not predictable from the life-story of his remote original Sir John Oldcastle (*c.* 1378–1417), High Sheriff of Herefordshire, who became Lord Cobham by marriage in 1409. Oldcastle steps into Holinshed in a role as remote as can be imagined from the reverend vice and vanity in years; he does not appear, moreover, until after the new-crowned Henry has banished his youthful mates. 'A valiant capteine and a hardie gentleman' in the French wars, he has been 'highly in the king's favour',[1] but is charged with Wycliffite heresy and condemned. Escaping from the Tower he hides in Wales, while his supporters are cruelly suppressed, but eventually he is captured and on Christmas Day 1417 is hanged and burnt.

The valiant Lollard could hardly have expected reincarnation as Oldcastle–Falstaff. Falstaff's biblical quotations might just possibly reflect such antecedents; moreover, Oldcastle was cast off by the King after early favour (some traditions date the rejection before, some after, the accession); and during his trial he confessed

that in my frayle youthe I offended thee (Lorde) moste greeuously, in Pride, Wrathe, and Glottony, in Couetousnes and in Lechery.[2]

But the resemblance is not strong. Oldcastle's posthumous story ran in two contrasting channels.[3] One, hostile to him, is that of

---

*From the Introductions to the new Arden Shakespeare editions of *The First Part of Henry IV* (1961), pages xxxix–xlv, and *The Second Part of Henry IV* (1966), pages lv–lxi. Copyright © Methuen & Co. Ltd, 1961 (pages 222–8 in this edition) and 1966 (pages 228–35). Reprinted by kind permission of the author and the publishers, Methuen & Co. Ltd, London.

anti-Wycliffite orthodoxy, and is found in the poet Hoccleve,[4] in popular political verses, and in chroniclers from Walsingham to Polydore Vergil. Thomas Fuller, in his *Worthies of England* (1662), defending Oldcastle as a forerunner of Protestantism, blamed 'the *Papists* railing on him for a *Heretick*' (II, 253) as the fabricators of his disrepute as a coward. His flight to Wales and consequent absence from Henry's later wars were misconstrued as pusillanimity; his Lollardism was taken for presumption, blasphemy, and even diabolical instigation; his friendship with the King was restricted to Henry's unregenerate youth; and from his name he was wrongly assumed to be old. The contrasting, favourable, tradition emerged with Tudor Protestantism and is traceable to John Bale's *Brefe Chronycle Concernynge ... Syr Iohn Oldecastell* (1544). This influenced Hall and was reprinted almost verbatim in Foxe's *Actes and Monuments*, later editions of which contained a long 'Defence of the Lord Cobham' and furnished the historical materials for the Munday–Drayton–Wilson–Hathaway play. By this tradition 'this most constaunt seruant of the lorde and worthy knight Sir John Oldecastell, the Lorde Cobham',[5] was a Protestant hero and martyr, 'a principall fauourer, receiuer, and maintainer of ... Lollards',[6] a scholar of philosophy and theology, a popular and virtuous leader, wild when young but a religious convert – 'his youth was full of wanton wildness before he knew the scriptures', says Bale – and not rejected by Henry until some time after the coronation. Bale, however, mistakenly endorsed the error about his age. These, then, are the conflicting stories, germs of Oldcastle the vicious reprobate and Oldcastle the virtuous martyr, the former incorporated in the crude anonymous farce-chronicle *The Famous Victories of Henry V* (1594?) and in Shakespeare's plays, the latter in *Sir John Oldcastle*'s hero –

> It is no pamperd glutton we present,
> Nor aged Councellor to youthfull sinne,
> But one, whose vertue shone aboue the rest,
> A valiant Martyr and a vertuous peere.

How Oldcastle came to be involved in stories of youthful riot is a matter of speculation. The syllogism may have been that the companions of the young Henry were scapegraces; that Oldcastle was a companion of the young Henry; and that therefore Oldcastle was a scapegrace. Professor Dover Wilson suggests that his rejection by Henry welded itself in the popular mind with that of the scapegraces, the more readily since according to the hostile tradition both occurred approximately at Henry's accession ('Before the Kings coronacion [Oldcastle] was forsaken of the Kinge,' says Tito Livio's translator[7]) and the 'confession' reported by Foxe might be an effective link.

Since the historical Oldcastle was certainly neither old nor unmilitary and (being a warrior) probably not fat, these attributes of Falstaff must arise otherwise than from history. In fact, several elements from the hostile tradition coalesced with features of the popular Morality Vice. Oldcastle's age (thirty-nine at death) was exaggerated by the interpretation of his name on which Shakespeare puns in the 'old lad of the castle' (*Henry IV, Part One*, I.2.41); but the Vice, too, was often the aged counsellor to youthful sin. The shortage of valour is derived from the hostile tradition, but it too was easily corroborated by the pusillanimity of Vices, parasites, and boasters. The 'goodly portly' figure is in neither history nor *The Famous Victories*, and attempts have been made to explain it. It may be Shakespeare's dramatic contrast, Dover Wilson suggests, to that of the 'starveling' Prince (II.4.240), whose lithe agility the chroniclers celebrate. Or something may come from *Woodstock*'s plump 'old turkey-cocke'. But here again the Vice has something to contribute, as will be seen.

Falstaff is indeed a rich amalgam, a world of comic ingredients. Source-seekers have proffered his components in great profusion. Of these the most important is the Morality Vice, the ensnarer of youth. Since Quiller-Couch proposed this in *Shakespeare's Workmanship* (1918) the idea has been amply elaborated, and John W. Shirley has excellently explored the relevant characteristics of Gluttony, the Gula of the Seven Deadly Sins and a favourite Morality-play tempter.[8] Vices often bragged, like Sensual Appetyte, or Ambidexter in *Cambises* (1569), or Lust, Sturdiness, and Inclination in *The Trial of Treasure*. They might sanctimoniously champion virtue; 'Vertue is mocked of euery man', laments Incontinence in *The Longer Thou Livest*. Collectively they share their features with the farce-clowns like Huanebango the braggart of

Peele's *Old Wives' Tale*, or the greedy cowardly Dericke of *The Famous Victories*, whom Falstaff copies in making his nose bleed with spear-grass (*Part One*, II.4.302). An Elizabethan audience would recognize in Falstaff the familiar Vice-qualities of gluttony, idleness, and lechery, and in Hal the youth in danger. Throughout Falstaff is referred to in Morality-idiom – iniquity, ruffian, vanity in years, beating Hal out of his kingdom with a dagger of lath, the abominable misleader of youth, the old white-bearded Satan; and in *Part Two* he is rejected finally (as prospectively in *Part One*, by Hal's soliloquy and many a hint) as the tutor and feeder of Hal's 'riots' (a recognized Morality-term), the old profane surfeit-swelled gormandizer. Hal's soliloquy (*Part One*, I.2.193 ff.) tells the audience both that Hal is not the hooligan of *The Famous Victories* (which, incidentally, is not at all Morality-influenced) and that he participates undeceived in the unyoked humours of idleness.

'Morality tradition' is a broad category. The various kinds of Vice-farce, with such conceits as clownage keeps in pay, furnish a wide panorama of aged, obese, gluttonous, wenching braggarts, comically outrageous in huffing, lying, thieving, and gormandizing. Somewhere in the picture are the *miles gloriosus*, with his bogus valour, and the witty parasite (both frequent in Plautine comedy), the fool, and the Elizabethan army officer often castigated for recruiting and other swindles. Enthusiasts have even sought Falstaff in historical persons – Tarlton the clown, Chettle the dramatist, and a certain Captain Nicholas Dawtrey. Neglecting these agreeable whimsies we may admit something, though with reserve, in the other identifications. The *miles gloriosus* boasted of courage but avoided combat, like Bobadill in *Every Man in his Humour* or Parolles in *All's Well*, and scholars have worked out his contribution to Falstaff. Yet since he was fatuous, humourless, and finally unmasked to derision we may agree with Maurice Morgann that elements of the *miles gloriosus* in Falstaff are so modified by wit and self-possession as to become something different, a mere trace of flavour in a succulent gallimaufry, like the *soupçon* of Basilisco in the soliloquy on honour.

As for the parasite tradition, this contributed something; Iago has been called the culmination of the fatal parasite, Falstaff of the comic.[9] Butt, wit, sponger, trickster, and mocker, this classical type was familiar to the Elizabethan stage in such figures as Mathew Merygreke in *Ralph Roister Doister* or Cariosophus in *Damon and Pithias*. But again the relationship to Falstaff is only tangential; Falstaff is a parasite but a benefactor too, and much else besides.

His quality as Fool, however, is more noteworthy, for he shares not only some of the Fool's superficial features – comic bragga-docio, inventiveness of idea, dexterity with words, mock moraliz-ing, deliberate mistakings, absurd actions – but also the Fool's deeper significance, as liberator from convention. In Miss Enid Welsford's words:

> under the dissolvent influence of [the Fool's] personality the iron net-work of physical, social, and moral law, which enmeshes us from the cradle to the grave, seems – for the moment – negligible as a web of gossamer. The Fool does not lead a revolt against the law; he lures us into a region of the spirit where, as Lamb would put it, the writ does not run.[10]

We cannot always live in that region, as the play makes clear, nor is its freedom, as some Falstaff sentimentalists suggest, more pre-cious than the network of law. But Miss Welsford does in fact admirably describe the effect Falstaff has upon our spirits.[11]

Falstaff as a whole is far greater than the sum of his parts; this Vice–Parasite–Fool–*Miles-Gloriosus*–Corrupt-Soldier is inspired by such humorous virtuosity as immeasurably to transcend such components. His whole nature is unified of paradoxical opposites, so that a man no more knows where to have him than he himself knew where to have the Hostess (III.3.125–6). Parasitical, he yet gives to life as much as he takes, and indeed provides amidst all his vices a vast salutary criticism of the world of war and policy. He is vicious, yet his vices are a tonic for human nature; he exploits his dependants, yet they remain indissolubly attached to him; he lies, yet would be dismayed if his lies were to be believed. He laments his age, corpulence, and lost agility, yet he behaves with the gaiety of youth, has intellectual legerity to offset his bulk, and is agile whenever it suits him. A reprobate, he yet quotes scripture for his purpose. Finally, is he or is he not a coward? No, say Morgann and Bradley: he is sought for in war, leads his men into danger, and philosophizes coolly on the battlefield. Yes, say Stoll and others: as Poins foretells, he runs at Gad's Hill and boasts afterwards; he hacks his sword, slubbers his garments, and is touchy when taunted; his Shrewsbury nonchalance is clown-foolery only; his ignominious stabbing of Hotspur is 'one of the accepted *lazzi* of the coward on the stage'; and his capture of Colville in *Part Two* is buffoonery, like Pistol's of Monsieur le Fer in *Henry V*.

This tiresome question need not have arisen had not Morgann rightly desired to vindicate Falstaff from the ignominious clowning he received on the eighteenth-century stage. It would have been quickly settled had not Falstaff's vitality confused critics as to the difference between dramatic and real persons. This multifarious material is not to be reduced to a single realistic formula. That Falstaff's panic at Gad's Hill is not put on there is no doubt. It is a foretold outcome of the trick played on him; the point of 'By the Lord, I knew ye as well as he that made ye' (II.4.261) is to show his resourcefulness in improbable excuse; and the surprised relief in 'But by the Lord, lads, I am glad you have the money' (II.4.269–70) is proof that he had thought the booty to be lost. The multiplication of buckram men does not mean either on the one hand that he expects to be believed or on the other that he has recognized his assailants and is pulling their legs: he is putting on the expected enjoyable show. And who, in fact, is 'he'? 'He', really, is the comic personality given a chance by the dramatist to revel in a comic role. The exaggerations are not to be explained realistically by the argument that so acute a wit cannot expect so absurd a yarn to be believed and is merely countermining the Prince and Poins for the trick he has detected: he has not detected it, but, like the brilliant stage-comic he is, he has an invention full of nimble and delectable shapes which he exercises on all possible occasions with the effect (eagerly expected by Prince, Poins, and audience alike) of landing himself in foreseeable quandaries and then unforeseeably extricating himself from them.[12] To schematize Falstaff's shotsilk variety into stable colour is absurd: his dramatic sphere of popular comedy allows a rapid shifting of attitudes. A real man who ran at Gad's Hill would not receive a charge of foot from his stampeder, nor would a dozen captains seek him out, nor even with Hal's connivance would anyone believe he had killed Hotspur. But the stage-comic frees us from the restricting congruities of real life. Professor Empson has put it (it is Dover Wilson's plea too) that 'the whole of the great joke is that you *can't* see through him, any more than the Prince could' – 'the dramatic effect simply *is* the doubt, and very satisfying too'.[13] Is Falstaff then inconsistent? Yes, if judged realistically. No, when taken, rightly, for what Empson calls his 'Dramatic Ambiguity', for the figure of dramatic comedy that he is, butt and wit together, equally amusing by his elephantine panic, exuberant fabrications, and comic aplomb in the midst of war. His philosophy of courage is, no doubt, to show as much or as little of it as circumstances required; he might observe, like the practical but not cowardly Bluntschli in Shaw's *Arms and the Man*, 'It is our duty to live as long as we can', and like Bluntschli he keeps in his holster something better than pistols. Yet Bluntschli would hardly 'roar' in flight, as Falstaff does (II.2.109), and the attempt to fit Falstaff into a formula of psychological realism must finally fail. Brilliant at timely evasions, he escapes this straitjacket as he escapes any other.

In other words, Falstaff, though immensely 'living', is not like any single real man. But he is symbolically like life itself; the large comedy of humanity is embodied in him. He expresses the indispensable spirit of fun. When he runs away, the fun is at him; when he does not run away, the fun is through him. The consistency lies not in the congruence of one action with another, but in the whole function of providing mirth and a liberating irreverence. Falstaff differs in amplitude but not in kind from the stage funny man who, without incongruity, is both knocked about and knocker-about. In the words Whitman wrote on himself, he is large, he contains multitudes. . . .

Falstaff, a modern critic observes, 'commits what Shelley was to call "the generous error", the error of those who try to live life by a vision of it, thus transforming the world about them and impressing upon it their own character. . . . His vision of life takes over whenever he is on the stage'.[14] This is true of *Part One*. But the situation in *Part Two* is more complicated.

He starts promisingly. Shrewsbury has done him good. Shakespeare discreetly avoids the too-open question, 'What did the King and court *really* think he had done there?', though in fact Morton and Lady Percy know that Hal, not he, killed Hotspur. There is an undefined impression that 'he hath done good service'; he is sent 'with some charge' to Prince John, to whom in fact he dispatches a letter. His service at Shrewsbury, the Lord Chief Justice admits, 'hath a little gilded over' his Gad's Hill exploit (a very grudging admission if Falstaff were really supposed to have killed Hotspur). Shakespeare has it both ways – Falstaff has killed Hotspur, and is being rewarded; he has not killed Hotspur, and nobody is fool enough to say he has. But at least Falstaff is tolerably elevated, entering with sword and buckler borne by his page; he seeks two and twenty yards of satin for his short cloak and slops (a lavish supply even for a Falstaffian girth); he is impudent with the Lord Chief Justice; he 'holds his place' so as to exasperate the Prince and Poins; he is sought by a dozen captains; and he deals masterfully with the egregious Colville.

Yet there is something ambiguous in all this. The insouciant mastery which floated him through *Part One* is not so certain. The Lord Chief Justice and Prince John, while not actually quashing him, show him as less than commanding. He cannot even best the Lord Chief Justice's servant. Since he thinks that the Prince is on his side, that the Lord Chief Justice is heading for disgrace, and that the laws of England are to be at his commandment, he is not perturbed. But the 'generous error' is in fact dangerous; *Part Two* is a play in which men destroy themselves by delusions. There are hints often enough that Falstaff's 'vision' is blindness, the ground under his feet hollow. As late as the end of Act V, scene 1, he expects to make Hal laugh heartily; as late as the end of Act V, scene 3, he 'know[s] the young King is sick for [him]'. This complacency is folly.

Shakespeare makes clear the Prince's separation from him. Almost as soon as Falstaff sets foot on the stage he is confronted not by Hal but by the Lord Chief Justice, to whom Hal is to entrust his own guidance and the enforcement of Falstaff's dismissal, and through whose agency the King has 'severed' Falstaff and Hal (I.2.191). But the severance is Hal's own, too; the rejection in effect takes place not as the play ends but as it begins. If made explicit at the outset it would seem too drastic after the high favour of *Part One*, but it is already under way. Hal is kept out of sight until Act II, scene 2; then he enters not with Falstaff but with Poins, in a state of chrysalis-uneasiness over his misspent time. He meets Falstaff only in the latter part of Act II, and in no friendly spirit. Throughout, every remark he makes about Falstaff is derogatory; he addresses him only three civil words – 'Falstaff, good night' (II.4.353) – the last time he speaks to him before the rejection scene. Ignorant of Falstaff's whereabouts, he must ask Poins whether the old boar feeds in the old frank. Neither he nor Poins knows who Doll Tearsheet is. And he dines not specifically with Falstaff but 'With Poins, and other his continual followers'. The spectators, like bystanders seeing most of the game, have every chance to read the danger signals, displayed in the relationships between the Lord Chief Justice, Falstaff, and Hal, in the marked coarseness of Boar's-Head life and indeed of Falstaff's witticisms,[15] and in the imminent dangers of anarchy. But Falstaff sacrifices his intelligence to his self-satisfaction; only when the blow falls does he sense that anything has changed.[16]

In other respects he has lost little of his verve. His mind is still able; he knowledgeably caricatures military theory and medical science (III.2.250–63, IV.3.85–112); he is familiar with Galen, the Bible, the Homilies, and literary fashions. His speech, if less elegant than in *Part One*, is not without virtuosity and Lylyan graces.[17] His wit still flashes so comprehensively that a commentator pursuing him with notes feels like a lepidopterist after not one butterfly at a time but a host. Even so, his increasing coarseness is noticeable, both in gross equivoques and in self-approval. Nor does he so readily outshine others. The Lord Chief Justice holds his own; the Hostess has most of the best things in II.1, and she, Doll, and Pistol are the main comic forces in II.4. Indeed, Falstaff's own humours must divide the honours of the title-page with Pistol's swaggerings (the 1600 quarto title-page reads: *The Second part of Henrie the fourth, continuing to his death, and coronation of Henrie the fift. With the humours of sir Iohn Falstaffe, and swaggering Pistol . . .*). In Gloucestershire, his superiority of wit is not more remarkable than Shallow's inferiority. He lacks Hal to bring him out. His mind operates, then, less refreshingly than in *Part One*, in ways touched with the gross, the patronizing, even the sinister. Proximity to the throne can be no place for him.

Still, one holds towards him a double attitude. Since he swindles Mistress Quickly and Justice Shallow, treats Hal cavalierly, and recruits his yokels for slaughter, he has been called 'the most pitiless creature in the play'.[18] As another critic observes,

he added hypocrisy to debauchery, cowardice and bragging impudence, and so, to accord with his profession of swashbuckler in chief, assumed a choler though he had it not.[19]

Yet the element of truth in these judgements does not reflect one's whole sense of what is going on. The moralistic strain of criticism which judges Falstaff's actions as if they were actions of real life is sounder than its opposite, which takes them in a gay separation from anything real, but it errs in neglecting the controlling context of tone and manner. Shakespeare has provided much besides mere judgement-by-the-letter-of-the-law. Realistically considered, of course, Falstaff's recruiting is disgraceful. Dramatically considered, however, its disgracefulness is relieved by the whole treatment, which invites enjoyment rather than indignation. One never supposes, somehow, that the recruits will come to harm. And in fact, since Falstaff arrives late at Gaultree, there is no harm for them to come to.[20] In real life, Falstaff's victims would suffer hardships and perhaps disaster: in the play, not only are they, like Falstaff himself, positively funny but they do not evidently suffer from their victimizing.

Yet, while keeping all this well within the sphere of the comic, the play does impose its responsible moral terms. One laughs at the comic aspect of Falstaff's misdeeds, but one is well aware that they disqualify him from a king's favour. He deteriorates not in artistic quality (not much, at any rate), but in the totality of qualities to be liked. One takes him in the tolerance of comedy when the results are comic; one condemns only when they threaten to be serious.

Playgoers have discussed Falstaff's dismissal for centuries. 'I don't know', Rowe commented in 1709, 'whether some People have not, in remembrance of the Diversion he had formerly afforded 'em, been sorry to see his friend *Hal* use him so scurvily.'

Johnson rejoined that since Falstaff 'has nothing in him that can be esteemed, no great pain will be suffered from the reflection that he is compelled to live honestly'. Yet Hazlitt much preferred him to Hal, and Bradley, admitting that the rejection had to come, regretted that it was done in public, in a display of Bolingbrokian 'hardness and policy'. For Professor Danby, Hal is a 'makeshift ideal' for the theme of 'Commodity', a brilliant façade before a vacuity of true feeling; 'to pseudo-fellowship in Hal', he comments, 'must be added pseudo-morality'.[21]

Shakespeare's problem was not wholly tractable. The Wild-Prince stories presented a licentious ribald miraculously converted, which was material rather for a romance than a history. A Wild Prince, on the other hand, whom his fellow nobles knew to be grooming himself for responsibility would contravene the chronicles and forfeit that dramatic emergence into virtue which was integral to the legend. Shakespeare effects a skilful compromise. Hal is reputedly dissolute but, as far as one sees him, harmless enough. He is aware of his destiny. While the crown is remote, and Falstaff's japes are innocuous, he enjoys the Boar's Head, though hinting that the revelry must end. As the accession grows nearer and Falstaff grosser, he avoids him. Three things make his course seem heartless in a way Shakespeare probably never intended: these are Hal's soliloquy (*Part One*, I.2.193 ff.), Warwick's declaration that Hal frequents the Boar's Head simply to recognize and disclaim vice (*Part Two*, IV.4.67 ff.), and the rejection speech. But these three need taking with care. Hal's soliloquy is a morality-manifesto rather than heartless policy, Warwick is providing a gloss to console the dying King, and the rejection speech is official rather than personal, a required public demonstration. The general tenor of Hal's evolution deserves respect. In Act II, scene 2, he jests uneasily to distract himself from the misery of his father's illness, and Falstaff's presumption affronts him. After a brief and indeed disapproving intervention at the Boar's Head he recalls his responsibilities, though since the chronicles leave the suppression of the Archbishop entirely to Westmoreland and Prince John he does not appear at Gaultree (and thereby escapes odium). His bearing in the sick-room is admirable, and his address to the lords is honourable. The opposed evolutions of Falstaff and Hal, rightly observed, will dispel any notion that Falstaff is scurvily treated; only the most careless reading could take the rejection as a melodrama prepared by a calculating Prince against a hoodwinked crony. As for the publicity which Bradley regrets, Falstaff's hubris positively demands a public scene; he flaunts his way of life for all to see, and boasts that it will be the King's, too. The public disgrace is the appropriate nemesis, and the punishment is lenient – temporary committal to a prison reserved for important notables who fell out of favour, followed by a life 'very well provided for', ten miles from court. Falstaff's pride is hurt, his overweening confidence deflated. But the 'fracted and corroborate' heart reported in *Henry V* is an after-thought irrelevant to *Henry IV*, occasioned by the change of plan whereby Falstaff was dropped from *Henry V* and had to be disposed of. 'Dickens', Sir Alfred Duff Cooper suggests,

> would have settled Falstaff down with a pension in a country cottage, with honeysuckle round the door, and a hospitable inn hard by, where the old gentleman, grown quite respectable, would have recounted tales of the riotous past, to the wondering yokels, and where the King would have paid him an occasional visit. But Shakespeare did not live in a sentimental age.[22]

In fact, unsentimental though Falstaff's dismissal is, Shakespeare provided a future for him at the end of *Henry IV, Part Two* not far different from that thus humorously described – though no Shakespearian Falstaff, one hopes, would grow 'quite respectable', whatever a Dickensian one might do. The rejection, in short, is necessary, well-prepared, and executed without undue severity.

'And yet', my friend Mr Dipak Nandy writes to me, 'might not something more be said? One asks why, despite all these considerations, one's feelings are nevertheless jarred. Why is there, in Morgann's terms, such a gap between one's understanding and one's impressions?' He makes three suggestions. First, the rejection dislocates not only Falstaff's self-esteem but our very 'taking' of him as a splendid performer in his own role. However reprehensible in real terms, he has appreciatively acted out the great enlargement of comedy, and 'the success of a role depends in large part on the acceptance of the role-player *as a role-player*.' Falstaff not only has been enjoyable, he has shown himself a virtuoso in relishing his part. 'I know thee not, old man' strips him bare of the gorgeous assumptions he has donned for our pleasure, and turns him into an aged cast-off: 'in rejection, the multitude of roles we call Falstaff seems to become suddenly humanized into a person; and this', Mr Nandy observes, 'I find pathetic'. Second, the terms of Henry's reproof – fool, jester, a dream he despises – though accurate in sense, destroy that balance of judgement so well held in *Part One*, by which Falstaff is a rascal and yet contributes wisdom to a world of harsh purpose. They invite us to assume the same tone, to accuse ourselves in the same terms, as Henry uses; and this we are wholly unwilling to do. To do so would in some sense be treachery to ourselves. So strict a rejection of what has pleased us may be the tribute duty owes to responsibility; yet it impoverishes our sense of life. And third, though the rejection is inevitable, its very necessity marks a narrowing (not less regrettable because absolutely requisite) in Henry himself. 'Are we not', Mr Nandy writes, 'witnessing the disjunction between the King and the man that the histories stress as, at moments of crisis, their kings have to confront in their own souls the realization that they are men no more? Is it not possible for the sentimentalists to argue that the sense of loss they feel at the rejection derives not only from the loss of Falstaff, not only from the decease of a human relationship, but also from the loss of something, some generosity perhaps (not in what he *does* to Falstaff, which is mild enough, but in what he *says*), in Henry himself, from the feeling that the transformation of Hal into Henry involves – and that "necessarily" – some sacrifice?'

This is said well; it reflects something of what we feel; and we cannot but regret that stroke which eclipses the gaiety of nations and impoverishes the public stock of harmless pleasure. Yet taking all in all – the seamier streaks, the dangerously predatory impulses, revealed in Falstaff, Hal's disciplining through grief, the noble idea of justice that dominates the accession, the need for unmistakable severance, and the comfortable leniency of the sentence – it is still possible to hold that Shakespeare *has* here achieved a balanced complexity of wisdom not inferior to that in *Part One*, the acknowledgement of necessity with its double face of grief and consolation;

that Hal has deepened, not narrowed; and that Falstaff (at a distence of ten miles) can fleet the time carelessly with his cronies, remedying the long consumption of his purse at the expense of the royal exchequer. His well-wishers need ask no more.

NOTES

1. Raphael Holinshed, *Chronicles*, reprint of 1807–8, III, 62.
2. John Foxe, *Actes and Monuments* (1563), page 266.
3. Thoroughly plotted by Wilhelm Baeske, *Oldcastle-Falstaff in der engl. Literatur bis zu Sh.* (1905).
4. Hoccleve, *Works. I. The Minor Poems* (EETS, Extra series lxi (1892), 8–24, 'Address to Sir John Oldcastle').
5. Foxe, op. cit. (1563), page 263.
6. op. cit. (1596 edition), I, 513.
7. cf. C. L. Kingsford, *The First English Life of Henry V* (1911), page 22.
8. 'Falstaff an Elizabethan Glutton', *Philological Quarterly* XVII (1938). In *The Castell of Perseverance* (*c.* 1425), the World, Devil, and Flesh lead Mankind 'with synnys al a-bowt'; Flesh is corpulent and accompanied by Gluttony, Lechery, and Sloth. In Medwall's *Nature* (*c.* 1486), aged Sensuality has Gluttony as an accomplice. In *The Nature of the Foure Elements* (1519), Sensual Appetyte under the guise of Friendship tempts Humanyte to the tavern, and in *Lusty Juventus* (*c.* 1540) the age-old Hypocrisy incites Juventus to lechery and self-indulgence. In William Wager's *The Longer Thou Livest the More Fool Thou Art* (*c.* 1586), Incontinence is as old as Idleness, 'parent of all vice', and tempts Man with food, wine, and girls: in Lupton's *All for Money* (1578), Pleasure is glutton and lecher, and Gluttony prompts to 'fine fare and gluttonie'. Ryot, in *Youth* (*c.* 1550), is thief and tempter to wine and women; *The Trial of Treasure* (1567) has one Gredy-Gutte – 'the cowe-bellied knaue', 'the great-bellied loute'. In *The Faerie Queene* (I.4.21–3) Spenser's Gluttony is, like Falstaff, 'Not meet to be of counsell to a king', 'Full of diseases', his belly 'up-blowne with luxury'.
9. E. P. Vandiver, 'The Elizabethan Dramatic Parasite', *Studies in Philology* XXXII (1935), 411.
10. *The Fool* (1935), page 317.
11. cf. C. L. Barber, 'From Ritual to Comedy', 24, in *English Stage*

Comedy, edited by W. K. Wimsatt (1955): 'In the theatrical institution of clowning, the clown or vice, when Shakespeare started to write, was a recognized anarchist who made aberration obvious by carrying release to absurd extremes'.

12. A. J. A. Waldock comments well to this effect in 'The Men in Buckram', *Review of English Studies* XXIII (1947), 16–23.

13. W. Empson, 'Falstaff and Mr Dover Wilson', *Kenyon Review* XV (1953), 223.

14. Robert Langbaum, 'Character versus Actors in Shakespeare', *Shakespeare Quarterly* VIII (1957), 66.

15. In chronicle-tradition, while loose in morals before his accession Prince Henry turned strictly continent on becoming king (C. L. Kingsford, op. cit., page xxx).

16. Bertrand Evans studies 'Shakespeare's devotion to a dramatic method that gives the audience an advantage in awareness, and thus opens exploitable gaps between audience and participants, and between participant and participant' (*Shakespeare's Comedies* (1960), page viii).

17. See I.2.6–28. C. L. Barber observes about the styles of Nashe and Falstaff that both deal in conceits elaborated with 'consciously specious plausibility', mock-heroic elevations, and formally marshalled argument (*Shakespeare's Festive Comedy* (1959), page 71).

18. J. F. Danby, *Shakespeare's Doctrine of Nature* (1949), page 84.

19. J. W. Draper, *The Humors and Shakespeare's Characters* (1945), page 38.

20. In *Part One*, where Falstaff's 'ragamuffins' do reportedly come to harm, or at least are humorously and improbably said by Falstaff to be all dead except two, one never sets eyes on them. They exist, rather, as creatures of Falstaff's comic fantasy.

21. Danby, op. cit., pages 85–90.

22. *Sergeant Shakespeare* (1949), page 85.

TEN

Henry V*

M. M. Reese

AFTER the sustained conflicts of the two preceding plays, *Henry V* is in the main a demonstration. The hero is no longer in the toils. The end has proved the man, and his victory over himself has been much more than a personal victory. Riot and dishonour have been put to flight, reason is passion's master, and England has at last a king who can physic all her ills. Because he has proved himself a valiant and chivalrous prince, and one who acknowledges the sovereignty of law and justice, the crown comes to him 'with better quiet, | Better opinion, better confirmation', and all the soil of the Lancastrian achievement has gone with his father to the grave. In *Henry V* Shakespeare celebrates England's recovered majesty through the deeds of 'the mirror of all Christian kings'.

A formidable body of critical opinion is hostile to this view. In general it is held that, if this really was what Shakespeare was trying to do, he failed to bring it off; his natural scepticism could not help revealing the essential hollowness of this idealized and unlikely figure. Obviously there is something in this. Shakespeare was much too conscious of the human pressures that weigh on a public man to believe that a whole reign – even a short one that enjoyed God's special care – could be conducted on this rarefied level, and he has allowed the human material to be transformed by the universalizing tendencies of epic. But the hostile critics have various kinds of objection to the play. They are united only in their dislike of Henry, and they find different ways of rationalizing their prejudice. Purely subjective notions paralyse their judgement, and they write

*From *The Cease of Majesty: A Study of Shakespeare's History Plays* (1961), pages 317–32. Copyright © M. M. Reese, 1961. Reprinted by kind permission of the author and the publishers, Edward Arnold Ltd, London.

as pacifists, republicans, anti-clericals, little Englanders, moralists, even as arbiters of etiquette, until one is astounded at the prejudice Henry has managed to arouse. In all the canon only Isabella, in *Measure for Measure*, has stirred so much personal distaste. In the meantime all contact is lost with Shakespeare's purpose and achievement. Dr Johnson wrote of the play without much enthusiasm, but at least he noted (with reference to Shakespeare's endless enjoyment of the joke about the warming properties of Bardolph's nose) that 'this poet is always more careful about the present than the future, about his audience than his readers'. The immediate effect in the theatre was what concerned him most.

Hazlitt went full-tilt at the play, branding Agincourt as a royal Gad's Hill and describing the Archbishop of Canterbury as a pander to riot beside whom Falstaff was only 'a puny prompter'. Henry made war on his neighbours because his own crown was doubtful and he did not know how to govern the country anyway. Hazlitt concedes that 'we like him in the play. There he is a very amiable monster, a very splendid pageant', to be admired rather as one gazes at a caged panther in the zoo. But objective criticism of the play was made impossible by the writer's Francophil republicanism. He admired Napoleon but not 'this star of England'. A hundred years later Mr John Masefield, in not dissimilar terms, found in Henry 'the knack of life that fits human beings for whatever is animal in human affairs': a back-handed compliment at the best, but almost the only one he is willing to pay to a man whom he reckoned to be 'commonplace'. Bradley, who could not stomach the rejection of Falstaff, allowed Henry a certain coarse efficiency but thought him to be inescapably his father's son, 'the son of the man whom Hotspur called "a vile politician".' The key to the reign is therefore to be found at *Henry IV, Part Two*, IV.5.178–225; and presumably there is not much point in reading *Henry V* at all. Granville-Barker found the play to be lacking in any 'spiritually significant idea': which is patently absurd, since in Shakespeare's time the wise government of states was one of the highest destinies to which God might call a man. But Chambers says much the same thing: 'Here you have a Shakespeare playing on the surface of life, much occupied with externalities and the idols of the forum. And with the exception of a few unconsidered words that fall from the mouth of a woman of no reputation, there is nothing that is intimate, nothing that touches the depths.'

More recently, and more soberly, Dr Tillyard has given Shakespeare credit for good intentions but concludes that he set himself an impossible task. Shakespeare's Hal, so warm and human, was irreconcilable with the copy-book hero of popular tradition; and Tillyard blames the sources for the fact that the king is a lesser person than the chivalrous prince who won Vernon's heart (*Henry IV, Part One*, IV.1.97–110). Mr Traversi finds human flaws in Henry's total self-dedication to the business of being a king, and, like Bradley, he feels the father's influence to be still pervasive. The coldly official manner masks a personal inadequacy of which Shakespeare was evidently aware.[1]

There is no means of persuading people to like Henry if they lack the inclination, but at least we should recognize what Shakespeare was trying to do and how he set about it. Popular legend gave him a paragon, as Tillyard says. It was sufficiently potent to cause Polydore Vergil to break off his mainly critical narrative and insert a most uncharacteristic eulogy. Hall, Daniel, Drayton, and Raleigh all came under Henry's spell, Hall in particular finding him the cradle of all the royal virtues: 'a king whose life was immaculate and his living without spot . . . a shepherd whom his flock loved and lovingly obeyed . . . he was merciful to offenders, charitable to the needy, indifferent to all men, faithful to his friends, and fierce to his enemies, toward God most devout, toward the world moderate, and to his realm a very father'. This was Shakespeare's feeling about him too; and it is important to remember that he did not accept the legend without examining it. In two plays devoted to the education of a prince he built up Henry's character so that men could believe in it, showing the human weaknesses as well as the dedication and conveying the magnitude of the responsibility by hinting at the personal sacrifices which it demanded. He does not allow us to think of Henry as an angel temporarily borrowed from above. The character gains its strength and conviction from all that has gone before, not from *Henry IV* only but from all the poet's earlier studies of kingship and society. In these studies he has shown us not only the sort of man the ideal king will be but also the roots from which he must grow; good government results from a complex of social and moral relationships, and *Henry V* is a play about England as well as about a single heroic man.

Is it a successful play? The proof is in the theatre; and critics who dislike the play may fairly be asked to give an honest answer to the question of what their response has been when – if they ever have – they have seen it acted on the stage. No play of Shakespeare's has such a simple, unvarying effect. It is absolutely proof against the perversity of directors. It is quite impossible to do anything 'clever' with it, and the only way of producing it is the way the author indicated long ago. Nor does it fail in its impact. In times of war and national danger men have been inspired by it; but even at ordinary times, when one perhaps goes to the theatre in no mood to be stirred by elementary heroics, the play's energy and its uncomplicated sentiment unite the audience in common surrender. In the theatre it is no longer possible to have any doubts about Henry himself. If Shakespeare had any secret reservations about the character, they are not apparent on the stage, where Henry is virtuous, strong, and gay, a born leader of men. It is quite evident that Shakespeare approves of him; just as, in his own dramatic terms, he approves of Isabella and does not approve of Shylock.

Of course the play's appeal and interest are limited, and this very limitation makes its unfailing success in the theatre the more remarkable. Technically it is a considerable achievement, since Shakespeare was writing in a mode that he recognized (and he admits it often enough) to be extremely difficult.[2] 'O for a Muse of fire.' He decided that the noble deeds of Henry V, which were of a kind to inspire wonder and imitation, could not be fittingly celebrated except through the medium of epic; and epic and drama are not naturally congenial to one another. The well-known admissions in the Prologue are not just an apology for the theatre's failure to accommodate marching armies: Shakespeare was quite ready to stage a battle when it suited him, and with no apology for the small numbers engaged in it. The Chorus was a device that he seldom used, and never so extensively as in *Henry V*. Its function here is to apologize for the unsuitability of any stage for the breadth and sweep of epic; but at the same time Shakespeare uses it with great boldness and ingenuity to make good some of the deficiencies he so modestly admits. He tells the story of the reign in a sequence of episodes, linking them by speeches in which the Chorus supplies gaps in the narrative and generally sets the mood for the following scene. This is a practical function of some value, as we can discover from those episodic chronicle plays where no such assistance is supplied. But the verse of the choruses, corresponding to the passages of heightened description which a narrative poet habitually employs, has the further function of establishing the epic stature of the hero.

Properly the hero's qualities should be established through the dramatic action, and the prominence of the Chorus, like the element of rhetorical strain often detectable in the verse, is a weakness that necessarily results from the use of the epic mode: Shakespeare was trying to do something that did not wholly belong to drama. His method was to illuminate his hero in a succession of facets. Dover Wilson calls them tableaux,[3] and they may be compared with magnificent stained-glass windows whose panels unfold a story. But tableaux and stained-glass windows do not move. Their nature is to crystallize an emotion, and it is a just criticism, so far as it goes, that the ritualistic style of the play confines the hero to certain rigid, one-dimensional attitudes. Henry's character is immediately established in the opening conversation between the two ecclesiastics, and it does not develop thereafter. Nor, despite the immense surface energy which keeps the play moving in the theatre,[4] is there any real conflict. Henry has risen above temptation, and there is nothing to excite us in his calm pursuit of an assured destiny. Doubts assail him only twice, when his bedfellow betrays him and when ordinary soldiers question the justice of his war. But even then – so it is said – the official manner does not relax. He always seems to be speaking 'for the record', and even in soliloquy he addresses himself as though he were a public meeting.

The familiar criticisms start from here. Henry is smug and hypocritical; or he exists only on the surface and is simply too good to be true. Then it is only a short step to more serious accusations, and Henry's behaviour is condemned by standards not in the least applicable to his time and state. It is easy to see how this has happened. Epic praises heroes and denounces villainy. It does not deal in light and shade, and its blacks and whites have a definition too simple for the give-and-take of ordinary life. Aeneas is always *pius*, Odysseus always πολύμητις, because the poet does not mean to complicate the fundamental issues. So with Henry: if in the play his virtues seem to be superhuman, this does not invalidate the seriousness of Shakespeare's purpose nor, within the restrictions imposed by his medium, the success of his execution. Henry is an appointed symbol of majesty, and the action of the play is directed with the most elaborate care to show him doing everything that the age expected of the perfect king.[5] If real life is not quite as simple as that, no matter. Human virtue is always muddied, or it would not be human; epic is the art that on special occasions transforms it into the ideal.

Shakespeare opens the play with two churchmen marvelling at Henry's recent conversion. 'His addiction was to courses vain, | His companies unlettered, rude, and shallow', and so on; but

> The breath no sooner left his father's body
> But that his wildness, mortified in him,
> Seemed to die too. Yea, at that very moment,
> Consideration like an angel came,
> And whipped th'offending Adam out of him.
>
> I.1.25-9

This does not mean that Shakespeare has turned his back on *Henry IV*. Spectators familiar with these two plays would understand the true character of the Prince and would know that there had been no unpremeditated change in him. But there is no reason why the two bishops should have known it too, and their assumption of a heaven-sent conversion is an effective and economical way of emphasizing the reputation that Henry now enjoys. It is the reputation that matters, not the manner of it; and it would be odd if the Church did not find in it the occasion for a certain amount of professional congratulation. In any case Ely does also allude to the explanation of Henry's behaviour that had earlier been given by Warwick:

> The strawberry grows underneath the nettle,
> And wholesome berries thrive and ripen best
> Neighboured by fruit of baser quality:

And so the Prince obscured his contemplation
Under the veil of wildness, which, no doubt,
Grew like the summer grass, fastest by night,
Unseen, yet crescive in his faculty.

I.1.60–66

They enter the King's presence and at once he raises the question of his claim to France. This is the crux of the play. Henry's detractors say that he had not forgotten his father's advice to busy giddy minds with foreign quarrels, and that he was base enough to seek the clergy's blessing for a war for which he had no better excuse than this need for diversionary activity, coupled later with his personal anger at the insulting message sent by the Dauphin. The clergy, for their part, sanctioned the campaign, and even made a handsome donation towards expenses, because there was a bill before Parliament to confiscate their temporalities.[6] If this is a just interpretation, Henry is beyond our pardon. The idea of the godly ruler fails at once, and all the later heroism and fair words and gallant comradeship in battle cannot gild the fault. Henry's reformation would be mere expediency, and Shakespeare's picture of him as the mirror of all Christian kings would be a shocking irony.

It is improbable that Shakespeare would have deliberately wrecked his play in the first ten minutes: not even in his so-called 'bitter' period was he as outrageously cynical as that. In fact we have only to read these two scenes carefully to realize that he did nothing of the kind, and two recent editors of the play[7] have convincingly argued that, however it may appear to us today, the French war was a righteous war which a virtuous king was bound in honour to undertake. Shakespeare deliberately departs from the sources in order to make this plain. Hall's untempered Protestantism, echoed in spirit by Holinshed, seized on the opportunity to accuse the clergy of seeking to divert the attack on their property by urging the King to conduct the anti-clerical laity upon a campaign in which, if God were just, many of them would be killed. Shakespeare will have none of this. In I.1 Canterbury says that he has offered money to the King. It may indeed be a bribe to ward off sequestration, but that is not how Henry receives it. He gives Canterbury the most solemn warning not to twist the facts when he pronounces on the English claim to France. To consult his spiritual advisers on a matter of this gravity was the correct thing for a king to do, and it is ironical that Henry's critics should have regarded it as a brazen invitation to the clergy to consecrate commotion's bitter edge. But Henry warns Canterbury of the dreadful responsibility that rests on him:

> For God doth know how many now in health
> Shall drop their blood in approbation
> Of what your reverence shall incite us to.
>
> I.2.18–20

Canterbury follows with his exposition of the English claim, more than sixty lines of it. It would be a remarkable audience that did not fidget, but we must remember that the English pretensions to the crown of France, for us long buried in a distant past, were by no means a dead issue when Shakespeare was writing. The loss of Calais was still in living memory, and Elizabeth had not in theory surrendered either this or any other French possession that was lineally hers. Dover Wilson believes[8] that Shakespeare's audience would have thrilled at this reminder that their claims on France had not been abandoned but only slept; and might indeed, if the hour produced the man, one day be revived. Henry V was such a man, and Canterbury assures him that his cause is just: a point on which Shakespeare has to satisfy us if we are to believe in his conception of the King. Historically Canterbury was quite right. The Salic Law had been in the particular instance a dishonest contrivance by French jurists to deny the claims of Edward III; and in addition to these claims Henry had also inherited the rights of his own Angevin ancestors. The present century has made us suspicious of the excuses invented to countenance aggression, but in feudal law Henry's war was justified.

Even so, he will not leave until he is satisfied that the kingdom is safe from the Scots. It is Henry himself who raises this point, showing himself to be aware of his duty to protect his people from attack; and he is rewarded by Exeter's assurance of the unity of the realm.

> For government, though high, and low, and lower,
> Put into parts, doth keep in one consent,
> Congreeing in a full and natural close,
> Like music.
>
> I.2.180–83

It is a wonderful evocation, especially significant in this context, of the harmonious relationship between Henry and his people, and it is followed by Canterbury's elaborate comparison between society and the hive:

> ... therefore doth heaven divide
> The state of man in divers functions,
> Setting endeavour in continual motion;
> To which is fixèd as an aim or butt
> Obedience; for so work the honey-bees. ...
>
> I.2.183-7

Its biological accuracy has been challenged but it is a classic statement of the Tudor theory of status. At its close Henry announces his decision to enforce his claims, and the French envoys are summoned to be made acquainted with it. They produce the Dauphin's gift of tennis-balls, a painful reminder of carefree days in the company of Falstaff. It is absurd to pretend that the French war was a personal vendetta to avenge this trivial insult. That decision had already been made, and in his reply Henry leaves the French in no doubt of the real issues.

> ... this lies all within the will of God,
> To whom I do appeal, and in whose name,
> Tell you the Dauphin, I am coming on,
> To venge me as I may, and to put forth
> My rightful hand in a well-hallowed cause.
>
> I.2.290-94

Actors of Henry tend to go through a certain amount of foot-stamping during this speech, but the text does not seem to warrant it. Henry is sarcastic, masterful, and icily determined; there is no evidence of lost control, and the chief impression given by the speech is that it is the Dauphin who is the irresponsible playboy now.

The next scene introduces us to the reprobates, but not to Falstaff. His presence was promised in the Epilogue to *Henry IV, Part Two*, 'If you be not too much cloyed with fat meat'. It seems, too, that the author went sufficiently far towards keeping the promise by including him in the original draft of the play, where it was he, and not Pistol, who ate Fluellen's leek[9]; and where he may have had a meeting with the King in the night before Agincourt that we should dearly like to have overheard.

It has been suggested that the Cobhams, not content with getting his name altered from Oldcastle, now managed to get him off the stage altogether; and so it needed nothing less than a royal command to get him back again in *The Merry Wives of Windsor*. But the influence of the Cobhams in these matters tends to be overrated, and they were seemingly powerless to prevent the use of their family name of Brooke as a *nom de guerre* for the jealous Ford. Falstaff's disappearance is also attributed to the departure of the comedian Will Kempe, who left the company at about this time. But it is by no means certain that Kempe ever played Falstaff: the part may have been created by Thomas Pope. Moreover, Kempe was still in the company when the Globe was built during 1599, being one of the small group of actors who shared the financial risk[10]; so it seems likely that he was available to play Falstaff if it had been required of him.

What then did happen to Falstaff? It has escaped notice that his omission may have been Shakespeare's deliberate artistic choice. The Epilogue to *Henry IV, Part Two* is suspect anyway. It contains two further paragraphs after the prayer for the Queen which should have closed the entertainment, and it is evident that there is more matter in the printed text than was ever spoken at a single performance. The promise that Falstaff should reappear seems to have been added at some time after the original performance: possibly for an appearance at court, in regard for the Queen's known affection for the character, or possibly to appease the public outcry at his most unpopular rejection. It may well be that, at the request of the company and to please the audience, Shakespeare genuinely tried to introduce Falstaff into *Henry V* but later abandoned him as alien to the spirit of the play.

If he had appeared in person, it would have been necessary to degrade him out of recognition – or else to diminish the conception of Henry that Shakespeare was trying to create. Shakespeare's eventual compromise is brilliant. Falstaff is present only to die one of the most moving deaths in all our literature. It is not just anyone who dies, and the emotion that this scene creates is born of our happier memories of him in his prime. It is hard to believe – and

Shakespeare could not make it harder, either for himself or for us –
that it is a better world in which this man has no place. The Arden
editor writes that 'the "finer end" that Falstaff made changes the
tone of the play, it deepens the emotion. . . . The play gains in epic
strength and dignity from Falstaff's death, even as the *Aeneid* gains
from Dido's death, not only because both accounts are written
from the heart with a beauty and power that have moved men's
hearts in after time, but because Dido and Falstaff are sacrifices to
a larger morality they both ignore'.[11] In the England of Henry IV,
Falstaff was a symbol and source of the corruption that he was
confident would still prevail in the following reign, but Shakespeare allows us to forget the dishonour that now dies with him.
'Dost thou think, because thou art virtuous, there shall be no
more cakes and ale?' There is a heavy loss in the death of so large
a morsel of our common nature, and Shakespeare gives us leave to
think, if we are so inclined, that there is something frigid and unnatural in the perfectly disciplined soul. He even has the audacity
to allow his hero to be cursed for ingratitude, by the honest
Gower as well as by the disreputable Nym. But the point is this:
the better we can be induced to think of Falstaff, and the more we
regret his absence, the higher is the tribute which, consciously or
not, we are paying to Henry and the larger virtue that he represents.

The country's unity demands a further sacrifice before Henry
sets out for France. The unmasking of the conspirators is not a
comfortable episode, but that kind of thing never is. It can never
be pleasant to see men bared to the soul. But the scene further
illustrates Henry's kingly qualities, in his willingness to pardon
the drunkard whose railing was offensive to his person but did
not harm his royal office; and then in his severity to the close friend
who had plotted to destroy him.

> Touching our person seek we no revenge,
> But we our kingdom's safety must so tender,
> Whose ruin you have sought, that to her laws
> We do deliver you.

> II.2.174–7

For the country's good he rises above personal affection and suppresses any impulse he may have to show mercy to men he had

loved and honoured. Their fate shall be according to the course of law.

But this is one of the few occasions in the play when we are admitted to Henry's inner thoughts.

> O, how hast thou with jealousy infected
> The sweetness of affiance!
>
> II.2.126–7

This is at the heart of his grief and disappointment. Breach of trust weakens the defences of society, and even while he is publicly denouncing the traitors he is on the rack of bitter self-questioning. He is moved to dwell upon the harsh realities that may lie beneath the 'glistering semblances of piety'. The fair face of unity may conceal a thousand other treacheries in men who seem to be dutiful, free from gross passion and constant in spirit. Scroop's fault strikes him as another fall of man, because of its implicit threat to loose all the hideous forces of appetite and anarchy. The speech, which many critics regard as an insufferable piece of sanctimonious ranting, exposes the tensions in which a king must live. The revelation of this treachery has opened up for Henry the gulf that separates his own conception of honour from the passions of the men he has to rule.

He derives genuine consolation from the thought that God has revealed the plot before it could do any actual harm, and this strengthens his faith in his mission as he leaves for France. Many things in his conduct of the war have been disliked because they have not been understood. He is a man well versed in 'the disciplines of the wars', and Fluellen's praise of him is not to be taken lightly. Where he seems to modern ideas to have been quite astonishingly insensitive, he was in fact directing the campaign according to the recognized principles of his age. Thus he begins by sending Exeter to give the French a further opportunity to avoid the whole bloody business. The justice of his cause, 'no sinister nor no awkward claim', is reasserted and France is warned to surrender

> The borrowed glories that by gift of heaven,
> By law of nature and of nations, 'longs
> To him and to his heirs.
>
> II.4.79–81

If the warning is not heeded, the King's reply will be 'bloody constraint', and the French will be responsible for all the innocent blood that will be shed. Before Harfleur Henry in person threatens terrible destruction if the town will not surrender. It sounds the utmost in hypocrisy to call the citizens 'guilty in defence' if they try to save their town from a foreign invader, but if in justice Harfleur was his by rightful inheritance, then they would indeed be guilty of impious defiance in attempting to withhold it from him. That is what the rules of war prescribed, and the effectiveness of Henry's highly-coloured threats does succeed in preventing bloodshed, so that in the end he is able to tell Exeter to 'Use mercy to them all'. At Agincourt his order to the soldiers to kill their prisoners has again been misunderstood, and Dover Wilson's analysis of the situation – which was historical – deserves to be carefully studied.[12] Henry's action has the immediate endorsement of Gower, who was a professional. 'The King most worthily hath caused every soldier to cut his prisoner's throat. O, 'tis a gallant King!' This is followed, again significantly, by Fluellen's enchanting comparison of Henry of Monmouth and Alexander of Macedon, and of the fish that swim in the rivers at both these towns. Then Montjoy appears to bring the French surrender to the leader whose determination and tactical insight have averted an ugly situation.

It may well be that no amount of explanation will make these incidents acceptable to modern taste. There are many matters on which Shakespeare's thinking is so utterly different from ours that reconciliation is impossible. It never seems to have occurred to him, for instance, to question the morality or wisdom of capital punishment as a social expedient: he lived in a world where this drastic medicine was probably necessary. Warfare similarly had a code of behaviour that was found to be satisfactory for the short-season campaigning of feudal armies, and the civil war of the seventeenth century was fought broadly by the same conventions as Shakespeare accepted for Henry V.

In any case these blemishes, if they are blemishes at all, do not spoil Shakespeare's wonderful picture of the King as he leads his tiny force to victory. This is no lay figure just striking the right attitudes. The battle scenes glow with the warmth and inspiration of a man leading his people in fulfilment of a sacred trust bequeathed to him by his ancestors. Already his personality has healed the bitter wounds of civil war, and from 'that nook-shotten isle of Albion' his armies come 'as fierce | As waters to the sucking of a gulf', the youth of England all on fire with his spirit. The French King fears his dreadful prowess, 'The native mightiness and fate of him' (II.4.48–64), and the scenes in the enemy camp, with their boastfulness and bickering and essential triviality, show by contrast the doom of a nation that has lost its soul. Weakened by disease and their losses before Harfleur, the English army limp through France with colours dimmed by 'rainy marching in the painful field', and here Shakespeare bids us remember the band of scare-crows that Falstaff led across the midland plain to Shrewsbury. But in the face of overwhelming numbers[13] the English are united by the King in that sort of fatalistic courage of which great deeds are born. In Henry's speech on the eve of battle Shakespeare rises unmistakably to the height of his epic theme.

> And Crispin Crispian shall ne'er go by,
> From this day to the ending of the world,
> But we in it shall be rememberèd.
>
> IV.3.57–9

The literal-minded hasten to point out that this prophecy has been disappointed: we no more remember Agincourt than we remember who Crispin was. But they are wrong. The English race have remembered Agincourt whenever the odds were long and the future dark and doubtful, and Henry superbly touches the strings that move men to be greater than themselves. 'How Thou pleasest, God, dispose the day.' Almost, in such a mood, it does not matter. This is the triumphant cry of one who has done all within the reach of man.

Henry's 'band of brothers' is composed of men who are free. They are human enough to 'have no great cause to desire the approach of day', and Falstaff's Boy is not the only one who would give all his hope of fame for a pot of ale and safety. But they would not be there unless they chose to be. Henry wants no lagging spirits, and if any have no stomach for the fight, he will find their passages home to the safety of their English beds. In a heroic hour there is no place for Bardolph, whose fire is out. In the whole army only Pistol asks for greater indulgence than perhaps we ought to give him, and Shakespeare has many ways of showing the single-mindedness and quiet comradeship of the men whom Henry leads. Fluellen, an indomitable cocksparrow, is given latitude to develop a richly idiosyncratic character within the framework of the honesty and loyalty that are his most significant virtues. The interlude that he plays with Gower, Jamy, and Macmorris offers, as Johnson very rightly said, only 'poor merriment', but these four men of different races are a further symbol of the unity and spirit that Henry has inspired. 'By the mess, ere theise eyes of mine take themselves to slomber, ay'll do gud service, or ay'll lig i'th'grund for it.' Finally, in a lull in the action before the stirring movement of the battle, three ordinary soldiers show the true nature of their loyalty in the very act of asking themselves why they give it.

This is an important episode in several ways. It demonstrates, 'as may unworthiness define', the royal leadership promised in the fourth chorus, and we see Henry comforting his troops, 'even as men wrecked upon a sand, that look to be washed off the next tide'. It is not done in a few empty phrases drawn from the cheap currency of military exhortation. Henry reasons quietly with his men, soberly admitting the dangers and conceding their right to hold the doubts and reservations they have expressed. It was a king's duty to feel his responsibility for the men he was leading into battle, and his claim on their obedience is complemented by his obligation to satisfy them that the cause is just and 'his quarrel honourable'. The relationship between king and subjects in this scene crystallizes Shakespeare's idea of majesty. All know their duty. The subjects owe obedience, for 'to disobey were against all proportion of subjection'; but 'if the cause be not good, the King himself hath a heavy reckoning to make'. The soldiers' blunt questioning moves Henry to a further examination of his conscience, and when he is alone he contemplates the terrible responsibilities of his office. 'Every subject's soul is his own': wherein he is luckier than the King, whose public conscience faces problems beyond the understanding of ordinary man. In Henry's speech on ceremony (IV.1.231–77) Shakespeare relaxes the epic mood to sum up his earlier reflections on power and the nature of kingship. We are back in the taverns[14] as Henry longs for the 'infinite's heart's ease' that his subjects are free to enjoy, and human feeling makes a momentary challenge to the austere disciplines of royalty. His recent conversation with the soldiers has reminded him again of the isolation which he has forgotten in the free-and-easy comradeship of the camp. But the moment of weakness passes, and Henry's acceptance of his burden is the more impressive for his admission of a personal sacrifice. His speech acknowledges the sleepless hours of care and service, and dismisses the pomps of office as the baits in which flatterers offer their deceiving poison. The scene closes with Henry committing his cause to God and praying that his father's usurpation shall not decide the issue of the coming day. In the course of some 320 lines he has shown almost every quality that Shakespeare thought to be fitting for a king.

Johnson believed that Shakespeare found himself short of material for the final Act, but Henry's wooing, so often criticized as heavy-handed and hypocritical, was in the accepted manner of the light-hearted gallant.[15] It is important to Shakespeare's purpose to have the righteous war crowned by a peace that unites the two countries, and of this new and wider unity Henry's marriage is the fitting symbol. Burgundy's lengthy declamation (V.2.23–67) urges the need for harmony, for war is not man's right condition. This play, which shows like no other the particular virtues that war can breed, also examines its horrors with penetrating disillusion. It has been hailed both as a glorification of war and as an exposure of its corruption and brutality. Both views are correct. Suffering, bloodshed, and cruelty are always implicit in the action; the foibles of the professional soldier are mocked, although not unkindly, in the blinkered pedantry of Fluellen; war's heroics are debunked in the response made by Pistol and his crew to Henry's speech before Harfleur; and Pistol stands also for the type of man to whom war brings the opportunity to line his pocket and acquire at the same time a bogus reputation as a hero (II.3.52–3, V.1.81–5). The desolation pictured by Burgundy is a final condemnation of war as destructive and unnatural, and the signing of an honourable peace is therefore to be regarded as Henry's concluding achievement.

But only through war could Shakespeare fully express the sort of man that he wanted Henry to be. As well as frailty and weakness, war develops special qualities. Possibly they are the highest virtues, possibly not; but at any rate they are particular virtues and they are valuable. Shakespeare insists on this in *Henry V*. In the ordinary way we come to know many things about Henry – that he is self-controlled and dedicated, superior to flattery, pious and God-fearing, and so forth. But war is the ultimate test of a country's unity and spirit, and the ultimate challenge to the men who rule it. This was the challenge that Shakespeare needed if he was to draw Henry in the fullness of his majesty.

It may not be a wholly convincing portrait: in the bold, bright colours of epic it is not always easy to recognize a human being. It is natural, too, to react against a surfeit of perfection, and without going to the extreme position of Henry's more implacable critics, many readers of the play have found him too coldly official for their taste. But Shakespeare's ideal king is a composite figure, and in Henry IV he found qualities of humanity and compassion that the stylized epic mode prevented him from revealing in the son. It is perhaps easier to admire Henry V than to like him. But an Elizabethan audience may not have had this difficulty, and it does not seriously weaken the effectiveness of the play that Shakespeare was intending to write. He brought his historical sequence to an end with a heartening picture of a society cured of its sickness and united under a prince whose own redemptive experience corresponded with that of his people. To an England living under the shadow of the Queen's approaching death, with all that this might mean, he offered this final assurance that under strong and disciplined leadership men had nothing to fear.

NOTES

1. W. Hazlitt, *The Characters of Shakespear's Plays*; J. Masefield, *Shakespeare*; A. Bradley, *Oxford Lectures on Poetry*; H. Granville-Barker, *From 'Henry V' to 'Hamlet'*; E. K. Chambers, *Shakespeare: a Survey*; E. M. W. Tillyard, *Shakespeare's History Plays*; D. A. Traversi, *Shakespeare from 'Richard II' to 'Henry V'*.
2. cf. the judgement of J. H. Walter in the introduction to the new

Arden edition, page xvi: '*Henry V* is daringly novel, nothing quite like it had been seen on the stage before'.

3. In the introduction to his Cambridge edition, page xii.

4. On the lower levels, obviously, the play was composed with great technical assurance. There is a conflict of a kind in the clashes between the English and the French both at court and on the battlefield; the two camps are excellently contrasted, and Shakespeare has found room for a rich variety of character and incident, all of it related to the central theme.

5. See J. H. Walter, Arden edition, pages xvii–xviii. Thus Henry is the intimate of scholars and divines and seeks the advice of wise counsellors; he banishes idlers, parasites, and flatterers, although he can unbend in the company of ordinary men; he is master of his passions and does not give way to lust or anger; he accepts all the cares of state, burdensome as they are, and recognizes titles and ceremony at their true rate; he has the sinews to protect his kingdom, and, if necessary, to conduct a righteous war, but at the same time he knows that war has many evils and he acknowledges his duty to see that it is not waged without real cause; personally brave, he raises the spirits of his men; he rules mercifully but justly, being ready to sacrifice his friends if they threaten the public safety; he maintains order and the country is united under him.

6. See I.1.7–19. A fairly comprehensive bill for the appropriation of ecclesiastical property had been brought before Parliament in 1410. It did not pass into law, other distractions coming to the clergy's rescue, but it was reintroduced at the Leicester Parliament of 1414.

7. J. H. Walter, Arden edition, pages xxiii–xxvi; J. Dover Wilson, Cambridge edition, pages xix–xxiv.

8. Cambridge edition, page xxiv.

9. See J. Dover Wilson, Cambridge edition, pages 113–16; J. H. Walter, Arden edition, pages xliii–xliv. The triumph over the spineless Le Fer (IV.4) is such a characteristically Falstaffian exploit that it would be difficult to believe that the scene was not originally written for him.

10. See M. M. Reese, *Shakespeare: his World and his Work* (1953), pages 212–13, 263–6. The original performance of *Henry V* may be dated with some certainty between March and September 1599, this being the time that Essex was in Ireland (V Chorus 29–32).

11. J. H. Walter, Arden edition, page xxvi.

12. Cambridge edition, pages xxxiii–xxxviii.

13. One against ten, Drayton says (*Ballad of Agincourt*, IV.3), but he

was claiming a poet's licence. The English had just over 6,000, the
French about five times that number.

14. The play's frequent references to Falstaff, like the reiteration of
the joke about Bardolph's nose, may indicate, as Johnson suggested, that Shakespeare was reluctant to part with him 'and has
continued his memory as long as he could'. But they have a more
important purpose in constantly reminding us what Henry has
given up.

15. Dover Wilson points out (Cambridge edition, page xliii) that this
is how most of Shakespeare's bachelors have gone about the
business of getting married. Except that he would have been much
wittier, it might be Benedick talking.

ELEVEN

What Is Shakespeare's *Henry VIII* About?*

Frank Kermode

DISCONTENT is the chief characteristic of all criticism concerned with *Henry VIII*, and it is not too much to say that a perennial incapacity to fit it into the shifting pattern of Shakespeare's life-work or to see it as a unified drama presenting distinct critical problems of theme and manner is responsible for the established habit of regarding it primarily as the centre of a merely scholarly dispute as to who wrote it, or who wrote which parts of it. I do not intend to hesitate over this aged argument any longer than is necessary to my theme; but since nearly all the criticism with which I am familiar regards the problem of authorship as inhibiting open discussion of that theme, it is essential to glance at the issue.

The notion that a good ear detects in the play stylistic variation so large that it can be reasonably accounted for only in terms of dual authorship is, I imagine, even older than Richard Roderick, who is given the credit of having first recorded it. We are warned, indeed, that good ears sometimes show remarkable disagreement among themselves, and are frequently, even on mature heads, full of echoes of a conservative schoolteacher's forgotten instruction; but I cannot think that this is a caution sufficient to make most readers abandon the view that the splendours of the collapsing Buckingham and Wolsey, so relaxed and elegiac, so formal and so unstartling, are not Shakespearian splendours. A quick reference to the most conventional scenes of *The Winter's Tale* reveals the absence of such syntactically liberal verse; there is no conventional languor in Prospero's farewell to magic. I, for one, am not persuaded that there isn't an authorship problem.

*From *Durham University Journal* n.s. IX (1948), 48–55. Copyright © Frank Kermode, 1948. Reprinted by kind permission of the editor of the *Durham University Journal*.

I am, however, well aware that what I have said lacks the validity so properly required in observations of this sort; the foregoing paragraph has a doubtful value as a subjective impression, but none at all (in isolation) as a contribution to objective truth. The issue is whether *any* observation of the internal 'evidence' can have any more general validity than mine. Dr Johnson's impression that the Prologue and Epilogue were not Shakespeare's was of precisely the same order as mine – *non vultus, non color* is the sum of his evidence, and the basis of his conjecture that the lines were the work of Jonson. Obviously such an issue could not be allowed to remain frankly at the mercy of conjecture, though in the absence of clear external evidence there was no way of avoiding exactly this kind of critical intuition as the *primum mobile* of all systematic work on the play; unfortunately its limitations as the starting-point of scholarly investigation were not invariably recognized.

This accounts for the famous investigation of Spedding,[1] almost a century ago. Perhaps it is the lack of general interest in the play itself which is responsible for the survival of Spedding's essay as a central work in the study of it. In this case the basic intuition on which all the conjecture was based was due to no less good an ear than Tennyson's; and this celebrated organ detected in parts of *Henry VIII* the accents of Fletcher. Spedding proceeded to demonstrate, by means of 'scientific' verse-tests of the kind just coming into vogue, that certain parts were indisputably by Shakespeare, certain others by Fletcher, and some more doubtful ones by Beaumont. His proof was pretty generally accepted, and, I suppose inevitably, gave rise to other work which credited Massinger with a hand in the play. It is precisely against the claims of the Spedding school that Professor Alexander argues in his contribution to the subject, of which more later. It is worth noting that Spedding, in taking up Tennyson's hint, discovered on reading the play that it was so patchy, discontinuous, and unshaped that he was compelled to assume that one author had completed another's work without really knowing what the primary intention had been. I believe that this assumption of Spedding's underlies the dearth of critical comment on the play itself; it is assumed to be of interest only in that it was a collaboration of such a kind that no unity of conception and design ought to be expected of it. Even Alexander, in disposing of Spedding's proof, does not seriously challenge its corollary.

On the very general grounds that laymen are nowadays rather better educated in the matter of statistics than they were even fifty years ago, most people would regard Spedding's figures with some suspicion. The figures with which he deals are by no means large enough to convince us that analysis of them can offer 'general formulæ which may be applied to any particular case considered'.[2] So that even if the methods by which Spedding attempted to lift his thesis beyond mere conjecture were considered to be adequately precise, it is no longer possible to agree that they produce universally valid results. The more particular argument which Professor Alexander attacks in detail is that of Hickson, who held that one definitive test was provided by the fact that Fletcher sometimes, but Shakespeare never, 'pauses upon a superabundant syllable'. The way to disprove this assertion is, of course, to produce examples of the phenomenon from indisputably Shakespearian work; and this is what Professor Alexander does, though it is perhaps worth noting that not all his examples are good ones. Too many of them are drawn from lines broken between two speakers; examples of this sort can be found early in the canon, are not evidence that Shakespeare was changing his habits, and are, I think, unfair. His sixth example –

> Would have him wed again.
>   If you would not so –

is surely perfectly regular; an elision only (you'd) is required. Compare this line, occurring among the triplets of Jonson's Prologue to *Epicene* –

> And though all relish not, sure there will be some
> That when they leave their seats ...

where there is presumably no doubt about the elision. It seems possible then (for others of Alexander's examples could be disputed) that it was not easy to collect many even in the later plays. Of course the Professor establishes his case, which is that 'the extra accented syllable is ... not unknown in Shakespeare's work', and the general pseudo-scientific structure which Spedding and his followers erected on that primary intuition of Tennyson or some other critic, such as themselves, has tumbled down. Nevertheless the intuition has precisely the same (limited) validity as it had before the assault. No amount of internal evidence could prove it right, and no amount will prove it wrong. And so, if it is profitless to talk about *Henry VIII* as an intelligible thing in itself unless single authorship can be proved (as Spedding assumed, and as Alexander assumed in confuting him), one might as well follow the tradition and give up at this point. But if we remind ourselves that Spedding accepted the view that the play was unsatisfactory and formless *a priori*, and argued that proved collaboration would account for this state of affairs, and that this was most improper of him, since joint authorship doesn't inevitably produce discontinuity, and certainly not to the bizarre degree that this theory postulates (one collaborator not knowing what the other one was up to) we may take enough comfort from this apparent illogicality to proceed on another but more reasonable assumption, that, as has been previously but inadequately asserted, the play is substantially what one man would have written, even if more than one hand contributed to it.[3]

As I have indicated, I sympathize with Spedding when he expresses himself thus of his sensations in reading a scene written in a manner quite different from the preceding one –

I felt as if I had passed suddenly out of the language of nature into the language of the stage, or of some conventional mode of conversation. The structure of the verse was quite different and full of mannerism. The expression suddenly became diffuse and languid. The wit wanted mirth and character. And all this is equally true of the supper scene ...

although I should not have used language so gratuitously pejorative. The manner is different; there is no need to go beyond that. It is with this that I have to disagree –

... throughout the play the king's cause is not only felt by us, but represented to us, as a bad one. We *hear*, indeed, of conscientious scruples as to the legality of his first marriage; but we are not made, nor indeed asked, to believe that they are sincere, or to recognise in his new marriage either the hand of Providence or the consummation of any worthy object, or the victory of any of those more common frailties of humanity with which we can sympathise. The mere caprice of passion drives the king into the commission of what seems a great iniquity; our compassion for the victim of it is elaborately excited; no attempt is made to awaken any counter-sympathy for *him*; yet his passion has its way, and is crowned with all felicity, present and to come. The effect is much like that which would have been produced by *The Winter's Tale*, if Hermione had died in the fourth act in consequence of the jealous tyranny of Leontes, and the play had ended with the coronation of a new queen and the christening of a new heir, no period of remorse intervening. It is as if Nathan's rebuke to David had ended, not with the doom of death to the child just born, but with a prophetic promise of the felicities of Solomon ... I know of no other play in Shakspere which is chargeable with a fault like this, none in which the moral sympathy of the spectator is not carried along with the main current of action to the end.

All the same, this is the kind of criticism which lingers over Falstaff, the fat lovable rogue, and calls Isabella a prig. It is almost enough to answer that the play was by both necessity and choice obliged to be reasonably historical. Anne was the mother of Elizabeth, and none of Katherine's woes could alter the fact. Wotton called the play (the play that caused the fire) by an alternative title, *All is True*; and the Prologue makes it plain that foolery must be absent from a stage displaying what is 'only true'. The time for taking liberties with the chronicles was past; and anyway this history was much too recent to be drastically rebuilt. But this suggests that the play is a pageant with no more form than chronology imposes, and I am sure it is nothing of the sort. It is a new kind of play, and very unlike the other histories, but not so unlike that they cannot help us to understand it. Long before drama replaced the Morality *rex* with the King of England, but all about him stood the incarnate agents of his and his land's good and evil. The Tudor king was God's deputy, and so, of course, were the kings of the history plays. But in every case there was something wrong with their title and their rule; they were punished, or their children's children were punished. Henry VIII, on the other hand, had nothing wrong with his title, nor with his rule (if Halle and the absence of judgement upon him may be believed), and as

God's deputy was a minister of grace. It is not he who rises and falls or merely falls for the instruction of the audience; it is the Queen and various great men under his rule. The play is concerned with the old tragic theme of the great man's fall, and the King has a special place in that theme; he is the centre of the drama (and therefore it is pointless to talk of having to get to know new characters at the end of the play) but he is not simply the old *rex* who was the owner of the vices and virtues doing battle about him; he is a representation of an exalted view of kingship fostered by the Tudors out of expedience perhaps, but accepted by James and his subjects as a natural law. If we recall that James himself is often (especially in court masques) practically equated with God, and that this is not to be written off as disgusting flattery, we may find it easier to believe that Henry VIII is represented in this play as exercising certain God-like functions.

The Arden editor got nearer than most to seeing what the play was about.

> In comparison with *When you see me you know me*[4] the play may be regarded as history, but it is rather a new 'Mirror for Magistrates' in the form of a drama, interspersed or interrupted by pageants. Those that can pity may, if they think it well, let fall a tear over the successive fates of Buckingham, of Wolsey, of Katharine; and for the sightseers there are the processions.[5]

No doubt the processions were conceived to meet a demand for spectacle, but they also have a simple function in the drama, which is to illustrate the circumstance from which the great ones fell. This is self-evident, and needs no labouring; the detail of the stage directions indicates further that all is true. It is in regarding the play as a collection of tragedies that Pooler came near to the heart of the matter. For this is a collection of falls (Miss Spurgeon conscientiously notes the iterative imagery of falling) and there are not three falls, but four, Katharine's, Buckingham's, Wolsey's, and Cranmer's.

The tragedy of Katharine is the one which has provoked most indignant comment in the critics. We are made to sympathize with her; she clearly doesn't deserve to fall; Henry himself confesses her virtue –

> That man i'th'world who shall report he has
> A better wife, let him in naught be trusted
> For speaking false in that. Thou art alone –
> If thy rare qualities, sweet gentleness,
> Thy meekness saint-like, wife-like government,
> Obeying in commanding, and thy parts
> Sovereign and pious else, could speak thee out –
> The queen of earthly queens. She's noble born,
> And like her true nobility she has
> Carried herself towards me.
>
> II.4.134–43

It is impossible to deny an element of hypocrisy in the King's character in this part of the play, or that he was too easily managed by flatterers. But this ought not to obscure the equal fact that there was reason in his stated motives for seeking the annulment, and that one of these, which would weigh powerfully with the Shakespearian audience, was the continued failure of Katherine to produce an heir. This was the reason, in so far as reason was needed, for the stage-fall of this virtuous queen. In fact, the purely historical reason – after all, she did fall – was enough for the dramatist's purpose.

The *Mirror for Magistrates*, itself the product of a long medieval tradition, had a numerous progeny.[6] The theme continued popular until well into the seventeenth century; and by the turn of the century, so Farnham assures us, it was beginning to show its vitality and adaptability once more by allowing a discreet sentimentality to creep into it, especially when it was concerned with the Falls of Women. The tendency is discoverable in Daniel's *Rosamond* of 1592. Women were more likely to be the passive agents of evil than men, and philosophical considerations of the working of Fate, the natural concomitants of the *de casibus* theme, could in these cases be suspended. So they are in Drayton's *Matilda* (1594), and the most powerfully sentimental of all such poems are Murray's *Sophonisba* (1611) and Sampson's *Fortunes Fashion* (1613) which concerns itself with the fall of Lady Elizabeth Gray, the queen of Edward IV. Sampson (whose work I have not read – it is very difficult to find) apparently treats his theme of injured innocence with a wealth of pathos, and Farnham believes that all this is symptomatic of the departure of the heroic spirit from literary tragedy, and its replacement by explorations of broken hearts and suffering womanhood.

Katherine's fall is surely exactly of this fashionable kind. She is presented happy and virtuous, confident of the King's attention, free-spoken and above all very much alive. At the prelates' inquiry she behaves much as Hermione does in *The Winter's Tale*; she firmly retains the sympathy of the audience which she won by her just forthrightness in the first Act. But she falls; there is no malice in the King when he considers it, and he sends her his good will before she dies. Griffith makes it clear that she deserves no reproach, and her death is heralded by a dance of blessed spirits. The whole scene in which the famous song is sung, and the death-scene itself, are full of carefully organized appeals to pity; the mood is elegiac; they are scenes of great beauty, but for all that they remain what are now known as 'tear-jerkers'. So were the poems of Murray and Sampson, practically contemporaneous productions; and this fall is the more pathetic in that it is *true*. Long before the *Mirror* itself had shown that British history was a rich store-house of *de casibus* exempla; no fiction could match history in this respect, for history shows what has happened and what therefore can and will happen again. Virtuous women fall; they are not without sin, and may be, as Katherine was, party to an offence perhaps incurring God's displeasure; but there is little suggestion in this kind of tragedy that the fall is deserved. Fashion has, in this corner of the traditional theme, ousted the customary moralizing and speculation. Katherine's ultimate beatitude is not in doubt; but on earth she fell from greatness, though a queen and a king's daughter, and a heavy spectacle it is.

The fall of Buckingham is a relatively simple affair. The spite of Wolsey is the cause of it, and the sufferer, though a good and learned man, is splenetic and undisciplined. The ultimate pathos of all such falls is heavily underlined in this play. Buckingham makes a noble end, in the tradition of English noblemen.

> For further life in this world I ne'er hope,
> Nor will I sue, although the King have mercies
> More than I dare make faults.
>
> II.1.69–71

When Vaux invites him to a barge fitting his great person, he replies –

> Nay, Sir Nicholas,
> Let it alone; my state now will but mock me.
> When I came hither, I was Lord High Constable
> And Duke of Buckingham; now, poor Edward Bohun.

II.1.100–103

Farnham's remarkable book makes us aware that the medieval view of Fortune and its connexion with doctrines of divine retribution were complicated and inconsistent. Fortune is sometimes a sporadic betrayer of her minions; sometimes she inevitably makes fall succeed rise. To ride her wheel was to make the whole circle; to fall rapidly from the topmost point into the mire. That was the more general view, but the first, that great men sometimes avoided falls, and wicked men punishment in this world, was also quite frequently proposed. The orthodox Elizabethan view, however, denied Fortune existence except as a figurative expression for God's providence. This was the view of Raleigh and Primaudaye[7] – tragedy was explicable in terms of a man's sins and justice operated inexorably in the sublunary sphere, for, as Aquinas held, the divine providence prevented anything from occurring by chance. The idea that, since good men fall and bad men escape earthly retribution, there is an element of chance, and that, in a disordered world-centre, the provisions of Fortune operate but fitfully, was rejected by the orthodox as Epicurean; it was, in fact, an aspect of that Pyrrhonism to which the Protestant temper was naturally opposed. The orthodox view, as is well known, lies behind the sin-and-scourge pattern of the earlier histories. An ancient belief, which, Battenhouse suggests, survived through Plutarch, complicated the issue a little by holding that since man is fundamentally responsible for his own acts his wisdom can prevent his fall. But such a belief would be offset by Calvin's (whose affinities with Raleigh and Primaudaye as above expressed are obvious) – that man is incompetent, through *the* Fall, to behave so. Sin is inevitable, judgement is inevitable. The orthodox position is strong; but the misfortunes of good men were an observable fact, and though even good men are sinful there is an obvious disparity between a

Buckingham or a Clarence on the one hand and a Wolsey or a Tresilian on the other. The *Mirror* itself, though much concerned with the idea that a great one rose by his crimes and perished by God's hand, did not claim that the just man would be free from effects indistinguishable from those of tragic retribution ('some have for their virtue been envied and murdered' it says, and perpetuates in some ways the old idea that against the cruelty of Mutability only the Stoic philosophy has a defence, regarding rise and fall and death itself as irrelevant. 'Wherein may be seen by example how grievous plagues are punished, and how frail and unstable worldly prosperity is found, even of those whom Fortune seemeth most highly to favour' – be they just or not, one might add). I am sure the fall of relatively just men (it may easily be conceded that no man may be absolutely just) formed a separate group of tragedies even when the idea this kind of tragedy best exemplifies – *de contemptu mundi* – was moribund. In some ways the fall of Buckingham is the male equivalent of Katherine's fall, but it is altogether more conventional, closely resembles the kind of fall experienced in the original *Mirror* by Clarence, and lacks the elaborate fashionable circumstances of the Queen's tragedy. The pathos is certainly there; against the splendour of masquing and procession Buckingham has become plain Bohun; but, of course, we are not mulcted of so much sympathy for him as for the Queen, and he falls as great men will as the heterodox wheel turns.

Wolsey certainly does not fall 'like a blessed martyr', and there is no difficulty in accounting for his tragedy in a perfectly orthodox way. He had been the protagonist of *de casibus* tragedy long before this play was written. The prose *Life* of Cavendish, a gentleman usher in Wolsey's household, deliberately shaped the Cardinal's incredible rise and rapid fall on the Boccaccian model. Endowed with nothing but brains and a capacity for learning, his master rose on Fortune's wheel to the positions of King's chaplain, Archbishop of York, and Cardinal, to Chancellor of the Exchequer and the most powerful man in the kingdom, lavishing a great fortune on luxurious furnishings and entertainments of all kinds; but all this incurred him the animosity of powerful men, and he was in an instant swept away. (The play with its device of the inopportune discovery by the King of Wolsey's private accounts is not here historical, for it borrows the tale from another fall, of a Bishop of Durham who made this error and was exposed by Wolsey.) Finally the fallen man dies, broken by sickness. Cavendish, whose work was still in manuscript in 1613, though the author of this play must have had access to it, emphasizes the odd fact that Wolsey's body was discovered to be clad in a hair shirt; and he makes it clear that in his view the Cardinal deserved his fame as well as his fall. In the play there is an obvious attempt in the speech of the gentle Griffith to do justice to the extraordinary magnanimity which was an aspect of Wolsey's obsession with power and greatness, but the author's animus is equally clear: Wolsey is associated with Rome, as Cranmer is with the Church of England; he calls Anne a spleeny Lutheran, whereas the well-disposed think of her as a jewel of worth. From Cavendish (to some degree aided by Campion) the conventional view of Wolsey probably derived. He was a great man, and fell greatly. So he is presented in the ambitious *Life and Death of Thomas Wolsey Cardinal* of Thomas Storer (1599) in which Farnham sees a prototype of the Elizabethan tragic pattern. Storer presents the tragedy as a clear case of rising, flourishing, and fallen greatness. In the play Wolsey is described as an example of purely malignant ambition meeting retribution not only through the discovery of his evil designs but from the accumulated animosity of the other lords who taunt him with his faults in a scene drawn in detail from Holinshed. Incidentally, it is the discovery of his traffic with the Pope which brings about his fall, and the fall was almost undoubtedly associated with the fall of the Roman Church in England. But it is basically as simple as the simplest and most orthodox falls in the *Mirror*, for Wolsey's acts of conspiracy and treachery are directly responsible for his tragedy, in that when they were discovered they provoked the just condemnation of the King, and also in that they roused the outraged earls who so gleefully accuse him (III.2). This, then, is the completely orthodox fall, in accordance with contemporary Christian moral philosophy, and in a sense all the others are variants of it.

The most curious of these is the arrested fall of Cranmer. This seems to me the only possible description of it. Associated with it is the merely adumbrated fall of Gardiner, which is the product of the operation of Mercy in its negative mirror-image, Justice. For Cranmer (whose piety is heavily emphasized in the first three scenes of the last Act) is evidently headed for the same kind of fall as Buckingham's; he displays exemplary resignation even before the event, exhibiting the humility and the traditional noble attitude of a man about to suffer. We are familiar with the use of the figure of Fortune's buckets from *Richard II*, and just as there is an element of this traditional imagery in the contrasting fortunes of Katherine and Anne, so there appears to be in the supposedly falling Cranmer and the overweening Gardiner. But the King, observing everything down to the indignities which Cranmer is made to endure, makes an impressive entry and, having by use of the ring-token made it clear to the enemies of the just cleric that he proposes personal intervention, redeems Cranmer from falling and indicates a displeasure with Gardiner and a recognition of his injustice which foreshadow retribution on this arrogant (and Romish) antagonist.

This royal act is an exercise of mercy; and there is a connexion between the part here played by the King and the role of Mercy in the earlier Moralities — that is, those written before the *tragic* theme usurped the form, and in which *homo* in his extremity is preserved from Hell by precisely such an act. It does not seem to be relevant to speak of inconsistency in the character of the King, nor indeed to posit some act of *depersonalization* as so many modern critics might; for there is nothing out of character in the exercise of divine grace by a Tudor or Stuart sovereign. Here Henry is God's deputy, and it is well known that this office was in Tudor political philosophy a property of all kings by divine law. Cranmer and the Church of England redeemed, it is proper that he should sponsor and prophesy over Elizabeth, the first personally effective Protestant monarch, and the fact that she could not have existed but for the tragedy of a good woman must not be allowed to detract from the pleasure the auditors are expected to feel at the end of the play, which is of course related to the happy dynastic progress of English history since that birth, a progress which might have been very different if Henry had not put away Katherine.

So the Arden editor is not far out when he suggests that this play is an anthology of falls, like the *Mirror*. It is, however, as I see it, necessary to count four of them. The last, Cranmer's, is different from the others. It shows that a man having risen may avoid a fall because Mercy (and perhaps Wisdom as in the Plutarchian theory) intervene. It is not that retribution ceases to function; Cranmer was undeserving the treatment of Wolsey. His fall would have been the kind which yields with any conviction only to the Pyrrhonist reading which was, though extant, heterodox. These four falls, all different, might well be regarded as an attempt to present in the closest possible interrelation as many entertaining variants on the popular theme as the dramatic convention permitted.

Nevertheless, one should beware of regarding the play as episodic. It is called *Henry VIII* and it is about Henry VIII. Notoriously, kings were men as well as divine agents. Here is a king susceptible to flattery, to adulterous passions, choleric and extravagant. His rejection of Katherine is influenced by some of those human flaws; but it is not quite unconnected with a proper kingly concern over the health of the state. The result is the tragedy of a good woman, a type well understood, and for which the dramatist had exemplars. Human justice lacks the certainty of its divine counterpart; so, in spite of a fair trial, Buckingham, not without sin, falls. The man who caused this tragedy falls as a result of his treachery in the treatment of the affair of the Queen; he knows very well what the moral of his tragedy is, and urges it on Cromwell at some length. 'Fling away ambition', he says, already seeing himself as an example or a Mirror. He was never happy until the fall occurred, for God has so disposed it that the evildoer has that in his own breast which destroys his peace. Here punishment is visited on the offender through the King; he is the agent of the divine retribution. As Wolsey falls in sin, Cranmer rises in virtue, and they clearly represent Popery and the English Church as much as they do great men vicious and virtuous. In his turn, Cranmer falls, and we have a pattern whereby to understand the nature of his tragedy; but there is no need for it; Mercy intervenes, and virtue is saved from such a tragedy by the King himself. The guilt or virtue of the King in respect of these happenings should be judged primarily by their fruits. These are the birth of a great queen and the establishment of the reformed church. It is unthinkable that these should be dismissed as the workings of chance; such a position would be both heterodox and treasonable. The play may be regarded as a late Morality, showing the state from which great ones may fall; the manner of their falling, be they Good Queen, Ambitious Prelate, Virtuous Prelate, or merely Great Man; and the part played in their falls for good or ill by a King who, though human, is *ex officio* the deputy of God, and the agent of divine punishment and mercy.

NOTES

1. See J. Spedding, 'On the Several Shares of Shakspere and Fletcher in the Play of *Henry VIII*', *Gentleman's Magazine*, n.s. XXXIV (1850), 115–24, 381–2.

2. A mathematician, quoted in Alexander's article, 'Conjectural History, or Shakespeare's *Henry VIII*' in *Essays and Studies* XVI (1930), 85–120. The argument is one with which Bernard Shaw has made many familiar.

3. Even Miss Spurgeon, in her British Academy Lecture *Shakespeare's Iterative Imagery*, allowed herself to be diverted into discussing the authorship problem. Few would share her conviction that her methods offer a valuable test of authorship.

4. Rowley's amusing play of 1605, which may be glanced at in the Prologue. It is, as Schelling says, the below-stairs view of the King. Will Summers is really the most important character. It shows Henry as bluff, choleric, but addicted to jests.

5. *The Famous History of the Life of Henry VIII*, edited by C. Knox Pooler (London, 1915), page xxx. See also the Prologue to the play, lines 5–7.

6. See Willard Farnham, *The Medieval Heritage of Elizabethan Tragedy* (Berkeley, 1936).

7. These doctrines are elucidated in R. W. Battenhouse's *Marlowe's Tamburlaine* (Nashville, 1941).

TWELVE

Shakespeare's Histories on the English Stage*

Arthur Colby Sprague

To the Elizabethans comedy and tragedy were classical forms about which there were accepted things to say. Histories were modern, popular, and wholly English. As such they were scarcely a subject for serious criticism, but their effect upon audiences in the public theatres did not escape comment. Turning to 'our domesticke hystories', Heywood in his *Apology for Actors* exclaims:

what English blood seeing the person of any bold English man presented and doth not hugge his fame, and hunnye at his valor, pursuing him in his enterprise with his best wishes, and as beeing wrapt in contemplation, offer to him in his hart all prosperous performance, as if the Personater were the man Personated, so bewitching a thing is liuely and well spirited action, that it hath power to new mold the harts of the spectators and fashion them to the shape of any noble and notable attempt.[1]

Nashe in a famous passage in *Pierce Penilesse his Supplication to the Diuell* speaks of the eager interest taken by audiences in the fate of such an English worthy as John Talbot, who after lying dead for two hundred years had triumphed once more upon the stage. And to Nashe this seemed a bestowal of fame where fame was due and a hope offered 'to aduentrous mindes, to encourage them forward'.[2] Heywood, again, was gratified by the extent to which unbookish playgoers had become learned in their country's annals. It was the aim of plays, he wrote, 'to teach the subjects obedience to their King, to shew the people the vntimely ends of such as haue moued tumults, commotions, and insurrections.'[3] Histories,

*Chapter 1 ('The Histories') of *Shakespeare's Histories: Plays for the Stage* (1964). Copyright © Arthur Colby Sprague, 1964. Reprinted by kind permission of the author and the publishers, the Society for Theatre Research, London.

that is to say, presented with the utmost vividness those ideal characters through whom poetry was supposed to teach. This presentation was commemorative – a glorious warring against Time. And, more directly, histories upheld order and set forth the woes attendant upon popular uprisings and civil strife. Shakespeare's familiarity with these ideas is beyond question, *Henry V*, not to go farther, illustrating the first and second of them to perfection.

With the coming of neo-classicism at the Restoration, Shakespeare's histories fell into critical disrepute. They broke the rules; were 'rather chronicles represented, than tragedies'.[4] Indeed, since they were bound by fact, there could be 'no Manner of Fable or Design in them'. It was absurd 'to huddle so many Actions, so many Places, and so many Years into one Play, one Stage and two Hours', as Shakespeare himself recognized when he wrote the *Henry V* choruses.[5] Then, too, his English princes except perhaps John (Richard II and Henry VI were 'at times little better than paltrons') could not qualify as heroes in 'a just composition'.[6] That the laws set down for tragedy and comedy were inapplicable to histories, since these dramas were neither the one nor the other, was a point made by Samuel Johnson.[7] It was long over-due.

On the stage, meanwhile, from the first years of the eighteenth century, the histories had been prospering. *The First Part of King Henry the Fourth* shared with *Hamlet* the distinction of being acted in London at least once every year till 1750.[8] *Henry VIII* was played frequently, as were such rediscovered works as *The Second Part of King Henry the Fourth*, *Henry V*, and *King John*. The mounting enthusiasm for Shakespeare was, on one side, an expression of national feeling, and plays like *King John* and *Henry V* contained plenty of claptraps when, as was now almost habitual, there was war with France. Even criticism was affected. For were not 'the rules' French and Shakespeare who broke them, an Englishman? 'The dramatic Poetry of this Country', one reads in the *Gray's Inn Journal*, 9 February 1754, 'is like our Constitution, built upon the bold Basis of Liberty'.[9]

As the danger to England grew greater, with the rise of Bonaparte, passages of a martial sort began to be inserted in the texts of some of the histories, notably in *King John*. There the added words were especially composed for the occasion. With more discretion, George Frederick Cooke, appearing as Richard III at Covent Garden, 15 October 1804, drew upon Shakespeare to improve Cibber. As a writer in *The Monthly Mirror* noted, the actor had 'judiciously introduced some lines from Shakespeare's text, extremely apposite to the patriotic sensations of the present moment. They are in the address to his army, on the approach of Richmond's forces'. And he quotes:

> Let's whip these stragglers o'er the seas again,
> Lash hence these overweening rags of France;
> These famished beggars, weary of their lives. . . .[10]

V.3.328–30

That the speaker of these lines was the vicious and tyrannical Crookback seems not to have mattered. Any stick was good enough to beat a dog with – and in their hearts a fair number of those who heard him rather liked Richard. Besides, Cooke may by the manner in which he read the lines have dissociated them from the character and made them his own. The applause which followed would certainly have been for him.

With Garrick had begun the domination of the English stage by a succession of great actors. For them, Richard came to be as inevitable as Hamlet, with Wolsey and King John likely to follow and Hotspur, Henry V, and Henry IV interesting possibilities. Falstaff was often consigned to a mere comedian, though Henderson, Cooke, and Phelps all appeared in the role; and Richard II, a discovery of Kean's, was considered unreliable. Indeed, except for *Richard III*, as Cibber had providentially refashioned it, the histories proved a little disappointing when one went to them for star parts. Constance and Queen Katherine stood high with tragic actresses but were also faulty. Commenting on the relative failure of *King John* to become popular in 1783, even with Mrs Siddons and her brother appearing together in it, James Boaden had no doubt as to where the blame lay. 'It was dangerous', he wrote, 'to show such a meteor as *Constance*, and linger two acts further, after she had disappeared. Such is the inconvenience of chronicle plays; passion demands one termination and history another.'[11] There were spectators who left the playhouse as soon as Mrs

Siddons finished. In *Henry VIII*, where a similar problem arose, the curtain sometimes fell upon the scene of Katherine's death, with the whole of the fifth Act omitted.

Patriotism, then, and the presence of roles attractive to players, had something to do with keeping Shakespeare's histories on the stage. To these was now added the exciting possibility of re-creating a distant time. 'Archaeology' reached the theatre by slow steps, as when in the 1750s Garrick dressed some of Ben Jonson's comedies 'in the old English Manner'.[12] Certainly audiences were ready to welcome the production of *King John* at Covent Garden, 24 November 1823; as certainly, this was an event of real importance. J. R. Planché, who was a better antiquary than he was a playwright, had been given sole charge of the preparation of the play which, on this occasion, was to be costumed in the fashions of John's own time. He was, in fact, to *produce* the history a long time before producers as such had been heard of. As might be expected, the stage manager took umbrage at the granting of such extraordinary powers to an outsider; and the actors were dismayed at sight of 'the flat-topped *chapeaux de fer*' of the twelfth century, which they were to wear. Would they not be 'roared at', in these 'stewpans', when the night came? So, indeed, they were, Planché writes,

but in a much more agreeable way than they had contemplated. When the curtain rose, and discovered King John dressed as his effigy appears in Worcester Cathedral, surrounded by his barons sheathed in mail, with cylindrical helmets and correct armorial shields, and his courtiers in the long tunics and mantles of the thirteenth century, there was a roar of approbation, accompanied by four distinct rounds of applause, so general and so hearty, that the actors were astonished.

And he adds, not without elation, that 'a complete reformation of dramatic costume became from that moment inevitable upon the English stage'.[13]

At the beginning of Victoria's reign the histories were still popular. Macready during his two brief periods of management produced *King John*, *Henry VIII*, and *Henry V*, the last-named with particular splendour. Phelps at Sadler's Wells did all the histories except *Richard II* – and, of course, the three parts of *Henry VI* – and did them with taste and devotion. Charles Kean revived *Richard II*, which his father had played, and gave several of the usual histories as well. At the Princess's Theatre, in his time, archaeology was carried to astonishing lengths and the appeal of the production came before that of the play, or even its star. (The lesser Kean never shone with a dazzling brilliance.) It was only after 1862, only when Phelps had left Sadler's Wells, that Shakespeare's histories fell into neglect. This fate they shared with many once familiar tragedies and comedies. Tradition in the theatre was under attack at innumerable points with the passing of the old repertory companies. Phelps himself seemed a little old-fashioned now. The archaeological productions, except, perhaps, those of Charles Calvert at Manchester, no longer aroused excitement. They were so expensive too! 'Shakespeare spells ruin and Byron bankruptcy' was a managerial saying of the time just before Irving. Irving, during his long years at the Lyceum, gave a dozen of Shakespeare's plays in all, but only two, *Richard III* and *Henry VIII*, were histories. It was becoming necessary to go outside London in order to see *Henry IV* or *Richard II*. At the Stratford festivals Frank Benson's young actors were particularly happy in Shakespeare's histories.

Several of Benson's productions have interesting connexions with criticism, connexions which will be better understood, however, if we turn once more to what was being written about the plays. Their 'irregularity' was rarely dwelt on after Johnson's Preface.[14] Rather, as in Schlegel's lectures of 1808, it was their epic reach. The eight linked histories beginning with *Richard II* and ending with *Richard III* formed a single great work, to which *King John* served in some measure as Prologue and *Henry VIII* as Epilogue. They were a mirror of kings and should be a manual for young princes to instruct them in the nature of kingship.[15] Still more nearly in the line of Elizabethan thinking is Coleridge's statement that in *Richard II* 'the spirit of patriotic reminiscence is the all-permeating spirit'.[16] England, it was decided, must be the hero of the whole series.[17] Only when the order in which the plays were written had been approximately determined came the familiar division into two great 'tetralogies', the earlier in time reaching forward to the advent of the Tudors, the later beginning tragically with *Richard II*.[18]

Walter Pater's essay 'Shakespeare's English Kings', probably the best known of all essays on the histories – unless it be Morgann's on Falstaff – was published in 1889. Early readers must have found it unconventional at least. Shakespeare, they were told, was concerned not with the history of the English people but with 'the sad fortunes of some English kings as conspicuous examples of the ordinary human condition'; with 'the irony of kingship', which appears repeatedly in these dramas but most conspicuously in *Richard II*. For the essayist's interest was strangely concentrated upon this unregarded play and its sorry hero. By comparison, a widely commended king was referred to almost slightingly. 'The popularity, the showy heroism, of Henry the Fifth, is used to give emphatic point to the old earthy commonplace about "wild oats",' Pater wrote – to the dismay, I take it, of many schoolmasters. Richard is 'the most sweet-tongued' of all Shakespeare's English kings, he goes on, 'an exquisite poet if he is nothing else, from first to last, in light and gloom alike, able to see all things poetically, to give a poetic turn to his conduct of them.' And he is, by implication, an actor as well, throughout the long ceremony of deposition in which 'Richard more than concurs: he throws himself into the part, realises a type, falls gracefully as on the World's stage'.

Benson with some misgivings gave *Richard II* at Stratford in the spring of 1896, to find in the chief character one of his happiest parts. In December 1899, when he appeared in it at Manchester the performance was memorably reviewed by C. E. Montague in the *Manchester Guardian*. Benson, Montague wrote, had brought out what criticism had obscured – the poet in Richard, 'the capable and faithful artist' in this 'incapable and unfaithful king'. That the reviewer does not so much as mention Pater is of no consequence. He had points of his own to make, and made them impressively. Few theatrical reviews can have had so definite and enduring an influence.[19]

In addition to sharing in the rediscovery of *Richard II*, Benson in the summer of 1901 put on six of Shakespeare's histories, at the Memorial Theatre, in the space of a single week – the 'Week of Kings', as it came to be called. The plays, given chronologically by reigns but with neither of the 'tetralogies' preserved entire, were *King John, Richard II, Henry IV, Part Two, Henry V, Henry VI,*

Part One, and *Richard III*. William Butler Yeats saw them all, in a vanished Stratford of 'quiet streets where gabled and red-tiled houses remember the Middle Age'; where throughout the day 'one does not see or hear an incongruous or noisy thing'. 'Partly', he writes, 'because of a spirit in the place, and partly because of the way play supports play, the theatre has moved me as it has never done before.'[20] In that phrase *the way the play supports play* and in the seriousness with which he takes the fulfilment of the Bishop of Carlisle's prophecy in *Richard II* (Shakespeare 'did indeed think it wrong to overturn a King, and thereby to swamp peace in civil war') Yeats is suggesting sources of artistic dignity in the histories which were only to be fully recognized years later.

Shakespeare's plays were being re-examined, early in the present century. An understandable reaction had set in against adulation. There were novel standards of dramatic technique to apply, standards based on the practice of modern masters like Arthur Pinero and Henry Arthur Jones. For whatever reason, the judgements pronounced on the histories were often severe. Thus, Tucker Brooke, though granting certain exceptions, writes that 'the species as a whole was a plebeian growth, fostered by unpolished and irregular stage conditions, bound to few if any of the rules of art'.[21] And of the two parts of *Henry IV* and *Henry V*: 'Had Falstaff been dealt with as summarily as Mercutio in ''Romeo and Juliet'', the trilogy ... would have lost immeasurably in human interest, but surely it would have gained in homogeneity.' As it stands, we are 'diverted from the state of Plantagenet England to Shakespeare's Gloucestershire and the streets of contemporary London'.[22] This sounds surprisingly like the pronouncement of some early eighteenth-century critic obsessed by the neo-classical unities. Lytton Strachey is more trenchant. *Richard II*, he writes, in 'The Claims of Patriotism' (1918), is not a historical play.

It is not concerned with constitutional questions, or with national questions, or with any attempt to represent a state of society in a past age. It is a study ... of the introspective and morbid temperament of a minor poet who happened also to be a king. Again, the vital parts of *Henry IV* are by no means historical: they are a presentment of the contemporary tavern life of Elizabethan London.[23]

Or there is John Bailey, five years later, who decides that Shakespeare's histories 'are rather fragments or chronicles than dramas proper: and the dramatist in him shows itself rather in the new power and life-like truth of the characters than in any such linking of them together as would have converted a succession of episodes into a single dramatic action'.[24]

Too frequently the histories were regarded as a kind of discipline to which Shakespeare had subjected himself in preparation for the greater work ahead. Yet the new approaches which criticism was to adopt were not unknown during these same years. Walter Raleigh refers to Shakespeare as 'a passionate friend to order'; Quiller-Couch would have us think of the *Henry IV–Henry V* plays as primarily concerned with the transformation of Prince Hal into King Harry, and even suggests that they have a 'Morality structure' and might be called 'after the style of a Morality title, *Contentio inter Virtutem et Vitium de Anima Principis*'.[25] The one critic looks forward to the work of E. M. W. Tillyard; the other is anticipating Professor Dover Wilson and *The Fortunes of Falstaff*.

The somewhat fuller understanding of the histories which we now possess has come about as a consequence, first of reading them more closely and taking seriously the links between one play and another; then of detecting in many passages the presence of certain ideas, about the state, especially, and about the recent past, which were current in Shakespeare's time. These ideas were simple in themselves and not in the least original with the dramatist. Rather, as Tillyard points out, they were 'political commonplaces' widely shared. Among them were 'the need for a strong, just, and clever king, for the maintenance of the political hierarchies in the state, for the loyalty and altruism of public servants, and above all for . . . harmony in the working of the commonwealth'.[26]

That the sovereign was God's deputy in a 'wonderful order' of 'angels and men' would have been accepted without question by Elizabethan readers of Shakespeare's works. This concept had an immediate bearing on the dispute with Rome. In Samuel Rowley's play about Henry VIII, *When You See Me You Know Me* (1605), Catherine Parr, disputing with Bishop Bonner, asks why the King and his people were to obey the Pope.

BONNER
  Because faire Queene he is Gods Deputie.
QUEEN
  So are all Kings; and God himselfe commaunds
  The King to rule, and people to obey. . . .[27]

King John comes to mind – or is it *Richard II*? *Richard II* takes
on fresh interest once we realize that the King has every right to
speak of himself as 'The deputy elected by the Lord'.

As for the interpretation of England's recent past, this had been
formulated by Tudor historians, by Hall, in particular, before
Shakespeare adopted it in two divisions of related plays, the one
ending with *Richard III*, the other beginning with *Richard II*.
Under Elizabeth – herself a vital symbol, an almost mystical being,
to the poets of her reign[28] – the advent of the Tudors seemed an
event immeasurably happy; one which had brought an end to the
confounding of order during the strife between the houses of York
and Lancaster. The sin of Bolingbroke, 'his ambitious crueltie,
that thought it not inough to driue king Richard to resigne his
crowne and regall dignitie ouer vnto him, except he also should take
from him his guiltlesse life', was the starting-point for all these
miseries. Thus were 'rebellious subiects' deservedly punished.[29]

The difference between our present attitude toward the *Henry VI*
plays and that of a generation or two ago is remarkable. To deny
these plays a central theme, as was formerly done, would be
absurd in the light of what we now know about them; nor are they
likely to be dismissed as formless. On the other hand, the merely
political aspects of Shakespeare's histories can be exaggerated. It
is hard to take seriously the difficulty experienced by a recent
scholar in understanding why *Richard II* should have been chosen
for performance on the eve of the Essex revolt: must there not be
'at least some doctrine' in it of a subversive sort, he wonders.[30]
As if the graphic reminder that an English king had been formally
deposed was not enough in itself to explain the choice! 'Even in
plays where the political interest is most evident,' writes Professor
L. C. Knights, 'it is never exclusive or, as it were, self-contained.
The implied question, What does this political action or attitude
mean? is invariably reduced to personal terms: How does this
affect relations between men? What kind of man acts in this way?'[31]

Shakespeare, it should not be necessary to insist, wrote plays and not treatises.

In the theatre, to return to the fortunes of the histories there, a new interest in Shakespeare dates from the 1920s and the work of Robert Atkins at the Old Vic and Bridges-Adams at Stratford. Familiarity came first. Old Vic audiences now saw all the plays, though with the three parts of *Henry VI* telescoped into two. There were gifted players and fine productions in those years, though they received less recognition than was their due; and performances still famous, like those of Gielgud and Maurice Evans in *Richard II*, Ralph Richardson's Falstaff, and Olivier's Richard III and Hotspur, were to follow. Two events particularly concern us. At Stratford in the summer of 1951, *Richard II*, both parts of *Henry IV*, and *Henry V* were all given, and the theory that these plays were so interrelated as to constitute an artistic whole was demonstrated to the satisfaction of many who saw them. At the Birmingham Repertory first, then (in 1953) at the Old Vic, the three parts of *Henry VI* in straightforward, spirited productions by Mr Douglas Seale won a quite astonishing degree of success.

On the whole, Shakespeare's histories have been fortunate. The steadying ballast of known fact in them has served to prevent the extravagances of critics, the fantastication of producers.[32] Except for Falstaff there has been little nonsense written about the characters; little of the confusion between art and reality which led A. C. Bradley to reconstruct the girlhood of Cordelia. Only in the over-eager pursuit of topical significances has criticism strayed into wild conjecture. On the stage, until well into the nineteenth century, these plays were given in better texts than either the tragedies or comedies. *Richard III* is the sole exception, and the stage version of *Richard III* was certainly preferable to that of *King Lear* or *The Tempest*. Some of the histories were neglected but most were not. Such stuffy and pretentious productions as those of Beerbohm Tree in England and Richard Mansfield in America came later – at the very close of the movement initiated by Planché.

NOTES

1. *An Apology for Actors* (London, 1612), B 4.
2. *Works*, edited by R. B. McKerrow, I, 212, 213.
3. Heywood, op. cit., F 3.
4. Dryden, in 'The Grounds of Criticism in Tragedy', *Essays*, edited by W. P. Ker (Oxford, 1900), I, 208.
5. Charles Gildon, 'Remarks', in Rowe's *Shakespeare*, VII (1710), 338, 347.
6. Theobald, taking up a suggestion made to him by Warburton (Shakespeare, *Works* [1733] (1773), III, 345).
7. Preface to Shakespeare's *Works* (1765); see also Elizabeth Montagu, *Essay on the Writings and Genius of Shakespear* (London, 1769 (1770)), page 55.
8. C. B. Hogan, *Shakespeare in the Theatre, 1701–1800* (Oxford, 1952), page 460.
9. On the stage, it should be remembered, French characters were not yet obscurely medieval but wore modern dress. Francis Gentleman tells a quaint story of how at a performance of *King John* in Portsmouth, during the Seven Years War, the actors who appeared as Frenchmen were pelted by tars in the gallery until they removed the white cockades which they were wearing (*Dramatic Censor* (London, 1770), II, 172; see also Boaden's *Kemble*, I, 279).
10. *The Monthly Mirror* for November 1804 (XVIII, 351). An '&c.' follows the quoted lines, as if Cooke had gone on with the speech.
11. *Memoirs of Mrs Siddons* (Philadelphia, 1827), page 220; cf. Thomas Campbell, *Life of Mrs Siddons* (London, 1834), I, 208.
12. See especially R. Gale Noyes, *Ben Jonson on the English Stage 1660–1776* (Cambridge, Massachusetts, 1935), pages 253, 254.
13. *Recollections and Reflections* (London, 1872), I, 56, 57 (see also Odell, *Shakespeare from Betterton to Irving*, II, 169 ff.). The playbill of the opening performance, which has sometimes been misdated, is reproduced in *Shakespeare Quarterly* XI (1960), 233, with a note on the production by Evelyn Richmond.
14. The feeling that these plays ought really to have been tragedies, the refusal, that is, to recognize their right to be judged as histories, has persisted. See, e.g., C. Knox Pooler (ed.), *Henry VIII* (London, 1915), page xxxii, and John M. Lothian (ed.), *Richard II* (Oxford, 1938), page 14. A similar impulse led *The Edinburgh Dramatic Review* (21 April 1824) to criticize the manager of the theatre for not displaying the green carpet – symbol of tragedy – in a performance of *Henry IV, Part One*. Did Mr Murray 'consider

the play to be a comedy', despite the death of Hotspur? (VIII, 179). For green carpets, see a delightful essay by W. J. Lawrence, 'The Evolution of the Tragic Carpet', in *Those Nut-Cracking Elizabethans* (London, 1935).

15. A. W. Schlegel, *A Course of Lectures on Dramatic Art*, translated by John Black (London, 1846), pages 419 ff. The direct influence of these lectures is discernible as recently as 1923 (cf. F. J. C. Hearnshaw, 'Shakespeare as Historian', *Contemporary Review* CXXIV, 728 ff.).

16. *Coleridge's Shakespearean Criticism*, edited by T. M. Raysor (1930), I, 143.

17. See especially William Watkiss Lloyd, *Critical Essays on the Plays of Shakespeare* (London, 1875), page 182. Sidney Lee opposes the epic idea in *Shakespeare and the Modern Stage* (London, 1906), pages 180 ff.

18. Richard Simpson, whom one thinks of first, it may be, as an early explorer of 'topical significances', makes repeated use of the word 'tetralogy' in discussing these two sequences of plays ('The Politics of Shakspere's Historical Plays', *Transactions of the New Shakspere Society*, 1874).

19. See pages 47 and 48 and cf. page ix [of *Shakespeare's Histories: Plays for the Stage*].

20. 'At Stratford-on-Avon' (1901) in *Ideas of Good and Evil* (London, 1903), pages 142, 143.

21. C. F. Tucker Brooke, *The Tudor Drama* (London, Boston, and New York, 1912), page 301.

22. op. cit., page 335. For the application to Shakespeare of the new rules for playmaking, see G. P. Baker, *The Development of Shakespeare as a Dramatist* (New York, 1907 (1916)); Brander Matthews, *Shakspere as a Playwright* (London, 1913); and pages 35 and 39–40 [of *Shakespeare's Histories: Plays for the Stage*].

23. *Characters and Commentaries* (New York [1933]), page 230.

24. 'Shakespeare's Histories', *The Continuity of Letters* (Oxford, 1923), page 59.

25. Walter Raleigh, *Shakespeare* (London, 1907 (1926)), page 191; Quiller-Couch, *Shakespeare's Workmanship* (New York and Cambridge, 1918 (1931)), pages 114, 115. For a detailed account of criticism and scholarship in this period, see Harold Jenkins, 'Shakespeare's History Plays: 1900–1951', in *Shakespeare Survey 6*.

26. 'Shakespeare's Historical Cycle: Organism or Compilation?', *Studies in Philology* LI (1945), 34 ff.

27. Malone Society edition, lines 2227 ff.

28. See an excellent book, *England's Eliza*, by Elkin Calhoun Wilson (Cambridge, Massachusetts, 1939).

29. Holinshed, *Chronicles* (1587 edition), III, 508, and cf. page 522.

30. Irving Ribner, *The English History Play in the Age of Shakespeare* (Princeton, 1957, page 158; London, 1965, page 155).

31. 'Shakespeare's Politics', *Proceedings of the British Academy* XLIII (1957), 118. See also Muriel Bradbrook, *Shakespeare and Elizabethan Poetry* (London, 1951), pages 123, 124.

32. The histories have not wholly escaped silliness and even travesty in their production. Terence Gray's *Henry VIII*, at the Festival Theatre, Cambridge, in 1931, would appear to have been a perfect instance (see Charles Rigby, *Maddermarket Mondays* (Norwich, 1933), pages 103 ff., and Norman Marshall, *The Other Theatre* (London, 1947), page 66). *King John*, as produced by Tyrone Guthrie in 1941 and by Michael Benthall at the Memorial Theatre in 1948, was disfigured by many absurd inventions. Guthrie's debatable *Henry VIII* at Stratford, a year later, seemed to me neither improved nor altogether spoiled by its moments of irresponsibility.

MORE ABOUT PENGUINS

Penguinews, which appears every month, contains details of all the new books issued by Penguins as they are published. From time to time it is supplemented by *Penguins in Print*, which is a complete list of all available books published by Penguins. (There are well over three thousand of these.)

A specimen copy of *Penguinews* will be sent to you free on request, and you can become a subscriber for the price of the postage. For a year's issues (including the complete lists) please send 30p if you live in the United Kingdom, or 60p if you live elsewhere. Just write to Dept EP, Penguin Books Ltd, Harmondsworth, Middlesex, enclosing a cheque or postal order, and your name will be added to the mailing list.

Note: *Penguinews* and *Penguins in Print* are not available in the U.S.A. or Canada.

Penguin Shakespeare Library

SHAKESPEARE'S HISTORY PLAYS

E. M. W. Tillyard

In this major study Dr Tillyard sets Shakespeare's history plays against the general background of Elizabethan thought – 'a scheme fundamentally religious, by which events evolve under a law of justice and under the ruling of God's Providence, and of which Elizabeth's England was the acknowledged outcome'.

In Part I he describes the religious, scientific, and political ideas current in Shakespeare's day and enumerates the historical and literary sources for the plays. In Part II Dr Tillyard examines the individual plays in two main tetralogies, with *King John* and *Macbeth* – 'the epilogue of the Histories' – handled in separate chapters.

'A most stimulating study of a somewhat neglected phase in Shakespeare's work' – *The Times Educational Supplement*

'Nobody who is in any way fascinated by the mystery of Shakespeare's life and achievement can fail to be interested' – Ivor Brown

Penguin Shakespeare Library

SHAKESPEARE'S TRAGEDIES

Laurence Lerner

Shakespeare's tragedies have always been fertile acres for comment and criticism. The same dramas which inspired a Keats to write poetry appealed to A. C. Bradley – or to Ernest Jones, the psycho-analyst – as studies of character; and where the New Criticism has been principally interested in language and imagery, other critics in America have seen the plays as superb examples of plot and structure. Most of Aristotle's elements of tragedy have found their backers, and – as the editor points out in his introduction – these varying approaches to Shakespeare are by no means incompatible.

In what *The Times Literary Supplement* described as an 'excellent collection' Laurence Lerner has assembled the best examples of the modern schools of criticism and arranged them according to the plays they deal with. With its 'Suggestions for Further Reading' and the general sections on tragedy, this is a book which will stimu-late the serious reader and do much to illuminate Shakespearian drama.

Penguin Shakespeare Library

SHAKESPEARE'S COMEDIES

Edited by Laurence Lerner

Laurence Lerner's anthology of criticism on Shakespeare's comedies follows the pattern of his successful volume *Shakespeare's Tragedies*. Once again he has collected together some of the best modern Shakespeare criticism, mostly written in this century, and arranged it to throw light on nine of the comedies. (He excludes the last plays and the so-called problem plays.) A general section on comedy includes passages from Ben Jonson and Meredith.

The contributors run from Shaw, Freud, and Quiller-Couch to Granville-Barker, Middleton Murry, Auden, and Empson, and to more recent critics such as C. L. Barber, Anne Righter, and Cyrus Hoy.

PENGUIN SHAKESPEARE LIBRARY

Other volumes available:

* NOT FOR SALE IN THE U.S.A.